SEVEN DEAI
The Dark Co. , ...
of the Soul

SEVEN DEADLY SINS
The Dark Companions of the Soul

This work is a Psychological Exploration
from a Jungian perspective of the
Archetypal Image of the
Collective Shadow of Man,
by way of the Mortal Sins

Anne Maguire

Free Association Books

Published in the United Kingdom 2004
by Free Association Books
57 Warren Street W1T 5NR

© 2004 Dr. Anne Maguire FRCP (London)

Die Deutsche Bibliothek – CIP – Einheitsaufnahme
Maguire, Anne
Die dunklen Begleiter der Seele : die Sieben Todsünden
psychologisch betrachtet / Anne Maguire. Aus dem Engl.
übertr. von Christa Polkinhorn-Umiker. – Zürich : Dusseldorf :
Walter, 1996
ISBN 3-530-40014-9

Alle Rechte vorbehalten
© 1996 Walter Verlag, Zürich und Düsseldorf
Satz und Litho: Jung Satzcentrum, Lahnau
Druck und Einband: Clausen & Bosse, Leck
Printed in Germany
ISBN 3-530-40014-9

British Library Cataloguing in Publication Data
A catalogue record for this book is available from the British Library

Produced by Bookchase (UK) Ltd

ISBN 1 853437 44 1

Printed and bound by Antony Rowe Ltd, Eastbourne

This book evolved following a series of lectures upon the nature of the Mortal sins, which was undertaken by the author at the C. G. Jung Institute in Zürich, over a period of years between 1988 and 1995.

DEDICATION

This work is dedicated to my brother Michael who suggested the subject, and my friends, Marie-Louise and Robert who gave me their constant support. Also to the Spirit of the wise Ibn Sina (Avicenna) who understood so well the Dark Companions of the Soul.

My sincere gratitude to Mrs Nancy Thomson who typed the manuscript.

In this in-depth exploration of the nature of those sins classed as being of a mortal nature, certain personal life histories relevant to the subject have been included.

It must be stressed that in order to preserve anonymity only the age, sex, marital status if appropriate and where relevant the occupation of the individual is supplied.

CONTENTS

PROLOGUE

As I approached the question of an introduction to this present work the world was encircled and engulfed in waves of shock and horror when evil, as a reality, burst upon the infants' classroom early one morning in a small peaceful school in Scotland. In a matter of minutes it took the lives of a host of tiny children and their teacher. Such an act of premeditated murder, apparently perpetrated by just one man, was described as universally evil. In itself it would seem that it defies an explanation. Implicit in the hideous objective reality of the darkness, already seeds of goodness were engendered in the spontaneous reaction from the collective heart of mankind. But the reality of the dark act of evil was etched indelibly and forever in human consciousness.

Any discourse at this present time upon the subject of the mortal or deadly sins brings to consciousness the ever present problem of evil, which now stands squarely before us, and from which there is no escape. Evil has become a determinant reality, and man's task is to learn to recognise its presence and to deal with it, remembering also, that to touch it may bring as a consequence the danger of the falling into its power. Recognition is our prime task.

Towards the end of his life C. G. Jung wrote these words. 'The old question posed by the Gnostics, 'Whence comes evil?' has been given no answer by the Christian world, and Origen's cautious suggestion of a possible redemption of the devil was termed a heresy. Today we are compelled to meet that question, but we stand empty-handed, bewildered, perplexed and cannot get it into our heads that no myth will come to our aid although we have such an urgent need for one. As a result of the political situation, and the frightful not to say diabolic triumph of science, we are shaken by secret shudders and dark forebodings; but we know no way out, and very few people indeed come to the conclusion that this time the issue is the long-since-forgotten soul of man.'[1]

It has been my endeavour in this tentative exploration of the archetypal image of the collective shadow to portray the importance and the recognition of the sins classified as mortal, which were carefully compiled by the Church Fathers of the Christian Church, many centuries ago.

These sins were regarded by those priests as deadly because of their innate nature. In their complexity and intermingling with one another they violate the divine law, they destroy the friendship of God and they cause the death of the soul. In those far off early days of Christianity man had no difficulty whatsoever in accepting the presence of his soul. Indeed, he was mortally afraid and with good reason as were and are primitive people today of losing it. As Jung has indicated both in his writings and teaching, the soul has long since been discarded, or forgotten, along with God whom the scientists have informed us does not exist. Today however few may realise it, but the soul of man is central to the important and pressing problem of evil.

Since the epiphany of the Christ child two thousand years ago, which ushered in the Christian era and those attitudes which have come to be regarded as Christian, it is now evident that further profound changes have occurred during the last two centuries. There is a tolerant liberality on the one hand which undoubtedly has its virtues, and a saccharine sentimentality on the other which has little to do with the principle of Eros or relatedness, but much to do with cold heartedness. Innate in this development is the problem of morality, or the dictates of a moral conscience which has now become a matter of individual opinion. Those long-held traditional sources of authority as objective standards of morality, appear to have become irrelevant and derelict, to a place outside the domain of individual ego awareness. Thus the grave loss of long-held shared values has now become evident in the collective. Such a profound change reverberates back to the individual whose personal moral stance is further destabilised. The result is confusion as to what is right or wrong. Individuals hesitate to hold a moral viewpoint which does not adhere to the collective opinion of liberal tolerance, even though in their hearts they realise that certain acts or instances of behaviour are morally wrong.

The pervasive fear of resistance to collective opinion permits the acceptance of such antisocial or sociopathic behaviour, which alas, then becomes integral to the general morality.

The emotional vicissitudes which beset the individual emanate from the soul, and as such are the responsibility of the individual himself. It is a fact which may seem strange to the reader, but in reality a great many diseases of both the body and psyche issue from unconsciousness, often deep unconsciousness of personal emotional storms which arise in the inner world. These can be likened to the raging solar storms which can be observed as

10

sun spots on the surface of the sun. Instead of realising that the emotional problem is an issue of the shadow personality an outer object is usually sought for condemnation. This may be observed quite frequently in the phenomenon of unconscious jealousy where the secret desire is to bring down the other who appears to be better placed than oneself. Perhaps a simple jealous sentiment against a sibling which is constantly in families, or a murderous jealous passion intervenes whose aim is to either annihilate the other's personality, or to kill the actual individual who is the cause of one's displeasure, sometimes perhaps simply by his presence. In all these instances the ego personality is almost always unconscious of the hidden emotion or intention.

Likewise with the ubiquitous emotion of anger. It may be present simply as a bad temper, a sulky resentment or a monumental murderous rage. In mass uprisings or revolutionary episodes it is frequently in evidence. In the present epidemic of the condition classed as 'road rage' the incipient anger may be expressed merely as a derisory finger gesture, or overtly in wounding or bodily harm committed on the highway. Pride may be perfectly justified and laudable in one's sense of self esteem, but can so easily become excessive in egocentric behaviour when the ego personality is totally unaware of the unconscious possession. Thus a stumble, a slip or even a sudden fall is often indicative that the individual holds himself too high, and must be brought down to earth in some way for his own safety.

The intrusion of lust or excessive physical desire with its enjoyable pleasures and excitement may bring an element of joyousness sometimes into the boredom of a long relationship, or a marriage which has lost its vitality. Equally it may also bring disaster to one or all parties concerned. Lust together with greed (which may include avarice) and gluttony require a physical appeasement, and are said to be sins of the flesh for this reason.

Indolence or accidie as leisure and relaxation is subtly seductive, but through unwillingness to earn one's daily bread one may slip easily into a sluggish inertia. The Church Fathers condemned accidie for its intrusion into matters concerning the spiritual life, that is attention to one's soul, prayers and meditation upon God in the religious orders. Today in respect of modern man's attention to the inner world one can safely without fear of contradiction make the same accusation of inertia.

In all of these aforementioned phenomena the question of presence rests upon a state of equilibrium. When the emotion or desire is excessive then it may be regarded as a mortal sin encompassing the potentiality for death of the soul. Excess in everything is dangerous for both physical and psychic life. At Apollo's shrine, the dictum was 'Moderation in all things.'

Centuries ago a profound intuition was contained in the apocryphal logion: 'Man if thou knowest what thou dost, thou art blessed: but if thou knowest not thou art accursed and a transgressor of the law.'[2]

The deadly sins are as archiac as man himself, and they give form to evil.

11

Today knowledge of what exactly constitutes the sins tends to be non-existent, misplaced, forgotten or discarded as having no substance. I make no moral judgement upon this observed fact which has presented itself to me time after time throughout many years of medical practice, both as a physician and analytical psychologist. Certain ailments of the body as well as dreams reveal with great clarity the presence of an unconscious and therefore unrecognised emotion, or the unawareness of a destructive attitude. Recognition of this unconscious content is vital for both psychic life and physical health. The task of the physician is to alert the conscious awareness of the patient to that which is the cause of his distress, and which in their wisdom the Church Fathers classed as being sins of a deadly nature. Today in the atmosphere of tolerant liberality one hesitates to use so strong a term for excessive anger, passion, rage, greed or indolence, but nevertheless, it is indeed a sin to be so cowardly that one is afraid to name the evil before one.

About a thousand years ago the Persian physician and philosopher Ibn Sinā wrote the following. 'Brothers of Truth. It is no-wise surprising if the Angel flees from evil, whereas the beast commits wickedness, for the Angel has no organ of corruption while the beast has no organ of comprehension. No, what is surprising is that the human being invested with command over his evil desires should let himself be subdued by them, while yet he has within him the light of intelligence. But truly, like to the Angel, becomes that man who stands firm under the assault of evil desires. But he whose strength does not suffice to drive away the evil desires that tempt him, that man does not even reach the rank of the beasts.'[3]

The myth of modern man which Jung realised on the East African Athi Plains, is that man's consciousness is 'indispensable for the completion of creation if it is not to go down to its end in the profoundest night of non-being'.[4]

Consciousness is requisite for understanding the reality of psyche and the soul of man. It is only in the individual that any change may occur, change does not issue from the collective or the mass. Thus the task of the individual is to endeavour to perceive the presence of, and to grasp the nature of his own soul. At the same time remembering that it has been said that egocentricity which is a necessary attribute of consciousness is also its specific sin, indeed it is regarded as the supreme sin.

Perhaps this work will aid the recall and realisation of the nature of those evils which the Church Fathers so long ago regarded as deadly, and which eventually prove to be fatal for the soul of man, and indeed may be so for mankind itself.

THE SEVEN DEADLY SINS

It is to Tertullian that we owe the recognition of the distinction between the mortal and venial sins, an African who it is believed was born in Carthage about AD160. He was a pagan who abandoned himself to the lascivious life of his city until about his thirty-fifth year when he became a Christian; becoming the first Christian theologian to write in Latin. His noble hearted zeal, his passionate temperament and the profundity of his religious understanding quickly led him to achieve a position of leadership in the early Christian community. He indentifies himself in his writings as a member of the laity, never having been ordained in the Carthaginian church. He described the soul by nature as Christian. 'Anima naturaliter Christiana.'

Mortal or deadly sins are such that wilfully violate the divine law, destroy the friendship of God and cause death of the soul. In this they differ from venial sins which though tending to injure the higher life do not of themselves involve eternal death.

Pope Gregory the Great (Gregory I) speaks of seven deadly sins and the catalogue is commonly notified by the catchword Saligia. This is composed of the following:

Superbia	Pride
Avaritia	Covetousness
Luxuria	Lust
Invidia	Envy
Gula	Gluttony
Ira	Anger
Accidie	Sloth

They are to be regarded as successive stages in the downward course of evil. Pride is the first as it is the source of all the others, selfishness or egoism is the root of all sin. In his Summa II (ii) Thomas Aquinas discourses with great fullness on these aforementioned sins as does St. Augustine the great authority on evil.

REFERENCES

1 Jung, C. G., Memories Dreams and Reflections, Routledge & Kegan Paul, London. 1963. Chapter XII.
2 The Book of Luke VI 4 (Codex Bezae).
3 Avicenna and the Visionary Recital, p. 187–188, Translated by Corbin, Henri. Spring Publications, University of Dallas, Texas, 1980.
4 Jung, Ibid.

1

THE DEADLY SIN OF PRIDE

Pride has always been regarded as the first of the deadly sins. Pride is the quality of being proud. To be proud generally means that one has a high or overweening opinion of one's own qualities, attainments or estate and it simply means inordinate self esteem.

When one feels intense pride one has the sensation of fullness in one's chest or one's heart appears to swell, and we do speak of 'swelling with pride'. Sometimes the emotion of being proud imparts the sensation that one's head has enlarged. The phrase 'a swollen head' is always indicative of a conceit at least or possibly an arrogance. Sometimes there is an accompanying physical sensation of the limbs becoming bigger, and one becomes 'puffed up'. One may thus speak of a state of 'puffed-upness' a not uncommon condition today. When an individual is seized by hubris or arrogant pride and is quite unconscious of ego possession, physical symptoms frequently reveal the condition. These are commonly head noises, clicking of the aural Eustachian tubes, ringing in the ears, slight unsteadiness of gait, sometimes mild dizziness or even severe vertigo. These symptoms are those of altitude sickness as when one climbs to the tops of mountains.

Sometimes if one observes one's own country or team winning some trophy or other in combative sport, one's body is suffused with a warm glow, a sensation of heat may pervade the limbs, the eyes may be observed to glitter or shine and the skin becomes moist. Perhaps the intestines may undergo rapid peristaltic movements which are followed by a sudden urge to defecate. All these physical reality sensations or changes belong to the affect of pride. One is affected by the emotion, and when one becomes aware of this fact the body is sensed to be bigger, the limbs warmer, the eyes moist and then one knows that one is in the thrall of the emotion of pride.

One may realise then that perhaps one is proud because the organism is excited.

Alas, the split in the psyche of modern man does not always permit conscious awareness of the presence of overweening pride, arrogance or hubris which may befall him. In his unconsciousness the physical is not always related to the emotional state.

As C. G. Jung has often said,[1] the feelings[2] of other people do not concern one in the least, and for this reason one observes that the differentiated feeling type usually has a cooling effect in the presence of conflagration or contention, whilst the emotional person heats everybody up because the emotion or the effect, be it joy, anger, fear, panic or pride is constantly radiating out from the activated complex of the one so affected. In the case of pride however, there is usually a certain quality of remoteness which lies behind the effect, it is a distance because there is always the sense of over-valuation. At the base it is a question of an increase in the self esteem of the subject.

THE SECRET PRIDE OF AN
UNASSUMING MAN

A middle aged man in good health was presented with vertigo. He sought the help of various physicians, and was eventually investigated by a prestigious department of neurological medicine. He was told that there was no organic cause for the disorder.

The vertigo always came without warning. He was usually overcome whilst in the street or going about his business as a financial advisor. It had only occurred indoors on one or two occasions. He never had any warning, and was always brought to the floor where he remained until the dizziness passed. Epilepsy had been suspected, but the symptomatology of his condition did not coincide with that of Grand or Petit-Mal.

He gave the impression of a quiet and rather unassuming depressed individual when he came for advice. He seemed anxious to create a good impression, and was clearly very afraid of the malady which had beset him. The story which he divulged was as follows. He had it seemed been happily married for seventeen years, and had two daughters of whom he insisted he was very fond. Suddenly one evening three or four years previously he had returned home to find that his wife had left him. There had been no warning or hint of such an impending disruption.

He and his daughters, who were in their teenage years, lived together for two years after the mother's departure and the subsequent divorce sought by the husband upon learning of his wife's adultery. He had never considered the reality of the total situation. He had been depressed, and was simply not aware of the grief of his children or the practicalities of house management undertaken by the elder child in concert with her studies for university entrance.

About a year after the divorce, and approximately some three years after the departure of his wife he met and married his second wife. The latter was a professional woman, extremely handsome, sophisticated and financially sound. After the wedding the couple and the two children moved into a large house. The elder girl left for university, and within a year the patient found himself to be completely dominated by the career-orientated wife. The elder daughter had a serious mental breakdown and disappeared completely from the family circle, whilst the younger child fell into a rebellion, and became very wilful.

It was exactly at this point that the symptom of vertigo intervened in the man's life. The situation was simply this. When out and about in the streets, and in view of bystanders and spectators he would be seized by an attack of dizziness and fall to the ground. Just as if he suffered mountain sickness at the top of a mountain or a high tower.

When questioned about his second marriage he stated that he adored his new wife, and that she was handsome and everything he desired in a woman. She would have been perfect except for the fact she never permitted him to exercise his own will. He went further to say that his wife believed that his daughters were like their mother, and he would be wise to let them live with her.

He had introduced a second wife into the home without prior or adequate thought regarding the situation of his daughters, or of their feelings. He had à priori disregarded their grief at their mother's departure. He was clearly overwhelmed by the fact that a handsome worldly rich woman had agreed to marry him, and had been flattered by her attentions which had gone far to assuage the inferiorities which had surfaced after his wife's desertion. He had it seems never really addressed himself to the question as to why his first wife had sought the arms of another man. In short he was suffering from a severe inflation, substantiated by several dreams in which he was up in the air and out of touch with reality. His malady was exactly the same as a physical attack of altitude sickness.

When he lay prostrate on the floor he was utterly helpless, and this physical state was witnessed by the collective. The intention of the unconscious was to bring him down to earth and to the reality of his being. He was required to reflect and understand his relationships with his first wife, to his daughters, and indeed to his 'prostration' at the feet of his second wife, for indeed it was just so. He had abandoned his elder daughter because he had rejected her splendid qualities which had kept the family together for the two years prior to the advent of the second wife. He was also called to the task of meditating upon the wilful rebellion of his younger child, and why the second wife wished to dispose of her.

The illness brought to light the onerous burden of his unconsciousness with regard to the fascination engendered by the ruthless nature of his power driven new wife. This was only possible by a difficult analysis of the integral character of his anima,[3] cold and ambitious with serpentine unrelatedness. He had inferior intuition and undeveloped feelings, and therefore his task was not easy. He was to suffer many years of vertigo before he was able to comprehend his own secret inner pride which did not permit him to recognise his gross inferiorities in the realm of psychic relatedness. The psychosomatic disorder brought it into the light of day, and in due course he came to accept it. This was in fact the symptom which did in the end save his life. Otherwise, had it not appeared, the covert vaunting ambition of the cold unrelated anima would have led him to hell-fire and destruction.

This hidden pride is often very difficult to discern particularly in those whose personae range from the shy to the deeply unassuming. In his case 'the fall' was to reveal his inner secret of the sin of pride.

ETYMOLOGY OF PRIDE IN THE
ENGLISH LANGUAGE

The word pride is derived from the late OE 'prȳde, secondary form (probably after 'prūd', Proud or ON 'prýdil) of 'prȳte', 'prytu', abstract sb. f. prū d, presumably on the model of such pairs as 'hlūd', loud, / hlȳd sound, noise, 'fūl' foul/fȳlp filth.[4]

The word proud derives from ME proud or pout which earlier had been prud or prut. The OF was prud or prod. The original OF was preu which gave rise to M.F. and F. preux as in 'preux chevalier'. Preux came to mean in the E – prow which meant valiant valour or prowess.[5]

One's unconscious self-esteem or high flown opinion of one's own sense of presence may be discerned most readily in one's sense of physical habitudes so apparent to others.

For instance, a woman may be secretly proud of her looks to such an extent that she constantly and surreptitiously glances in the looking glass in order to observe and admire herself. A man of normal masculinity may repeatedly withdraw a comb from an inner pocket to smooth his hair. These unconscious mannerisms on the subject's part contain a quality which is outré and evidences secret pride.

Pride may reside in the self satisfaction of one's attainments accrued either through birth or merit, and revealed in a certain smugness of speech and bodily expression. Such is the way of inordinate self-esteem.

Jung said frequently that he always felt disinclined to congratulate one when hearing of a success. He knew that soon there would be the necessity to commiserate with ill fortune. It is a law that if one becomes inflated or puffed up with oneself, either with the accomplishment of success, beauty, attainment or even perhaps one's valour, just as surely one will be beset with ill fortune of one sort or another. There is immense truth in the statement 'pride goeth before a fall'.

One may observe this most acutely in the medium of the television screen. An individual achieves success either in the sporting world, the domain of the theatre or in Government. In the ensuing joy perhaps he stumbles, slips or falls because his attention to reality has wavered. At once the warning is that pride has overtaken him.

One of my patients suffered from a great many physical difficulties throughout the early years of her marriage. To her great sorrow she had never been able to bear a child. The analysis uncovered a great inner fear that if she did have a child she would die from one of her physical maladies leaving her child motherless. When she became conscious of this inner fear she was overjoyed to find herself pregnant. Eventually she was delivered of a beautiful healthy child. Her joy and her pride knew no bounds. It became apparent in the way she spoke of the pregnancy and the parturition that she believed that she alone had accomplished this miracle.

Then one night she dreamed that she was walking along a cliff path. On the right side there was a steep rock face which led down at right-angles to the sea. Suddenly in the dream she became aware that without any warning she was falling down into the sea. In her fear she grasped at a tree and was able to save herself. At that moment she awoke.

Together we decided that the dream was a warning. She was treading a dangerous path, and there was a real possibility that she might fall as the dream indicated. She agreed to exercise caution in her every-day life and to become conscious of the fact that the gift of her child came as a blessing. She had been blessed by an act of Grace. Her hubris was in fact quite unconscious, and that is why Jung was disinclined to congratulate success. One is usually quite unaware that one's ego-consciousness has been seized by one's proud, if not conceited and unrecognised shadow personality.[6] Very often one is quite simply not aware of one's overweening self esteem.

My patient, after the birth of her child was a modest person, but her shadow was quite the opposite. She had become too high up and inflated. Ego-consciousness had seized all the glory and taken full responsibility for the conception and birth of her child. She considered herself secretly to be a miracle worker, and had forgotten the realm of the gods. Indeed she had seized the mantle of the divine.

A scientist had some success with her researches which had been accepted by a prestigious scientific society, to which she had been invited to address. Her work was appreciated widely by her peers, and although she was a modest woman she admitted that she had felt very pleased with herself. Her shadow was however of a different calibre. She dreamed the following dream which revealed to her the salient fact that alas she had been seized by conceit.

In the dream she climbed to the top of a hill and suddenly had a good view of the countryside. At the same time she became aware that she was in a farm yard. She began to move her arms and realised that she was making the movements preparatory to flying. (Fledglings flap their wings to promote muscle strength in preparation to flight.) At that very moment of realisation she crowed like a cock – a fledgling cock.

The dream said it all. A cock bird, be it a farmyard cock, a cock robin, a cock pheasant or a turkey cock they all signify pride. The symbol of portrayal par excellence is the pride of the peacock.

There is a myth concerning the robin redbreast. He became very conceited because he found he could fly very high indeed. He decided to fly to the sun, and did so. As he descended through the downward slanting rays of the sun he became hotter and hotter and found that his throat was burned. That is why the robin today has a red breast. (Indeed it must be the first example of a 're-entry cosmic burn'.)

THE COCK AS SYMBOL OF PRIDE

There are such phrases as 'cock of the walk', or 'cock of the heap' which impute a certain self-aggrandisement.

The cock is a solar bird and is the animal of Asklepios the Greek god of physicians, and so by the same token the cock is also the bird of the physicians. It is the task of the cock to greet the sunrise which is established at the moment when the first ray of sunlight shoots forth over the eastern horizon. He cries out in welcome and awakens the world to a new day. As such he is a light bringer or an illuminator.

He can only achieve this if he has a vantage point. It is easier to see the sun rise from an elevated position, be it a hen coop roof, the upper tiles on a barn or a tree. The cock is therefore regarded as a rebirth animal, and is also associated with resurrection (the birth of the new day and the resurrection of the sun). He is also the bird of Hermes-Mercurius, Mithras and Apollo all associated with light as light bringers.

The cock signifies vigilance. It has a remarkably vigilant eye, a characteristic associated with heights or points of vantage. A proud man or woman carries the head high, and the glance issuing from the alert or attentive eye seeks to prevent the too close approach of others. There is always a degree of isolation or remote hauteur attached to this proud and vigilant eye.

The heights associated with the cock are usually mounds, hills, crags, towers, spires or any good lookout point. The enemy of the bird is the basilisk, and as the cock signifies the dawn and also optimism, the basilisk represents darkness and death.

Before Socrates' death his last words were 'Sacrifice a cock to Asklepios.'

By this it is thought that he meant that death was the cure for life. The cock's sacrifice indicated the safe entry into the beyond for Socrates after his death as he made his exit from the world of reality. It would signify the sacrifice of ego, and by the same token egoistic superiority, and consequently any innate residual pride.

In the Nordic tradition the cock is the awakener of the dead whose sleep is ended each morning in Valhalla, The Hall of the Slain in Gladsheim, which means the Abode of Joy. His name is Gollimkambi the Cock of the Golden Comb. It was thought that when the dead were interred in the barrows or great mounds still seen all over the Nordic areas of Europe, they lived on in these extensions of the Underworld.

The dead were said 'to die into the hill' which is under the domain of Gollimkambi. This belief is extremely ancient, and is encountered throughout the Celtic world where it was prevalent for countless centuries. Just as the Ancient Egyptians also believed that the sun went down into the underworld, and only after a great struggle did it emerge again the next morning bringing the new day. It is the same idea of the eternal return. The Norsemen believed that one could hear the clatter of ale-horns, and sometimes see the fires which blazed there during the night.

In an Eddic poem, the Svipdagsmal, Mimir's tree the Mimameith stretches its branches over all lands. No one knows what roots are beneath, and few can guess what will fell it. Not fire and not iron. This is the tree of Fate, it is the tree of life. On its highest branch stands the cock Vithofnir glittering like gold, and shining like lightning ever watchful.

If Vithofnir is the same bird as Gollimkambi who re-awakens the dead heroes in Valhalla each morning, then the top of the Mimameith must be in Asgard. This golden bird's watchfulness from the great height of the World Tree was the terror of the enemies of the gods. Since the cosmic tree is the origin of all life the cock is thus the protector and guardian of life, as the indicator of the presence of danger in the form of darkness, (unconsciousness) and death.

By announcing the sun the cock chases away the dark spirits of the night, and is thus a destroyer of demons. He also symbolises confidence because of the certainty with which he announces the break of day. There is indication here of the danger inherent in unconscious hubris.

A modern woman was so bound up with the minutiae of daily life I wondered if I could get beyond the fierce animus which guarded her against life. Suddenly one night she dreamed that she heard a cock crow, and she perceived a vast tree outside her house. She had seen the giant Sequoia trees of North America, and she believed the dream tree was bigger. She felt humbled in its presence.

Behind the murderous animus,[7] was the Self,[8] symbolised by the vast tree. The cock which crowed in the dream was reminiscent of Vithofnir or Gollimkambi, and the crowing announced the dawning of a new consciousness for the woman and a rebirth into life. The imprisonment by the animus which had brought her ceaseless problems and an onerous burden

21

was at last overcome. The dream envisaged that her difficult life situation was her fate, and which she had to accept. It belonged to the slow developmental process by which she was to become a conscious individual. The woman had been totally animus possessed, but the dream image brought an awakening experience with the entry of the Self into conscious life.

In Tibetan Buddhism the cock has a nefarious character. His position is at the centre of the Wheel of Life (together with the pig and the serpent) as one of the three poisons. His significance is desire, (attachment, covetousness and thirst]. There is always a secret greed or desire hidden in pride, a desire to be on top, first, the best or a longing to be the most beautiful or clever and so on.

In Europe the image is not quite the same, the cock is usually representative in image form of pride, but associated often with anger. The baleful eye and the upright ruddy coxcomb. He also signifies explosions of desire as in the Tibetan Buddhism. Anger is associated chiefly with the robin redbreast (cock robin) and the turkey cock. It is a form of angry pride or perhaps proud anger.

In Greek Mythology Leto gave birth to Apollo and Artemis, the children of her union with Zeus. A cock appeared as an accoucheur to assist in her delivery. This is how the cock came to be associated with Zeus, Leto, Apollo and Artemis the solar gods and goddesses. He often indicates the jealous pride of Leto. The golden verse of Pythagoras advised that the cock should be nourished and not sacrificed. He is consecrated to the sun and moon, both luminaries. In spite of Pythagoras' injunction the cock was assiduously sacrificed to Asklepios.

The cock as psychopompos leads the soul to the Beyond where it opens its eyes to a new light. The equivalence of a rebirth.

This quality is precisely why the cock is the bird of Hermes-Mercurius the Gods' messenger whose domain is the three levels of the cosmos, heaven, earth and hell. Associated with Apollo, Asklepios and Hermes the idea of the cock as a healer arose. Later on in Christianity, because of his association with heights and his watchfulness in times of danger, he was placed on the church spires as a weather-vane to chase away demons and jinns. He became a guardian spirit against the perils of the soul.

It was fitting that the unconscious chose the fledgling rooster as the central point of the woman scientist's dream. As a woman she was not proud or conceited, and she knew that although her work was good she could not take the credit for ownership as her researches had come from the unconscious, and by the grace of God. However her animus thought differently. He regarded himself as a proud rooster who could fly to heaven. Alas!

The dream compensated this deviation, and pointed out to her that although she was not in hubris her animus was momentarily 'caught'. The unconscious aimed to achieve the proper balance by showing her the presence of a proud animus!

In the English language there is a splendid nursery rhyme which illustrates conceit.

    'Humpty Dumpty sat on a wall
    Humpty Dumpty had a great fall
    All the King's Horses and all the King's men,
    Couldn't put Humpty together again.'

Humpty Dumpty was an egg-shaped fellow, and because of his shape he rolled off the wall as he was off balance. Here we are shown Humpty's fate all too clearly. It may be that Humpty Dumpty stems from Hump and Dump with an intrusive 't'. 'Humpt and Dumpt.' It means a short dumpy hump-shouldered person. In the nursery rhyme Humpty Dumpty was described or had the image of an egg (the fruit of the union of a cock with a hen]. In the English pantomime Mother Goose, the egg, or Humpty Dumpty became a favourite character. It is also applied to a drink composed of ale boiled with brandy. Such a powerful drink rendered the imbiber 'legless', and therefore he rolled like an egg or fell down. In any event composure was shattered, and pride dispersed. One was filled with brandy spirit and overcome. An apt description of pride. The inability to stay on the wall signifies the sureness of fate for Humpty Dumpty which lies inexorably in the wake of the proud ones.

One may speak of this inordinate self-esteem when it is exhibited in attitude or bearing. The 'proud gait' of pregnancy, a medical term for the imbalance caused by the weight of the child's body in the mother's, is also compounded by the mother-to-be's pride in the achievement of her pregnancy. It is the prerogative of the royal personages to hold the head high with the back very straight. The same proud bearing and conduct of self is found in the dancers of the corps de ballet. In all of these there is a certain rigidity, arrogance and haughtiness. These words describe exactly the meaning of 'pride' which was held in the Middle Ages.

There is also the meaning of a consciousness, of what is befitting or due to oneself or one's position. This may be a good quality, 'honest' or 'proper pride' is then spoken of. It can also be applied to misapplied feeling when we then speak of 'false pride'.

Since the end of the sixteenth century a phrase has been in common usage in the English language. It is 'to take pride in'. One hears this phrase about a good housewife, a keen gardener, a skilful sportsman, or one who takes pains with his book-keeping, hand-writing or scholarship. It indicates the presence of a high satisfaction, or elation derived from the appropriate skill or expertise. Justified certainly, but pride nevertheless. The balance has to be sought. This is why Ch'EN (modesty) No.15 Hexagramme in the ancient Chinese I Ching Oracular Book of Changes has such an excellent augury.

Sometimes pride is in a possession, a house, a name, a wife or mistress. One sees this where a man showers his wife or mistress with clothes, jewellery and luxuries, obtaining immense satisfaction in the adornment of his pride of possession. Here there is usually an anima projection on the part of the man, and in many instances it is to the inner anima that the outer gifts are unconsciously dedicated. One may perhaps perceive in such of these acts a proud or vain anima secretly at work behind the scenes.

These are personal and individual examples, but one may also speak of the young men of a country as the 'pride of its manhood'. Sometimes in speaking of a particular year which has been noted for an exceptional vintage, the number (of the year) replaces the sense of pride. One may say this of a vintage year for wine, that is '79, or a vintage car in the sense of a prestigious proud-bearing time or possession. You see how difficult it is to separate oneself from pride, and achieve a balance of justifiable pride and an excess which always leans towards a dangerous imbalance.

In pride there is also the implication of magnificence, splendour and pomp enfolded in an act of display. It has to be exhibited or seen.

Before the last Shah of Iran abdicated and had to flee for his life he gave a sumptuous, and indeed, stupendous party in conjunction with France. All the wealth of the Court, and the splendours of French creative artistry and style helped to provide a display of outstanding magnificence and opulence.

It seemed however that the contrast between the regal pomp and arid surroundings of immense poverty was particularly shocking. Sadly this overt pomp and majesty was superseded almost immediately by the annihilation of the Shah as Emperor only to be followed by his early demise.

Such words of description which come to mind for this kind of display are: impressive, spectacular, magnificent, splendid and also 'pomp and circumstance'. In all these words is a suggestion to rank above others, and finally to supersede one's own humanity, and perhaps approach the realm of the gods.

Pride as a self-regarding passion, or sentiment of self love, is associated in popular speech with several related qualities of the selfish disposition: egoism, conceit, vanity and arrogance.

Conceit as such is an exaggerated form of self satisfaction, whereas arrogance is an attitude of presumption which arouses resentment, or hatred in others. A vain person is always at pains to show off his supposed superiority to others, and is forever seeking the good opinion of the world.

Egotism is a habit of self regard affecting mind, manner and speech whereby the individual concerned becomes vastly intrusive. It is not at all difficult to spot the egoist, generally. He or she usually shoulders his way to the front of a gathering. He dislikes to listen overlong to others, but wishes to insert a comment a phrase or a monologue whenever possible. His speech is littered with 'me', 'my' and 'mine'. Sometimes however, there is a concealed but monumental pride in the apparently modest, or abjectly humble person who diffidently remains at the back, and by refusing to participate eventually draws all attention to himself.

Pride mirrors an habitual self isolation or conscious independence. It encompasses a perversity of will often indifferent to the opinions and favours of others. Frequently it tends to repudiate ideas of obligations, and unlike vanity generally does not engage in competition with others. Sometimes the most insidious pride may be connected with independence or equality, and 'is frequently a law unto itself living on the deference and administrations of others, but singularly indifferent to either blame or praise. One of the most despicable features of pride is the indifference to the sufferings of others'.[9]

In analysis it is difficult to overcome pride, moral censure is helpless, and only scorn or ridicule can remove it.

THE HIGH MINDED MAN OF ARISTOTLE

In the famous characterisation of the high minded man, Aristotle[10] explains that he is not only worthy of great things, but that he holds himself worthy of them.

His estimate of his own merits is independent of the verdict of others. If he holds himself to be worthy of great things when actually unworthy of them he is vain, while he who underestimates his own worth is mean-spirited. High mindedness then is a mean between vanity and want of spirit. It is in fact a lofty type of pride which is its own star. It is without the sense of duty or moral obligation. Its motive is honour, and it owes nothing to the instinctive sense of right.

External honour is the best thing that the world can give to the high minded man. He is glad to confer a benefit, but ashamed to receive one. If he does receive a benefit he will wipe it out by doing a greater. He will remember those whom he has benefited, but not those by whom he has been benefited. He will be in want of no one, and he will serve any readily. He will be proud to the great and prosperous, and lenient towards the lowly. He will not aim at the common objects of ambition, only for great honour or deeds will he strive. He will be open in friendship and hatred, disdaining timid concealment, contemptuously straightforward, really truthful but reserved and ironical towards the common people.

Indifferent to the praise and censure of others he will bear no malice and be no gossip.

On the whole vanity is better than mean-spiritedness which is to be condemned for its lack of energy.

Aristotle condemned calculated insolence as a form of pride.[11] 'Butcher Insolence has its roots in want of reverence, and want to self knowledge, and is the expression of a self-centred will recognising no power outside itself, and knowing no law but its own impulses. This ignorance in the Greek tragedy is the deepest source of moral evil.'

THE HIGH MINDED WOMAN

A modern woman in her late middle age may be described as a high minded woman. She is of excellent character, and is well known for her unfailing sense of fair play and justice. She does not gossip, and through the years has come to represent decency and fair play in her community. She has a fair minded animus.

She lives by the pen, and her works as an author extol the virtues by which she lives. She detests everything that is mean minded or spiritually impoverished.

Over a period of years it has come to my notice that although she is unduly proud of her right thinking and fair mindedness, she is disinclined to accept any form of criticism, be it quite mild. Any such criticism must always be explored at once, analysed and if possible annihilated. She has two great passions, her aforementioned sense of justice and the 'roman policier', the thriller.

Some time ago a friend with whom she was dining was late, and did not explain adequately the reason for her delay, nor did she apologise sufficiently. This ruined the dinner for the high minded lady.

She was alone in a huge city, it was night time, and it seemed to be foggy. The street lights were hazy in the fog, and she was unsure of her exact location. She came to a central place, and became aware that a figure was observing her closely. It was the figure of a man, and as she turned and moved away she saw out of the corner of her eye that he had followed her 'like a shadow'. Wherever she went he was there. He was in her words sleazy, and down-at-heel, and he looked dangerous. She felt afraid in the dream. Suddenly she knew that he was a private detective. This gave her a shock and she awakened at once.

In previous dreams a similar male character had appeared with nondescript clothes, a seedy air of decrepitude and a certain malevolence.

This strange rather frightening figure in the shabby clothes was the antithesis of her high minded animus. The dream had it seemed resulted from the emotion engendered by the real or imagined insolence of her friend. She herself was never insolent to others, and she could not abide it when she was subjected to it.

Although the mysterious figure was not insolent he was simply present, and there. Moreover he followed her. A detective who is said to be a private one is usually hired by someone to track down a criminal or uncover a crime. In any event it is quite in order to state that the person observed is under suspicion.

She described the haunting quality of the city in fog as similar to that described in some Charles Dickens books, and the character reminded her of those in his novels.

The woman objected strongly to those who proffered opinions which did not tally with her own. She was unwilling to accept criticism of her dislikes, and secretly she believed that she was always right.

The analytical task was to enlarge her ego-consciousness by integrating the dark side of her personality. It was a monumental task as it is for all women. This strange Luciferian figure in her dreams which frightened her, reminds one, of Jung's description of Hermes Mercurius the god of the alchemists. Mercurius as the prima materia appears in many forms. This dream revealed the beginning of the individuation process,[13] for Mercurius is the beginning of the process, the process itself and the goal.

He is a mediator like Hermes, and both a 'Servator and a Salvator.'

This woman was afraid of the follower, but he was also a leader, for Hermes is the great psychopompos. She secretly denigrated the figure as shabby, seedy, seamy and down-at-heel. Hermes is the god of the under-world, and he runs with all. He represents the archetypal image of the collective unconscious, and therefore is all things.

My analysand was altogether too high up, too proud and because of her pride, insolent – of which moral sin she was quite unconscious. The projection was therefore always found outside. Others were then it seemed insolent to her. She was on the one side too light, seized by a moralising Christian animus, but the dark and devilish side lived a secret life of its own, unhindered by reproaches, and uninhibited by moral censure because unknown. The only outlet possible was in the attraction to the detective stories in which she indulged herself, and in the bouts of punishing cruelty which she inflicted upon her friends and colleagues for real or supposedly real misdeeds against her person.

She had to learn to suffer for the conscious awareness of her failure in psychic relatedness. She had to realise that Hermes is both 'fair and unfair', 'just and unjust'.

Arrogant pride is described as hubris. It means an awesome or over-weening arrogance of pride in oneself. In Greek it means both 'pride' and 'lechery'. Both words are associated with penile erection. Hubris was said to be the sin of Lucifer, and the phrase 'Luciferian pride' means arrogant pride, that was the malady which beset the high minded woman, for indeed she was at base an ill woman, her soul was ill. She had an arrogant pride in perfection, and there was undoubtedly a strong masculine overtone, unbecoming to a woman.

Patriarchal gods particularly punished hubris, especially when the sin occurred in a lesser being, a mortal or a demi-god.

The ancient feast of the original Hubristika of Greece was an Argive Feast,[14] Lederer: a 'Feast of lechery' featuring orgies of transvestism. Men would castrate themselves during the feast, and throw their genitals into the gardens of women who had to provide them with clothes. By assuming the womens' tunics and veils they believed they donned the magic power of women. Christianity later was to condemn all forms of transvestism because of its implication that men acquired power through connection with women, whether it was a sexual connection or a masquerade. Not only was it an encroachment into the feminine realm but it was also a crime against the principle of masculinity. The sin was therefore twofold.

Many years ago when I worked as a dermatologist at one of the foremost teaching hospitals in London, I was responsible over a long period for the dermatological therapies required by a great many transvestites. In the course of endocrine treatment to encourage the growth of secondary sexual characteristics upon their bodies they developed skin problems of various kinds.

I came to know a number of these men fairly well, and I found that they flaunted their newly found femininity with an apparent and overt arrogance, but which was in fact unconscious. The voice, the gesture, the clothes and the demeanour were all rather flamboyant. Alas many paid a tragic price for their hubris, since a number died young from neoplasia due to hormonal therapy.

From the word hubrizein, which means lecherous behaviour, came the Roman word hybrid describing a child of a Roman father and a foreign mother. According to the old matrilineal law of inheritance, it was dictated that a child was a slave or a freeman according to the status of the mother, slave or free. The father's status was irrelevant. Similarly amongst Jews, in the case of mixed marriages or hybridisation a child of a Jewish mother was a Jew, but a Gentile if only the father was Jewish.[15] Ochs.

PRIDE IN THE OLD TESTAMENT

In the Old Testament, pride is condemned as self exaltation manifested by the wicked and foolish exacting swift retribution.

'For the day of the Lord of Hosts shall be upon every one that is proud and lofty, and upon every one that is lifted up, and he shall be brought low'.[16]

'Pride goeth before destruction and a haughty spirit before a fall.'[17] 'Thus saith the Lord. After this manner will I mar the pride of Judah, and the great pride of Jerusalem.'[18]

The punishment for pride lies in downfall, humiliation and even death.

The evil of pride is revealed in the character of certain outstanding individuals, to name a few, Absolom, Joab and Saul. But perhaps it was in the life of Nebuchadnezzar that the portrayal of pride is clearly defined.

NEBUCHADNEZZER, THE KING OF BABYLON

In the 7th century before the Christian era, King Nabu-kudurri-usur (Nebuchadnezzar II) was the great King of Babylon, he was the King of Kings, a title held by the last monarch of Ethiopia, King Haile Salassie.

Nebuchadnezzar ruled over the kings of all the vassal states under the dominion of the central state. In the second year of his reign, he had conquered the whole of Mesopotamia and Egypt. He had then in his possession the whole known world.

Roux[19] quotes the following words relating to Nebuchadnezzar's conquest of the Lebanon whereupon he acquired an inexhaustible source of timber. The pride of achievement is self evident. 'I made that country happy by eradicating its enemies everywhere. All its scattered inhabitants I led back to their settlements. I achieved what no former King had done. I cut through steep mountains, I split rocks, opened passages and I constructed a straight road for the (transport of the) cedars. I made the inhabitants of Lebanon live in safety together and let nobody disturb them.' All of this is true, and one senses the pride in achievement.

It was after this that it is believed that overwhelming dreams came to him. He had two, the first dream slipped away at the moment he awoke. He realised that the dream had great power, and consequently he was very distressed when he realised that he had not been able to grasp it before it eluded him. He called up his advisors who included magicians, astrologers and finally Chaldeans, those remarkable magicians and wise men of Ur.

The King told them to make the dream known to him. This suggestion by the King to his advisors reveals the pride behind it. However, he declared that if they did not, he would cut them to pieces and cast them upon the dunghill. If on the contrary they complied with his request he would then bestow riches.

The wise men were truly so, and the Chaldeans explained to the King that no man on earth could do this for the King. Moreover, they informed him that no ruler should ever make such a request to his astrologers and magicians. He was asking them to undertake the impossible and read the mind of deity, since dreams are messages from God. At the time of Nebuchadnezzar, Adad the son of the supreme god Anu was the Lord of heaven and hell. He was this characterised as the god of lightning and storm. It was this god who was to be considered.

The Chaldeans explained to the King that only the gods whose dwelling in not with the flesh could perform such a task which he required of them. This wisdom was to fall on foolish ears. The King did not listen. It reveals to us precisely the folly inherent in those caught in pride. A folly of which the victim is usually unaware. Nebuchadnezzar caught in hubris set himself as high or higher than the gods.

The King did not accept their suggestions and commanded that all the astrologers, advisors and magicians should be destroyed at once. Not included among the wise men, but confined to the dunghill nevertheless, was Daniel. He was a young Hebrew captive connected with the royal family, and already, albeit young in years, noted for his sagacity, profound prudence, learning and religious constancy. Moreover Daniel had a deep understanding of dreams. Daniel was sometimes known as Belteshazzar, which means the Lord's leader. The name was given to him by the prince of Nebuchadnezzar's eunuchs.[20]

When Arioch, the captain of the King's guard, came for him, Daniel begged to be granted an audience with the King. To support his request he boldly suggested that he would give an interpretation of the dream, which Nebuchadnezzar had not been able to seize before it escaped him. Daniel meanwhile consulted with his friends, and then asked God to reveal the secret of Nebuchadnezzar's dream.

That night he was blessed, and by the grace of God the secret was revealed to Daniel in a night vision. He thanked God and went to see the King. This is what he said to him.

'There is a god in heaven that reveals secrets and maketh them known to the King Nebuchadnezzar what shall be in latter days.'

He then described his own vision sent to him in the night. 'It was of an immense image of terrible form. The head was of fine gold, the breast and arms of silver and his belly and thighs of brass. His legs were of iron, and his feet were part iron and part clay. Then a stone was cut out without hands, which smote the image upon his feet that were of iron and clay, everything was broken up and blown away by the wind like summer chaff. The stone that smote the image became a great mountain and filled the whole earth.'

Daniel interpreted the vision for the King in the following way. He told him that the head of fine gold was his own person. He explained the destruction as the downfall of the kingdom which was to come in future years. He described the meaning in the stone which smote the image as the beginning of a Kingdom which God would set up, which would stand for ever and which arose from the eternal stone, which in the vision filled the whole earth.

The vision clearly indicates the utter destruction of the King and all that he commanded under his power. He had risen too high, he had forgotten his human roots and he was caught in hubris and believed himself to be above God.

THE HEAD AS SYMBOL

Arrogance is signified by an uplifted chin and a proud carriage of the head. Since the head plays such an important part in the sin of pride it is useful to examine the symbolism of this part of the body.

What does the head enfold as symbol? It represents the residence of the mind, the intellect and reason. It is the means by which an individual human or animal is recognised. It is the receptacle for the senses permitting orientation to both the outer and inner world of objective psyche.

It represents authority, knowledge, spirituality and leadership as both a chief and patron. Anciently, particularly amongst the Celtic tribes, whom the Romans believed to be the bravest of the brave, warriors' heads were believed to have apotropaic qualities. It was for this reason the head was cut off and either preserved or carried on the dagger belt. Generally captured heads were offered to the divinity in gratitude for courage and preservation of life.

In Daniel's vision of the Nebuchadnezzar dream the head was of fine gold.

For a moment let us examine 'gold'.

GOLD AS SYMBOL

It is the most precious metal and has the highest virtue. In Chinese the character 'Kin' represents both gold and metal. It has the brilliance of light, and it is said in India that gold is the mineral light. In certain mythology the flesh of the gods is said to be gold (e.g. Pharoahs), always the ikons of Buddha are of gold signifying absolute perfection. The same thing is found in Byzantine ikons, which are said to reflect the celestial light. A widespread and extremely ancient belief is that gold is born in the earth. The primitive Chinese character 'Kin' which I have mentioned is evocative of underground gold nuggets.

KIN OR JIN

Three united lines of a triangle suggests amalgamation.

Two nuggets of gold in the earth.

Gold or Metal.

Gold therefore would be the product of the slow gestation of an embryo or its transformation. It is the perfection of vulgar metals.

The Chinese symbolic colour for gold is white the colour of the earth, not yellow. Transmutation therefore is a redemption.

Golden light is generally the symbol of consciousness, it is essentially 'Yang' of the Chinese. Amongst the Aztecs gold was associated with the new skin which covered the earth in Spring time after the seasonal rains. That was the god Xipe-Totec the 'Our Lord the Flayed' associated with skin diseases and the symbol par excellence of rebirth. He was always known as 'The Golden One'.

Finally the is the mythical serpent of the Ural Mountains who was called the 'Great Earth Serpent' or the 'Great Rearer'. But his other name was Master of the Gold. It usually appeared as a crowned golden serpent, sometimes it was a brown-skinned man with black eyes and hair, clothed in yellow. It was said that wherever he passed gold was deposited, and that if he was angry he would take it elsewhere. Everything freezes on the passage of his being, even the fire, except in winter when he permits a little warmth and snow falls.

This association of the chthonian nature of gold illustrates a very widely held and widespread belief, accordingly gold, the precious metal par excellence constitutes the most intimate secret of the earth.

Of all the metals it is the most esoteric because of its purity and resistance to deterioration.

Gold which stands for the highest value can also produce the most immense pride, and today in our materialist society it is given pride of place. Sadly today the base and the knowledge are confused. Also today the rational conscious intellect has taken pride of place divorcing us from our instinctual feeling life. With such consequences as cannot yet be rightly comprehended we worship a metaphorical 'golden head', and the Self, the archetype of wholeness is forgotten. The world of the gods in man's consciousness no longer holds pride of place.

The cult of the god Hermes, divine messenger of commerce and thieves in ancient Greece, created an awareness of the ambivalence of gold, represented by his two faces. This was a symbol of the mysteries hidden from the eyes of common consciousness. The priests hid the gold, symbol of the light, from the profane, as such secret knowledge was not for everyone. Today we know that this secret knowledge is self-knowledge – the 'inner gold'.

Now after this long diversion we will return again to Nebuchadnezzar. Daniel's vision was interpreted by him for the King and then he was appointed as the King's magician-priest. Nebuchadnezzar thought himself to be very great indeed, time passed and then he had a second dream. It was a dream typical of those who climbed too high. He dreamed of an enormous tree growing up to heaven and casting a shadow over the whole earth. (remember the King had conquered the whole known world).

But then a watcher and holy one from heaven ordered the tree to be hewn down, its branches cut off and its leaves shaken so that only the stump remained. That he should live with the beasts and his human heart be taken from him, and a beast's heart be given to him.

Only Daniel proved to be adequate and courageous enough to interpret this immense dream. He wanted the King to repent of his pride, his avarice and injustice, otherwise the dream would come true.

Again the King did not heed. He ruled over all the lands, and was proud of his great powers. Then a voice from heaven cursed him and repeated the prophecy of the dream. There was no escape, and no possibility of salvation. It all happened as foretold, Nebuchadnezzar was doomed. Jung[21] 'He was cast out to the beasts and became like an animal himself. He ate grass as the oxen and his body was wet with the dew of heaven, his hair grew long like eagles' feathers and his nails like birds' claws. He was turned back into a primitive man and all his conscious reason was taken away because he had misused it. He regressed back even further than the primitive and became completely inhuman. He was Humbaba[22] the monster himself.' All this symbolised a complete regressive degeneration of a man who has over-reached himself.

Such a dream that came to King Nebuchadnezzar was a compensatory one. It was indicative that something had gone wrong, the unconscious had turned against him. He was at variance with the unconscious condition. He had succumbed to his powerful ambition, and was entrapped in hubris. So he had to fall, and he did by a regression to a non-human state. Such a fate was fitting because he had long ago thrown off his human condition, and was walking in the realm of the gods. The gods however are jealous gods and they are quick to observe and punish hubris. Punishment is never slow in coming if warning dreams are ignored or rejected.

Hubris as noted in its original Greek meaning of the word, implies wanton violence arising from the pride of strength, or passion. Included in the meaning are riotousness, licentiousness and insolence. There was in Nebuchadnezzar's personality a wanton violence in his passion for power which became interwoven with his pride.

A modern man had committed murder because he wanted the money which his colleague had earned and saved over many years. In their youth the two men had been involved in a sordid business which had brought immense profit. The murderer was impecunious, the colleague was not, and so therefore the latter was a rich man. In the prison cell the murderer had a dream. It was this. He was swinging on a vast swing which spanned the high heavens, and he was delirious with the sensation of a kind of god-like power which he held over the earth below him as he swung to and fro and beneath the planets in the vast dome of the stellar domain.

The murderer had lost his humaness and had entered the realm of the gods where it seemed he was to swing for all eternity, and yet was still in life. This was the tragic fate of this man who was invidious, a thief and a murderer – possessed by the dark side of deity. His hubris brought him to the prison cell where his physical body would remain for the rest of his days.

THE WOMAN WITH THE CRIMINAL ANIMUS

A woman in her late middle age, dreamed as a young woman some forty years or more before, that she observed a swelling appear in the earthen floor of the room in which she was seated. The swelling began to shake and

33

pulsate and suddenly in ruptured with the emergence of a human head, the face of which she described as being indescribably evil.

In the years which followed she was to become a ruthless domineering and brutal woman. Her children and grandchildren were to suffer the consequences of her personality. One of the chief aspects of her life was that she took enormous risks and entered into areas fraught with danger. She met men who lived in the criminal underworld, and seemingly without thought entered into unsavoury liaisons.

It was in fact the animus which led her into these dangerous areas. He does this frequently leading women into alliances which destroy. There is a violent hubris engendered in such animi. In the case of the woman he had a kind of crazy bravura, a devil-may-care attitude which led her to take grave risks in the dark areas of sexuality. The woman believed herself to be unassailable, and thought she could go anywhere, do anything and take innumerable and singular risks. As a master of the underworld the animus led her to believe she was a goddess. Women with a certain type of father complex are prone to this developmental attitude.

With her the feminine was repressed, and she was no longer human in her attitude. I was reminded of the great primitive goddess, Coatlicue of Mexico, and the Indian Kali. Zimmer[23] describes the great temple to Kali, and the immense festival held in the spring time to promote the refecundation of nature. He described the place as the bloodiest temple on earth, it was a kind of slaughterhouse, for the goddess was due the life blood of thousands of living creatures. This was the 'hideous' aspect of the goddess. But in her positive and non-terrible aspect Kali is a spiritual figure that for freedom and independence has no equal in the West. On her higher level stands the 'White Tara' symbolising the highest form of spiritual transformation through womanhood.

The fact that the woman somewhere considered herself to be a goddess was a compensation. It was through her eventual understanding of the spiritual side of the feminine that a transformation was possible.

PRIDE AND THE CHRISTIAN ETHIC

In his first letter to the church at Corinth, Saint Paul[24] advises that love is always patient and kind, and free from arrogance and self conceit. In the New Testament, the conception of love in its supreme revelation of Christ's humanity opened the way to the understanding of the moral defectiveness of pride. The ethical nature of Christianity shows a change in the highest Greek thought in its evaluation of those virtues which play such an important rôle in the life of Christ, meekness, humility and tolerance.

It is precisely in the human character of Jesus that a new criterion of pride is found. For Him the soul of the individual was endowed with an intrinsic and eternal worth. When this is accepted, Christ's conception of the brotherhood of mankind invests the needs and rights of one's neighbour with a new dignity; thereafter His warnings against self assertion, self-advertisement and egocentricity become completely understandable in the light of this profound concept. Pride is a complete contradiction of the Christian idea of unselfishness, and stands condemned by the general spirit of Christian ethic.

Saint Augustine[25] defined the unpardonable sin of pride as a state of mind consisting of 'a desperate and impious obstination in sin, with a proud refusal to humble oneself before God'. In his analysis of the causes of sin he linked 'superbia' (pride) with 'voluptas' and 'curiositas'.

Likewise Thomas Aquinas[26] also regarded pride as a mortal sin, but he believed it was the first and most serious of all sins. The first because every kind of sin springs from it, and the most serious because it involves non-subjection to God. It is of course the most difficult sin to avoid because it feeds on one's virtuous side so that in the last analysis one may become proud of one's humility. Thomas Aquinas understood pride to evolve because there was an essential defect of love from which all moral evil ensued.

THE DIVINE COMEDY

The Divine Comedy by Dante is a mine of information concerning the darkness of the human soul, and in particular is a praiseworthy discourse on the deadly sins. Dante Alighieri was born in 1265 in Florence of the minor nobility.

Because of political unrest he was forced to leave Florence and go into exile. For the rest of his life he was a wanderer. He lectured, he explained his ideas and he produced minor works. Then out of his sorrow, his studies, his dissatisfaction with political life, his observation of his peers and the world at large came his poem The Divine Commedia, arguably the greatest poem of the Middle Ages. This poem was completed later in life in Ravenna where he took asylum. He died with great honours in 1321.

In this poem Dante deals with the mortal sins, the sinners who commit them, and the way in which they expiated them. For a deeper understanding of the sins, and of their meaning this poem is invaluable. It is as relevant today as it was 700 years ago.

Perhaps nowhere is danger inherent in the sin of pride so clearly portrayed as in Dante's Divine Comedy. Like Saint Augustine and Thomas Aquinas before him, Dante gave Pride the first place amongst the seven deadly sins. On the first terrace of Purgatory[27] Dante meets with those who represent the pride of race, the pride of achievement, and the pride of dominion. They are depicted weighted down with heavy weights, whilst reciting the Lord's Prayer for both themselves and for those they have left behind.

As they leave the Souls of the Proud, Virgil the Leader of Dante in the Purgatory calls the attention of the Pilgrim to a series of carvings in the bed of rock beneath their feet. These are examples of the vice of Pride, of the haughty who have been brought low. Those who are exalted in their self esteem, and suffused with hubris do not need to wait long since retribution is always swift, and comes with a catastrophic suddenness.

Amongst those whose images were committed to the bedrock were Satan, Briareus, Nimrod and Niobe. It is worth while exploring the fate of the above, all alas caught in arrogant pride. Leaving Satan until the last, 'Briareus pierced through by the celestial thunderbolt heavy upon the ground was frozen to death'.[28]

Briareus or Agaeon in Greek myth was one of the three hundred-armed, fifty-headed sons of Ouranos (Heaven) and Gaia (Earth). Because of their strength, Zeus called for his assistance when the Titans attacked Olympus. When the Titans were defeated and thrown into Tartarus, Briareus and his brothers were detailed to guard them. Other accounts make him the opponent of Zeus and one of the assailants at Olympus who after his defeat was buried under Mount Etna. The multi-headed, and multi-limbed creatures were the Hecatoncheires, representing the gigantic forces of nature which appear in earthquakes and other convulsions of nature. They are ever ready to erupt, but must be limited and confined for order to be restored.

Nimrod,[29] as the mighty hunter of the Lord,[30] that is a copy of the Lord of the Hunt whom the Greeks called Orion, and the Canaanites Baal-Hadad. In the poem it is said 'I saw the mighty Nimrod by his tower standing there, stunned and gazing at the men who shared in Shinar, his bold fantasy.'

Nimrod (Orion) the son of Poseidon lived with Artemis, for he like her was also a mighty hunter. This displeased her brother Apollo, and one day when Orion was swimming in the sea, Apollo challenged his sister to shoot a black object bobbing about in the sea with her bow and arrow.

Artemis immediately took aim and hit it squarely, thus killing her lover Orion. In her grief Artemis placed Orion in the stars. One simply cannot place oneself upon an equal footing with the gods without retribution. The gods are jealous of their divinity. Apollo it would seem resented and was jealous of his sister's companionship with Orion. He knew the prowess of his sister as a hunter, and so he set the trap. Orion had usurped his place in his sister's affection, and had risen too high.

In the Old Testament there is a reference to Nimrod.[31] Assyria was called the land of Nimrod. Like all Assyrians he was a mighty hunter. He built the city of Ninevah and Sumer together with other cities. The beginning of Nimrod's kingdom was Babel in the land of Shinar. Babel being Babylon, and Shinar is Babylonia. The hubris which would fill the breast of Nimrod as he gazed at his vast and indeed immense achievements, would impart a certain godliness, so his downfall like Nebuchadnezzar was already in-potentia.

In the poem it is said of Niobe, [32] 'Oh Niobe I saw your grieving eyes, they wept from your carved image on the road, between your seven and seven children slain.'

Niobe was the Queen of Thebes and had much to be proud of. Her husband was a great lyre player. He excelled at this, and his music was so sweet that the very stones joined themselves to make the great palace at Thebes. Niobe's father Tantalus ruled over a mighty realm. Moreover, she had fourteen beautiful children, seven boys and seven girls. She did however boast of her supreme happiness, and this was to pave the way for her destruction.

When the sorceress Manto bade the populace to honour Leto and her divine twins, Apollo and Artemis, Niobe appeared dressed in a gown of golden thread. She had likened herself to Apollo himself by adopting a garb of the colour of the sun. Her radiance was equal to that of the god, but she was angry and refused to honour Leto and the divine pair. She enquired of the surrounding throng, 'Why do you set up altars to Leto and not to me?[33] Is not my father Tantalus the only mortal who ever ate at the board of Zeus? My mother Dione is a sister to the Pleiades. My father's father is Zeus himself.' Here clearly is hubris.

As a mortal, she had allied herself to the divine brother and sister, whose father likewise was Zeus. Her words constitute a statement of her arrogant pride. Meanwhile on Delos, Leto informed her children of her disdain for insolent mortals, and beseeched them to preserve her holy altars. They obeyed at once. They found the seven sons of Niobe participating in practice races to improve their horsemanship. The eldest was struck in the heart by an arrow, and soon all his brothers like him had fallen to their deaths.

Niobe did not want to believe that the immortals had so much power. Even then she was reluctant to bow her own proud head. Reduced to grief and sadness she stood with her seven daughters by her seven fallen sons. At the sight of her daughters she thought, 'I still have them.'

At the moment she saw all her daughters fall to their deaths as had their brothers. As she sat in stillness with the dead she turned to stone.

Niobe challenged and disdained the gods. She became in her mind the equal, and then the superior of Leto. For that act of hubristic insanity she paid the greatest price.

From the events which befell these souls in Purgatory it can be seen without the slightest shadow of a doubt that pride really does 'come before a fall'. The mighty are reduced. The crime is to go against or set oneself above a god. In psychological terms it is the meting out of a dire punishment for hubris engendered by ignorance or of identification with the Self. The balance of the opposites is disturbed. The mantle of deity, adorned so lightly and without a consciousness of wrong-doing must be discarded for a human attitude – a modesty of place. Otherwise, in either instance, disaster overtakes a mortal.

In life one can see sometimes all too clearly, how soon the recipient of an accolade an honour or a prize, falls victim to a catastrophe. Usually there is an initial faltering, a stumble or an error of judgment, which marks the début of unconscious possession not usually perceived by the subject. The falter or the error or judgment must be seen as an endeavour to restore equilibrium.

THE MYTH OF LUCIFER

To return to the poem of Dante. It is said of Satan[34] 'I saw on one side, him who was supposed to be the noblest creature of creation, plunge swift as lightning from the height of Heaven'

Satan or Lucifer, was God's first born, the son, who was the sun of the morning, the beautiful shining one who defied God. He set himself up as God's equal, he tried to usurp him, and was cast into Hell-fire for it. Satan or Lucifer was God's beloved son.

There is only one reference in the Old Testament[35] to Lucifer:

'How art thou fallen from heaven
O Lucifer son of the morning.
For thou has said in thine heart,
I will ascend to heaven. I will
exalt my throne above the stars
of God. I will sit upon the mount
of the congregation in the sides of
the north. I will ascend above
the heights of the clouds.
I will be like the most High'.

In the English language there still is in usage (although now used rarely) the saying 'as proud as Lucifer'.

Lucifer is the name for the planet Venus, when it appears in the sky as the morning star, just before sunrise. Lucifer means 'Light bringer'. The morning star has always been regarded as a god who announced the daily birth of the sun. The Canaanites called him Shaher. The Jewish morning service called Shaharit, still commemorates him.[36] The morning star had a twin brother, the evening star Shalem who announced the daily death of the sun, and spoke to him the Word of Peace, 'Shalom' (Hebrew). In Arabic the word Salaam has the same meaning. Jerusalem means the House of Shalem,[37] and the two gods were worshipped there.

Shaher and Shalem were the same as the Dioscuri of Greek myth, the Heavenly Twins, Castor and Pollux, born from the World Egg of Leda. In Persian sun worship they were represented as the two torch bearers, one whose torch pointed upwards, and the other downwards. The stars it seems were pointers to the sun, and acted as markers to its diurnal progress.

It is believed that Shaher and Shalem were the children of Asherah. In extreme ancient times, an asherah was a post or sometimes a tree, and was symbolic of the goddess of nature. In matriarchal times, she embodied the great goddess mother Asherah in Canaanite worship, later in Hebrew religious worship she was the companion of Jahweh.[38] As the companion of the Hebrew god she was believed to be the womb of the world.

In a Canaanite myth the morning star covered the glory of the sun god himself, and tried, it is said to usurp his throne. He was however defeated, and cast down from heaven in a bolt of lightning, into the abyss or the pit.

The pit was the same as Helel, or Asherah, the god's own mother, or bride, and his descent as a lightning serpent into the pit represented the fertilisation of the abyss by masculine fire from heaven. Lucifer, whose name means the bringer of light, embodies a power to illuminate and create increased consciousness. By its very nature however it also contains the power, not only to create, but to destroy, and the descent signifies initially the enveloping darkness of the unconscious.

Frequently a creative individual may suffer unaccountably a sudden alarming and persistent depression, which appears superficially to be without causal effect. Often, just as suddenly as it appeared, it disappears to be replaced by a creative work on the part of the individual. The depression is in these cases the precursor of the creative effort. At the time it signifies the engulfing (and dangerous) darkness of the pit, the unconscious world.

To return to the descent of Lucifer into the pit of Helel or Asherah. It signifies an hieros-gamos, a sacred union. The light bringer challenged the supreme solar god by seeking favours of the mother.

The word hubris as has been noted contains ideas of arrogant pride, and also sexual passion. It was the aim of the sacred kings to be espoused to the goddess to become one with supreme deity. The image of Lucifer appears to have become merged with Satan, the Hebrew name for the immortal serpent Sata father of lightning. In Jesus's[39] own words he states 'I beheld Satan as lightning fell from Heaven'.

In his letter to the Ephesians, Saint Paul[40] mentions the fact that 'the prince of power of the Air was linked to the children of disobedience'. Lucifer as the prince of the morning, God's most beautiful angel was thrown out of heaven with his followers because he wished to wrest the throne from God. He put himself not simply as high as God, but higher because he believed that he could displace, overthrow and demote Him. It is understandable that God's displeasure was incurred. The essence of disobedience is for ego-consciousness as a directed will to refuse to submit to a higher authority.

Lucifer as the morning star means Christ as well as the Devil. Thus he shares the attributes of both. As does the figure of Mercurius Duplex standing behind them, so the enigmatic Lucifer has qualities and attributes of each. Christ[41] says of himself, 'I am the root and offspring of David, the bright and morning star.' Lucifer as God's most beautiful angel is 'God's opposing will.' He is a shadowy figure, but suffused with inner light.

As Jung says[42] 'Without this will there would have been no creation, and no work of salvation either. The shadow and the opposing will are the necessary conditions for all actualisation. An object that has no will of its own, and capable if need be of opposing its creator, and with no qualities other than its creator's has no independent existence, and is incapable of ethical decision.'

Many years ago a young girl of ten or eleven years was brought to me. She was highly intelligent and very lovely to look at. She was totally under the domination of her mother, a beautiful and imperious woman. The mother recognising her daughter's intelligence and beauty set about finding the best music teachers, dancing instructors and educationalists.

The child became my patient before I became an analyst, and for a long time I did not perceive the real problem.

Undoubtedly the ambitious and authoritarian mother loved her child and the child in return was devoted to her mother, and above all wished to please her. At about the age of ten years the girl was beset by an obsessive-compulsive disorder. Contained in it was a complex ritualisation of repetitive patterns of behaviour. The trigger which set off the ritual behaviour was an exceedingly negative thought directed towards the mother.

The compulsive obsessive behaviour lasted for two years. During that time she was able to examine aspects of her own behaviour and that of members of her family. Slowly it came to me that this little girl had a secret; it was a monumental desire to succeed in everything, to be the best in everything. However the situation clarified, and it became apparent that the Luciferian hubris belonged not to her, but the mother.

It was not possible to discuss the nature of my thoughts with either the child or her mother. The problem of evil was certainly not a subject for discussion in the doctor's consulting room in those days, nor may I add is it today.

Standing behind the obsessive-compulsive personality one finds the hubris, often medically termed today as malignant narcissism, which simply means monumental overwhelming pride. Since such pride is at the root of evil it is not at all difficult to understand why such great ecclesiastical minds such as Saint Augustine and Thomas Aquinas proclaimed pride to be the first among the sins. Often the individual is part of a familial participation mystique, and there may be 'une folie a deux', or 'trois' as the case may be. Also circumspection is required when cases of apparent excessive obsequious humility present, as was encountered in the character of Uriah Heep.[43]

As Jung has indicated, it was Lucifer who understood the divine will struggling to create the world, and who carried that out most faithfully. For by rebelling against God, he became the active principle of a creation which opposed to God a counter-will of its own.

The young girl with the ambitious mother had her own will, to oppose her mother, usurp her and overcome her. She was then forced to face two opposing wills in herself, to please, and then to anger her mother. This was the conflict. In this severe phobia the rituals emanated to keep the hideous thoughts away, because they were too terrible to bear for the obedient child. Until the day came when the thought was faced, and the illness eventually passed away as the child began to suffer consciously.

At no time was evil discussed, but my own deliberately unrevealed consciousness of the situation acted as a lodestar.

Scott Peck[44] in an excellent work surveys this problem of evil from the aspect of serious obsessive-compulsive disorders.

In a letter to Victor White on the question of evil, Jung[45] said, 'In practice you say nothing when you hold that in an evil deed, is a small God; there is a big Evil and a little bit of Good. In practice you just cannot deny the reality of Evil. On the meta-physical plane you are free to declare what we call 'substantially evil,' and is in metaphysical reality a small Good. But such a statement does not make sense to me. You call God the the Lord over Evil, but if the latter is not real he is Lord over nothing: not even over Good because He is Himself, as the Summum Bonum that has created only good things and which have however a marked tendency to go wrong. Nor does evil or corruption derive from man since the serpent is prior to him – whence evil?' Jung continues, 'The necessary answer is: Metaphysically there is no Evil at all; it is only in man's world and it stems from man. This statement however contradicts the fact that paradise was not made by man, nor did he make the serpent. If ever God's most beautiful angel Lucifer desires to be corrupt, his nature must show a considerable defect of moral qualities, like Yahweh who insists jealously on morality and is himself unjust. No wonder that his creation has a yellow streak.

Does the doctrine of the church admit Yahweh's moral defects? If so Lucifer merely portrays his creator, Yahweh's immoral behaviour rests on biblical facts. A morally dubious creator cannot be expected to produce a perfectly good world not even perfectly good angels.'

He continues, 'On a practical level, the privatio boni doctrine is morally dangerous, because it belittles and irrealises Evil, and thereby weakens the Good because it deprives it of its necessary opposite, and there is no white without black, no warm without cold, no truth without error, no light without darkness. If Evil is an illusion, Good is a necessary illusory too. That is the reason why I hold that the privatio boni is illogical, irrational and even a nonsense. The moral opposites are an epistemiological necessity, and when hypostatised they produce an amoral Yahweh, and a Lucifer, a Serpent and Sinful Man and a suffering Creation.'

What is the meaning of such a pride as Lucifer's? Passion is apt to raise a human being above himself. The raising up causes him to be removed from his earthliness, he rises above his place on earth, and as a consequence he rises above his mortality, he becomes godlike. We see this time and again with those who have a huge success in life, and also those with minor degrees of achievement.

On a minor scale I looked after a man who won a fortune in a lottery. I met him when he was twenty-nine years old, when he came under my care. I at the same time was twenty-seven years old. He was dying when he was admitted to hospital and did so within a few days. He and I sat together in those last days, and he told me that when the fortune fell into his hands at twenty-seven years of age he began 'to fly', that is what he said. He bought a house, cars and a yacht. He gave parties and he drank and drank and drank. In two years he had irreversible cirrhosis of the liver, and died from haemorrhage of the oesophageal varices which were sequelae of alcoholic poisoning. What a terrible fate! He became over-burdened with a Luciferian inflation, an arrogant pride, and as it were he challenged God's dominion, 'he flew'. He left his earthly reality, a common enough fact concerning all addictions, be it alcohol or drugs. With his money he felt like a god, he could buy, and do everything he wished. He forgot his humble earthly self. In other words he became superhuman, and therefore non-human like Nietsche's Superman, and he destroyed himself. His liver self-destructed, and he could no longer remain in life.

You will recall Dr. Jung's story about the woman who came to see him after she had murdered her friend by poisoning her, and then she married the widower. But he died, her child left her, and then her dogs and horse died. She had lost touch with her reality, and her life as a human being was destroyed. She had usurped God himself by taking life. In both of these instances one perceives an invisible but monstrous pride which turns the human person into a veritable monster. In both of these cases, and in all cases of such hubris there was a deep unconsciousness.

The longing for the highest may be legitimate in itself, but the sinful presumption and inevitable corruption lies in the very fact that it goes beyond fixed human boundaries. As a human individual one is limited to one's earth-bound reality.

Through excess of longing a being can draw down the gods, or in Jungian psychology – the Self, upon him and into his passion. He seems to be raising himself up to deity, but in doing so he loses his human nature and is destroyed as a human being.

Alchemy which flourished for 1700 years disappeared in the 17th century when the rise of rationalism occurred. The Alchemists searched for the Elixir of Life, or the Lapis, the stone of wisdom. C. G. Jung was able to substantiate his concept of the Collective Unconscious by his prolonged alchemical studies. There was the alchemical idea of the 'ignis gehennalis', the central fire, which situated at the centre of the earth was vast and raging, and which had gathered itself together from the rays of the sun. It is called the Abyss of the Nether world, and it is said there is no other fire to contain the sun's heat. Jung states[46] 'It is in this central fire that the Mercurial serpent dwelt, the salamander whom the fire does not consume, and the dragon that feeds on the fire for he it is that overcomes fire, and by fire is not overcome, but in it amicably rests rejoicing therein.' Jung continues 'Through this fire is a portion of God's spirit, it is also Lucifer the most beautiful of God's angels, who after his fall became the fire of hell itself.'

In this idea one begins to perceive the torture and the torment of the damned, those who have disobeyed and refused to submit to God. It is also the torture and torment of the realisation of one's shadow on the personal level, and later on the deeper and collective level. The shadow roots stretch down into the profoundest depths of the collective unconscious, where one encounters absolute evil. That is the ignis gehennalis – or hell fire.

Lucifer, the Devil, Yahweh and also the Greek Zeus were associated with the lightning flash. The alchemists used the liberating flash of lightning as a symbol for unconscious luminosity. It is symbolic of sudden enlightenment, foresight or hindsight. It is the point where one realises, or comprehends a hithertofore unconscious content. It is symbolic of a sudden unexpected change if psychic condition. Ruland[47] speaks of 'the gliding of the mind or spirit into another world'. Such a change is like a rebirth, it is a revivification or a liberation from the darkness. The lightning flash has the power to transform. As Lucifer fell he knew his separateness, his otherness and also his similarity to God, who had until then contained Lucifer.

In the psychology of Adler the term 'godlikeness' is used to characterise certain essentialities of the power psychology attached to certain neuroses.

Jung[48] states that, 'analysis and conscious realisation of unconscious contents engender a certain superior tolerance thanks to which even relatively indigestible portions of one's unconscious character can be accepted. This tolerance may look very wise and superior but is often no more than a grand gesture that brings all sorts of consequences in its train. Two spheres are brought together which before had been kept anxiously apart. After considerable resistances have been overcome the union of opposites is successfully achieved at least to all appearances'.

As Jung explains, the apparent overcoming of the moral conflict gives rise to a feeling of superiority which may well be expressed in 'godlikeness', or it may be that another may perceive himself as a helpless object, who dons the mantle of 'godlikeness' in suffering. Jung explains this as a subtle kind of inner pride that also has its perils. In exploring this term of 'godlikeness' Jung states that insight and understanding widens the field of consciousness and brings a revelation of much that was unconscious before. This knowledge gives a superiority of knowledge which the subject believes will help others, and this causes him to become arrogant in his attempt to be well meant to those who find such intrusiveness to be perhaps annoying.

The most one can hope for is that consciousness of the presence of hubris is realised before an individual is overtaken by a catastrophe, before he or she is brought down to earth. First of all comments from family, friends or peers must be accepted, and such words as conceited, over-bearing, ambitious, self-seeking, proud or superior should be noted if applied to certain persons, or oneself.

It is important to watch one's dreams, to ascertain whether one is out of reality, above oneself or beyond oneself. It is vital for the continuance of life to become aware of it, for the consequences may demand the ultimate penalty. Accidents may be a trivial mishap, a fall down a staircase, or a stumble upon a polished floor. On the other hand it may be a fearful even mortal accident. All of these indicate a desire on the part of the unconscious psyche to achieve a balance between the ego-consciousness and the instinctual world. Since individuals so affected are above themselves, the accident brings them to a level compatible with their human state.

So often one perceives someone elected to high office or having reached the pinnacle of achievement, slip or fall in what seems to be a trivial accident that may have a serious outcome for the subject. It is not out of order to assume that the achievement of high honours is usually accompanied by a sense of satisfaction and pleasure with oneself, for the sin of pride may enter the tiniest crevice or niche in a personality.

It is the unconsciousness of pride as a sin wherein lies the trap, and which leads to downfall. In life, creative gifts, the health required to achieve and the ability to work, the luck which is a necessary accompaniment of life are bestowed by the Fates, and by the creative powers of the unconscious. As such they are God-given, but this fact is not usually registered since modern man finds it difficult to stoop so low and humble himself before a higher Being. It should never be forgotten that egocentricity is sinful.

So the accident of the fall, the slip, the stumble is a means whereby ego-consciousness is informed of its abnormal and unacceptably high level; equilibrium must be restored. If the individual becomes aware of his potentially dangerous state, this knowledge is like a lightning bolt of illumination. He senses at once his 'godlikeness', and if he should feel a fear and a sense of humility, then perhaps the proverb 'Pride goeth before a fall' may not be realised in the subject's life.

REFERENCES

1 Jung, C. G., Collected Works, Vol. 18, para 46.
2 Feeling. Definition: One of the four functions. It is a rational function which evaluates the worth of relationships and situations. Feeling must be distinguished from emotion, which is due to an activated complex.
3 Anima. Definition: (Latin 'soul') The unconscious feminine side of a man's personality. Personified in dreams by images of women. A man's anima development is reflected in how he relates to women.

4 Oxford Dictionary of English Etymology, Ed. by C. T. Onions, Oxford at the Clarendon Press, 1966.

5 Partridge, E., Origins, Etymological Dictionary of Modern English, Routledge, 1958.

6 Shadow. Definition: The unconscious part of the personality characterised by traits and attitudes whether negative or positive, which the conscious ego tends to reject or ignore. It is personified in dreams by persons of the same sex as the dreamer.

7 Animus. Definition: The unconscious masculine side of a woman's personality. Identification with the animus can cause a woman to become opinionated and argumentative.

8 Self. Definition: The archetype of wholeness and the regulating centre of the personality. It is a transpersonal power which transcends the ego.

9 Mill, J. S., Essay on Liberty, London, 1859, Chap. 51.

10 Aristotle, Nic. Ethics, Iv 3 (Ed. Grant), Encyclopaedia of Religion and Ethics, Vol. X, p. 276, T & T Clark, Edinburgh, 1918.

11 Butcher, S. H., Some Aspects of the Greek Genius, London, 1904, p. 109.

12 Dream. Definition: A dream represents an unconscious reaction to a conscious situation.

13 Individuation. Definition: The conscious realisation of one's unique psychological reality, including both strengths and limitations. It leads to the experience of the Self as the regulating centre of the psyche.

14 Lederer, Wolfgang, Fear of Women, New York, Harcourt Brace Jovanovitch, 1968.

15 Ochs, Carol, Behind the Sex of God, p. 96, Boston Beacon Press, 1977.

16 Old Testament, Isaiah 2, 12.

17 Ibid., Proverbs 16–18.

18 Ibid., Jeremiah 13, 9.

19 Roux, Georges, Ancient Iraq, George Allen & Unwin Ltd. 1964, Chap. 22–23.

20 Old Testament, Book of Daniel, Chap. I, 7 & IChap. II.

21 Jung, C. G., Collected Works, Vol. 18, para 246.

22 Humbaba. Definition: Elamite God of the Babylonian epic poem 'The Gilgamesh Epic'.

23 Zimmer, The Indian World Mother.

24 New Testament, Corinthians I 13:4.

25 Epistolae & Romanus Inchoata Expositio 'Saint Augustine' W. Montgomery, London, 1914, p. 198.

26 Aquinas, Thomas (Summa Torinus Theologiae II ii qu 162 5–8).

27 Dante, A., The Divine Comedy Purgatorio Cantos X.XI.XII. Library of Congress Cataloguing in Publication Data (Dante Alighieri 1265–1321).

28 Ibid., XII Verses 28–30.

29 Ibid., v. 34.

30 Old Testament, Genesis 10:9.

31 Ibid., Micah V 6.

32 Dante, A., The Divine Comedy, Purgatorio Canto XII, Verse 37.

33 Schwab, Gustav, Gods & Heroes (Myths & Ethics of Ancient Greece), Pantheon Books, New York, 1946.

34 Dante, A., The Divine Comedy, Canto XII, Verse 25, Purgatory.

35 Old Testament, Isaiah 14/12–14.

36 Patai, Raphael, Myths and Modern Man, Prentice Hall, 1972.

37 Hays, H. R., The Beginnings, p. 85, New York, Putnam, 1963.

38 Hooke, S. H., Middle Eastern Mythology, Penguin, 1963.

39 New Testament, Luke 10: 8.

40 Ibid., Saint Paul, Letters to the Ephesians 2:2.
41 Ibid., Revelations 22:16.
42 Jung, C. G., Collected Works, 11 para 290.
43 Dickens, Charles, David Copperfield.
44 Scott Peck, M., People of the Lie, Simon and Shuster, 1985.
45 Jung, C. G., Letters Vol. 2 p. 60, Routledge & Kegan Paul, 1973.
46 Jung, C. G., Collected Works, Vol. 14 para 632.
47 Ibid., Vol. 9 Pt. I para 534n 7 Ruland (Lexicon 1612).
48 Ibid., Vol. 7 para 224.

2

THE DEADLY SIN OF ANGER

Anger or Ira is a primary emotion and needs to be experienced in order to be known. It has a distinct quality of its own, different from that of any other emotion. Not only is it not derived from other emotions, it does not even presuppose experience of them in order to give it its being. It does however enter itself into other emotions and it may be allied with affects which are distinctly malevolent.

A middle-aged male patient of mine had been married for many years to a woman who was both artistic and house proud. She would not permit a comfortable chair in her house because the lines of such were usually out of keeping with her strict sense of style. As a consequence the patient had never had a comfortable place to sit in his married life. It was a fact that he did not 'sit well' in the marriage. When I asked him if he felt anger against his wife, he said that he loved her, and did not feel anger. I told him the following story in order to illustrate the reason I had asked the question.

Another married couple had lived together for almost a quarter of a century. The wife was exceedingly devoted to housework, and their home was impeccable. Each night when he arrived home from work he opened the door to the sound of his wife's voice. Her greeting was, 'Take off your shoes.' It was followed by, 'Put on your slippers.' This the man did, then after washing his hands he entered the dining room where his place was laid, and at once his evening meal was put before him. Never was there a word of greeting on her part, or a word of complaint on his. After twenty-five years of this repetitive behaviour there came a night when he entered the dining room and at the moment that his wife placed the tea-pot on the table the pattern changed.

The man picked up the tea-pot and hurled it through the plate glass picture window with such force that the outline of the shape of the tea-pot was retained with the handle and spout perfectly defined.

The man, without a word, turned on his heels left the house and disappeared. Three days later he was found by the police in a tavern in a mountain village. After a two day bout of drunkenness he was quite sober when discovered, playing cards with some peasants.

The anger of twenty-five years exploded in that emotional act of furious violence which projected the tea-pot into space, and became his gateway to freedom.

ETYMOLOGY OF THE WORD ANGER

For a moment let us look at some of the words which imply the presence of anger. We have irritation, vexation and pique. All words describing a moderate form. A degree of anger to the point of bitterness is enfolded in the words antagonistic and alienated. When one's feelings are aroused quickly we may speak of an inflammatory reaction, whereas a violent explosion of rage is often said to be an eruptive anger. Outburst is a common descriptive word for such. A feeling of anger arising from a sense of injury is often described as upset, distress, or a grievance against someone or something. A display of anger, bitterness or ill-will, and sometimes vengeance is described by the word animosity. Other adjectives being acrimonious and rancorous. Animosity, spiteful malice, bitterness and ill feeling are always expressive of the anger of animus-anima interchanges, and animii possession. A feeling of anger due to disappointment or failure is described as chagrin. This always enfolds a feeling of shame, and sometimes guilt. Ill temper, irritability or moderate anger are found in the word asperity.

To be angry includes the ideas of being irate, wrathful, indignant or riled. Mutual accusations of anger are described as recriminations. Angry criticism is an expression of outrage, fulminations, vituperation and invective. Angry speech is alluded to as a harangue, a tirade or a diatribe.

One can be furious, seething, enraged, incensed, livid or rampageous. All words meaning intensely angry. A peevish anger is querulous or curmudgeonly. An easily provoked anger is irascible, cantankerous or splenetic (on a short fuse in modern parlance). Splenetic is to do with the spleen. The French word for anger is colère, and has given us choleric and bilious both words related to a choleric or angry nature with the meaning of irascible or peevish.

A mild to moderate nature may be described as crotchety or disgruntled.

From such a range one perhaps begins to see the size of the problem of this ubiquitous and often unrecognised emotion.

Too many people hide their anger as has been seen, banishing it to deep within themselves. It then builds up to an explosive outburst, a tantrum or

48

a bout of crying. Sometimes when patients or analysands come in and immediately start to cry or sob, it is useful to search the dreams for signs of latent or covert anger.

An old nursery rhyme which I learned when I was isolated in my nursery at six years of age is as follows:

'Cross patch, draw the latch
Sit by the fire and spin,
Take a cup and drink it up,
Then call your neighbour in'.

A cross patch is disgruntled, crotchety, rancorous or just angry. Undoubtedly it was my own childish state of mind at that time otherwise I would not have remembered the rhyme after all these years.

In an Italian painting I observed a figure which personified anger. It was a youth with rounded shoulders, sparkling eyes, a round puckered brow and a sharp nose with wide flaring nostrils. He was armed with a boar's head as his crest from which issued fire and smoke. He held a drawn sword and a lighted torch. There is a animalistic fury in the flaring nostrils, as one finds in a bull or a stallion. The pinched features are those of bad temper, the fire, the smoke and the lighted torch are ready to spread the conflagration, and indicate illumination. The boar is the animal sometimes drawn depicting blind instinctual rage. The sword symbolises the preparedness to fight, in order to protect oneself or kill the other. Symbolically the sword also means discernment and is thus the pointer towards disidentification with the emotion.

THE ANATOMY OF AN EMOTION

In the study of emotions, one invariably finds that the word 'emotion' is applied when it concerns a condition characterised by physiological innervations. The physiological part of the emotions can be measured, but not the psychic component

The James-Lange[1] theory of affect is helpful. This theory is composed of that of William James and C. G. Lange. Affect is the same as emotion, an emotion is an affect.

It is so called because emotion is something which 'affects' one. It does something, it interferes with the life process. Emotion as Jung[2] said is 'the thing that carries you away, you are thrown out of yourself, you are beside yourself'. For example, one is cooking dinner and a telephone call brings disturbing news, or a letter arrives which brings something of a distressful nature. Suddenly one loses oneself and burns the dinner. Ego consciousness is seized by the emotion, gripped and possessed, one is at once thrown out of one self or carried away. It is as if an explosion had moved one away from oneself, a volcano has erupted and one is thrown into another place.

That is what occurs when an emotional possession intrudes into a life.

There is quite a tangible physiological condition which can be observed at the same time.

It is always important to differentiate between feeling and emotion. Feeling is a function of evaluation, it is a rational function if it is differentiated. When it is not it just happens, and then it has all those qualities appertaining to it which may quite simply be described as unreasonable. Conscious feeling is a rational function of discriminating values. The difference between feeling and emotion is this. Feeling has no physical or tangible physiological manifestations, whilst and emotion is always accompanied, and indeed characterised by an altered physiological condition.[3]

To hark back to the James-Lange theory of affect, one is only ever really emotional when one becomes aware of the physiological alterations of the general physical condition, in other words the body 'speaks'.

If whilst driving a motor car one decides to overtake the car in front when a clear view presents itself, all should be well. But if suddenly whilst overtaking another car appears directly ahead, and is seen making its way towards one the first priority is to get out of the way. Therefore one either accelerates to overtake or slows down to drop behind. On reaching safety and only then a sensation of warmth spreads through the body, the drumming of the heart sounds loud in the ears, a weakness pervades the limbs and giddiness or actual faintness may occur. At that moment one becomes aware of bodily changes, that is the time one realises that one was in a tight spot and was very afraid. One had felt fear, but also anger at oneself.

This phenomenon can be observed in all kinds of situations in which one becomes emotional. Such emotions which predispose to the aforementioned changes are fear, panic and anger, although others may do so. These are affects, one is affected. Jealousy when accompanied by rage presents such a phenomenon so described, and a sudden shock occasioned by a startling surprise can cause the same disturbance.

When one is angry the blood is felt coursing to the head, the face becomes red and the body feels as if it is swelling up. The breathing becomes laboured, the voice rises and is often shrill. Then when these changes are perceived one knows one is angry, really angry. Watch a cat, she may be deeply asleep, suddenly she is aware that something is not as it should be, perhaps her resting auditory acuity picks up a slight sound or she smells a strange or unusual smell. At once she is awake and fully alert to the presence of potential danger. Perhaps it is another cat treading on her territory! Her fur stands on end, she swells in size, her tail becomes enormous and usually her body is stock-still. Then suddenly she is aware that she is angry and so she emits a deep-throated growl, but only then when the bodily changes have occurred. With a human being, before the physiological changes intrude one only knows that one is going to be angry, but when discomfort intervenes then one is angry. That is the locus where one is caught in one's own anger, possessed by it and thrown out of oneself. Jung declared, 'Immediately you realise that you are getting angry you are twice as angry as before.'[4]

When one becomes aware of anger there is often a simultaneous conviction that someone, (or an object sometimes) has purposely made one angry. When one has a feeling it is by no means the same because one is in control, and the situation is calm. For example, perhaps in analysis a dream portrays a serious unconscious situation in an analysand's life. At once on my part perhaps a negative feeling arises. Perhaps I do not like the situation or the analysand's behaviour, but because there is no malice or ill-will there is therefore no emotion on my part, anger is not part of the event. I can then explain that I do not like the situation represented in the dream, or the analysland's reaction to it. So all remains quiet.

But, if in the course of conversation with a colleague or friend an altercation arises bringing spitefulness or vindictiveness then one becomes angry, and has an emotion. When something is said quietly even in a potentially hazardous situation both the recipient and oneself is usually spared an emotional eruption because there is coolness between the opposing parties. On the other hand emotions are highly contagious. They are the real carriers of mental contagion.

If one is in a crowd which has become for whatever reason emotionally activated either through fear, panic or joy, then one simply cannot help oneself from being caught up in the emotional storm. This is the basic cause of the uprisings, rebellions, strike, violence and football riots. Quiet discussion of rights and wrongs does not lead to conflagration. It is the sudden emergence of an emotional outburst in one or more individuals which lights the fuse, and then like wildfire the contagion becomes uncontained and overwhelming, and suddenly everybody is in it.

As Jung[5] has said, the feelings of other people do not concern us in the least and for this reason we see that a person with differentiated feelings has a cooling effect, whilst the emotional person heats everybody up. The fire, which is anger or the affect is radiating out from him. He may be likened to a constantly sparking fire. The flame of that emotion is visible in his face, and in the faces of those who are affected by it. By sympathy the sympathetic nervous system of others (and one's own if one is present) becomes disturbed, and after a while the same signs are visible in others. This does not happen with feelings, only with emotions.

I was told by someone who had listened to, and indeed was present at Adolf Hitler's speeches prior to the Second World War that he charged the atmosphere. Apparently he always entered the stadium looking pale and tense. He began to speak in a quiet way, and gradually by means of his intuition he was able to pick up the mood of his audience. Then be began to be heated and spoke more confidently, and finally with immense passion. His emotionality became pronounced, and then the whole stadium was on fire.

Few could in those days resist the seduction by the persuasive emotionality of the demagogue, Hitler.

If a feeling value is overwhelmingly powerful it will indubitably become an emotion at a certain point.

Imagine oneself sitting quietly in a chair reading, listening to music or doing nothing. Suddenly a feeling besets one's tranquillity, it gets pushed aside, only to recur with a stronger intensity. Then a feeling of anger is perceived. Undoubtedly the first realisation was accompanied by fear, since fear may precede anger, but not necessarily. The feeling of anger was perhaps engendered by a word read in a book or newspaper, a musical sound, or a thought which comes to one out of the blue. One is reminded of a slight, a denigration, or perhaps a loss. A complex has been touched and the primary neutral reaction goes on into overt anger and suddenly one is furious. Emotions are not made, they appear.

When anger has been unexpressed over a period, as often occurs in marriage, a love relationship or family situation, the anger is no longer contained in consciousness. It is either suppressed or repressed. In the place of this non-acceptance or non-recognition of the emotion is a feeling of discomfort or malaise. Usually it combines fear and also guilt. The discomfort points to the fact that something is amiss. When it eventually becomes chronic a melancholy or a depression is usually described as the ailment. In such a situation there is always a sense that one has behaved in a way which is unsatisfactory, or one has a sense of failure, au fond, there is shame because the anger has never been recognised consciously or expressed.

Of all the organs of the body the organ of the skin is the complete mirror of unexpressed unconscious rage. One is able to visualise certain inner psychic complexes by the pattern of the skin disease as it develops in certain human beings. For instance in Atopic eczema, the redness, the lichenification, dryness and scarification which presents in this disorder reflects the dry anger engendered by the rejecting aspects of the mother complex.[6]

A woman patient came to see me because she suffered from severe chronic depression which had lasted for more that twenty years. She complained that she 'always felt depressed'.

She had also a physical problem, her nose was permanently red with an acneid condition as if she was an alcoholic, but she did not drink alcohol. It came to light that the marriage which had produced four apparently satisfactory children was in fact unsatisfactory in itself. The husband it seemed idolised the children, and the wife had become jealous of them. She had of course realised the jealousy but could not overcome it, try as she may. During her analysis an unusual fact emerged, the husband apparently had never given the wife a present in her whole married life. He gave her the obligatory engagement ring when they became affianced, but nothing else. She had never received a flower, a bonbon or a birthday card. This woman was the mother of his children, the conjugal partner and the producer of his comfort. The adored children on the other hand were given presents by the father and lavish parties to celebrate each successive year of their lives.

The woman at first was unaware that she had a fierce and mounting anger. She knew she was jealous of her children, and felt remorse and shame, but she never consciously realised that the basic problem was anger towards the unfeeling brutal husband. When the disfiguring illness began, some twenty years earlier she noticed that each day she felt at some time or other depressed.

The nose is the organ by which all animals smell out enemies, possibilities for courtship, food and danger in all kinds of forms. The human world has lost to a great extent this ability, but in dreams and in the language of the unconscious the nose is symbolic of the function of intuition. The woman in fact was an introverted sensation type, and intuition was her inferior function.[7] The symbolic meaning of the red nose in her case was that unconsciously her intuition, that is her unconscious perception, was indicating to her an inner anger of considerable force. Fortunately with support she was able to recognise and integrate this justified instinctual anger, and with this recognition came the conscious realisation of her husband's true nature towards her, his lack of sympathy and absence of human feeling. She made a complete recovery within the next few months, and the depression did not recur. It was essential that she integrated the latent anger into ego-consciousness.

The long standing non-recognition of anger as I have described often leads to depression, and eventually to permanent changes in the body. Although the original somatic manifestations may be present first in the organ of the skin, if the anger is unresolved other organs are often affected, such as the musculo-skeletal system and the haemopoetic system (the blood system). It is clear that when inner organs become afflicted that the unconscious problem is slipping into deeper psychic layers, and becoming less accessible to consciousness.

Another of my analysands whom I knew over a period of several years was married in her late twenties. She herself was of Anglo Saxon lineage, well educated, with a strong Christian upbringing. Her husband was Hindu, of impeccable education and from a high-born family. Undoubtedly they fell in love, and the marriage produced several children. Soon after the first child was born she, the analysand developed a red nose, and again she like the previous woman did not partake of alcohol. Eventually she was greatly disfigured by the nasal condition and sought therapy.

The analysis unearthed a powerful animus in her psychic hinterland. She was guided in the analysis to understand this overwhelmingly intolerant and judging unconscious being who made incessant demands upon her to judge, belittle and denigrate her husband's religious ideas. She tried to make him a Christian, and socially at least in order to please her he became one it seemed. Yet the animosity remained and as the years passed the anger increased but was repressed savagely. This Christian lady for reasons of respectability refused to believe that she was capable of such an immoral stance towards her husband. She never accepted that anger was the cause of he red nose. She went of to develop a malignant disease of the spleen, the organ which symbolises anger par excellence, and died at a comparatively early age. At base her real problem was one of love.

Possibly all mental processes cause slight physiological disturbances but are so transient or ephemeral that there are no available means as yet to demonstrate them.

There is a scientific and very sensitive method to measure emotions or their physiological components by means of the psychogalvanic effect. This method was first published early this century by Jung[8] as a means of demonstrating unconscious complexes. It is based on the fact that electrical resistance of the skin decreases under the influence of emotion. It does not decrease under the influence of feeling for one can have an intense feeling without physiological alteration. As soon as it occurs one becomes possessed, dissociation results and one is as Jung says 'thrown out of your house, and the house is free for the devils'.

The Word Association test is a tool of immense potential in those cases where psychic dissociation is the pertinent problem. It might be helpful to recapitulate the procedure of the experiment.

The test in which the organ of the skin played the vital rôle as psychic mediator was developed by Jung when he worked as a psychiatrist at the Burgholzli Psychiatric Hospital in Zürich at the turn of the century. In the test, words were pronounced to the subject who was to reply as quickly as possible with the first word which presented itself. A series of pairs resulted, called associations. The called word was known as the stimulus word, and the reply was the reaction. It was found that certain words connected with some emotional complex produced an effect on the galvanometer whilst indifferent words did not have any such reaction. Jung concluded that only stimuli with emotionality induced a deviation in the galvanometer. He enquired into these disturbances in reaction, thus making the test a valuable method of investigating the deeper roots of mental illness. It was this test which led to the recognition of the complexes, and to the discovery of the unconscious, independently of Freud.

I would like to illustrate the great value of the psychogalvanic effect in a case of a woman with repressed anger.[9]

She presented with an area of baldness on the top of her head, not unlike the tonsure of a monk. She wore a wig to cover the red shiny hairless skin which she called a transformation. The baldness was due to a severe skin disease called Chronic Lupus Erythematosus, which had begun when she was young and had progressed inexorably.

She brought me a dream which had upset her very much. In the dream her doctor who had treated her for many years was endeavouring to take her temperature by pushing a mercurial thermometer right down her throat and was choking her to death. On awakening she found that her mouth was full of blood. She explained to me that although in the dream her doctor whom she liked did not realise it, but he was killing her.

It was this dream which caused me to approach her illness in a different way. Instead of providing the standard dermatological therapy I suggested that she undergo an analysis using her dreams to guide us in the process. She agreed at once and it was decided to undertake the Word Association Experiment with her, at the début.

During the test she faltered on the stimulus word 'marriage' and in the re-run of the test could not recall the former lapse. These results were interesting and totally unexpected. The Word Association Test had touched at the heart of her problem. The marriage was the problem, and for twenty-seven years she had kept the secret to herself. Such a secret is isolating and severs human contact. In a strange way the baldness concealed by the transformation hair piece was a reflection of the inner situation.

She was twenty years old when she married, and the only child of the marriage was conceived during the honeymoon. During that period she also learned that her husband had been unfaithful to her prior to the marriage during the engagement, and also during the honeymoon itself. As soon as she realised that her husband was a philanderer the skin disease began on the scalp. Each time throughout the subsequent quarter of a century, when her husband was unfaithful a further extensive exacerbation of the disease process occurred.

Eventually she sank into long periods of depression. The analysis which she underwent provided a life line for her, the depression lifted, her continuous melancholic state gradually cleared, and the destructive skin process was at last controlled. A series of dreams indicated the presence in her unconscious psyche of a brutal animus, who tyrannised her. As the unconscious mind of woman, the nature of the animus is perceived in a woman's dreams, and by projection is encountered in the outer world. As her inner guide and psychopompos he had led her first into a marriage where she was a prisoner, and then whilst still his captive she met the doctor who in reality had tried it seemed with good intentions to cure her and almost killed her.

It appeared that she was hypnotised by her husband much in the way as a rabbit before a cobra. Outwardly she gave the impression of a kindly gentle woman. On closer inspection a different picture emerged. Although it was true she feared her husband and hated his infidelities the cause of her real terror lay within. It was a long time and with considerable difficulty that she came to realise the negativity of her thoughts as the animus entered from the unconscious through the open door of her inferior thinking function, feeling was her first function. The hideous nature of such thoughts was intolerable to her bovine Christian consciousness, and not to be accepted as were the flames of raging anger ever burning in her unconscious psyche. Anger was activated each time the infidelity complex associated with her husband's behaviour was touched.

In submitting to the tyranny of the negative thoughts of the animus the woman had set her face against her instinctual feminine nature, and had come to treat herself in the same denigrating and churlish manner as did her husband over the years, in outer reality.

What was required of her was a transformation of attitude. The dissociated anger connected with her marriage had to be recognised, accepted and integrated. Furthermore she was required to act, and stand by her feminine self. Her justified anger was that of a woman spurned.

In conclusion the woman had never permitted herself to recognise the anger she held for her husband. Her animus persuaded her through terror to accept the brutish nature of the man she had married. She was too cowardly to stand up to the inner figure, and also the outer one. The unexpressed anger therefore constituted a mortal sin. A monumental crime had been committed against her inner feminine being and she permitted it. This is why the destructive nature of the disorder became visible in her body and on her skin so that she could see it, and understand the true nature of the damage she had allowed to her person and her spiritual self.

Here there was no creative fire burning in her psyche, but a consuming destructive rage. This Christian woman was in fact a sinner and her sin was mortal for her soul.

The woman's dream, the analysis of her dreams, and the subsequent recovery permitted me as a physician to observe the rôle of unrecognised rage in this particular type of dermatosis.

PHYSICAL MANIFESTATIONS OF ANGER REVEALED IN BODILY DISEASE.

When anger develops, tightness of the jaws can be observed with clenching or grinding of the teeth. The neck tends to be shortened since the shoulders become elevated and the head appears to shrink into them. The back sometimes has a hunched appearance in the upper part, with rigidity of the intercostal muscles which affects respiratory excursion. The lower back may be held stiffly and the gait is often observed to be stilted with short steps. Sometimes a rhythmic clenching and unclenching of the fists, with the elbows held in a semi-flexed position also is occasioned by this emotion. Very often the elbows are folded so that the arms are held akimbo in order to protect the body.

The overall appearance of the physical contour is at odds with the aggression and hostility of the affect. Such an appearance is suggestive of a protective attitude against an unknown outer 'enemy' whereas in reality the enemy as a malevolent shadow is usually within.

If an angry reaction or a state of anger is realised and dealt with either by verbal expression or an act of violence, the body in time reverts to its former normality. If however, as is often the case, consciousness of its presence is unrecognised the changes in the physical attitude or stance may become habitual.

The early Greeks, Hindu peoples and the Hebrews believed that there was breath in the heart as well as in the lungs. Such a belief is understandable in view of the compact nature of the bronchial tubes and the lungs enfolded round the heart and its vessels. This together with the fact that the heart on its left side was always found to be empty after death substantiated the theory. I mention this because of the connection in language between breath and emotion. We do say that we 'gasp in surprise', 'yawn with fatigue', 'sob with grief', 'laugh with glee', 'fume with rage', (cigarette smokers take note) 'boil with anger', 'hiss with rage', or 'spit with rage' and so on.

Bearing in mind that when one weeps profusely or cries alone in the night there are always deep inspirations of breath and slow exhalations, particularly in the long wailing cries of anguish. A child's sobbing in characterised by a series of short inspirations of a convulsive nature, its body is wracked with deep tremors as it fights for its breath. In all these instances, in grief, fatigue and sorrow there is always an element of anger present to a greater or lesser degree. When a child sobs it is always anger. You may say, 'but the child is upset', to be upset is to be angry. This should be remembered for ourselves as adults.

One of my analysands, a middle-aged woman of an apparently serene nature had great problems in her life. She could never say 'No', to anyone. She always agreed to undertake the most onerous of burdens, which she carried out for others. She did not complain, she always 'did her duty'. She could never accept that a great many of her internal complaints, in particular problems with her gastrointestinal system were due to unexpressed anger.

Then one night she had a particularly vivid dream. She dreamed, and the image was of great clarity that she was in a child's bedroom. It was a well lit room and in the centre was a child's cot painted white. In the cot was a small child, a girl of three or four years of age standing, gripping the rails of the cot in a furious rage. The child's face was scarlet, the eyes glistened with tears, and the body was convulsed with wracking sobs. The child had smashed a pillow filled with goose feathers against the cot rails and the pillow had become torn. From the tear there erupted thousands of goose feathers which filled the air. When the analysand awoke she was suffocating and could hardly breathe because it seemed that the feathers had been inhaled into the mouth and nose, and had got into the eyes. As she woke up she recalled that the glittering tear filled eyes of the child were her own eyes.

The feather is really the equivalent of the hair. In the avian world the feather represents for the bird the hair in the mammalian world. The feather with its lightness and immateriality is symbolic of truth. Maat, the

Egyptian goddess symbolic of truth, was represented by a feather, she was the personification of the basic laws of all existence; she embodied the concepts of law, truth and world order.

In the chapter of 'The Weighing of the Heart' in the Egyptian Book of the Dead, the heart of the defunct must weigh no more than a feather.

This procedure took place in the Judgment where Osiris sat with forty-two Assessors, each Assessor representing one of the Nomes of Egypt and the Underworld. In front of Osiris a balance was set up. In one pan of the balance was placed the Feather of Truth, in the other the heart of the dead man. The God Thoth stood by to register the outcome, and Anubis the 'Lord of the Hallowed Land' (the necropolis) who as the god of the dead and embalming was represented as a recumbent black jackal on tombs.

The dead man accompanied by his Ba stood in front of Osiris in order to make his confession.[10] This confession was later written down.[11] The dead man lists the things he has not done, he denies that he has slanderously spoken, lied, gossiped, cheated, blasphemed, masturbated, stolen, committed adultery or killed. It is usually described as a 'Negative Confession.'[12]

The dead man then waited whilst his heart was weighed in the balance against the Feather of Truth. If the Feather weighed down the heart or if the balance did not move the man had made a true confession. But if the heart was heavy because burdened with guilt, and weighed down the Feather, the defunct was pronounced guilty.

To return to our middle-aged woman with the dream of the angry child. She sees herself in the eyes of the child, a raging angry little inferno of fury. That angry child lived still in the psyche of that middle-aged woman. It was unacceptable, and had been sealed off so she was unaware of the torment in her soul. On awakening after the dream she found herself to be choking with the feathers, goose-feathers. Seb the father of Osiris and Isis was symbolised by a goose, and was called The Great Cackler. He guarded the tombs of the dead and had great underworld connections.

We might say that the woman was being choked by the truth, and the truth had a certain underworld quality. It contained something dark and hidden, and we will not be far out if we suspect it is hidden in the heart, and is connected with the fire in the heart.

The dream of this woman shows that inside was a small suffering child, caught in such an intensity of anger which could only be described as murderous rage. The adult personality revealed in the calm demeanour was that of a dutiful selfless woman inclined to put the needs of others before her own.

As a child she had adapted to a difficult family by obedience to the whims of her parents. She was not permitted freedom of expression in her childhood, and the furious inner child remained trapped as the years passed into adulthood.

She had perforce to learn slowly and painfully to love herself, but first she had to realise that she had continued to neglect her own desires like an obedient but angry child. When eventually she achieved this she found her neglected creativity and lost her gastro-intestinal illness. Many such problems which affect the stomach, duodenum and intestinal canal stem from repressed anger extending over many years.

The negative emotion residing in the heart had to be liberated and realised in consciousness. It was only then, she told me, that for the first time in her life she felt she had 'a light heart'. The sin which she had committed against the Self was absolved.

Features indicating anger include tensions of the hands and jaws. The rigidity of the hands, the clenching or unclenching, and the grasping of the thumb all indicate anger, as is the rhythmic contraction of the masseter muscles of the jaw. Clenching of the teeth and grinding during the day or whilst asleep are also indicative of rage. Heart rate and respiration are always accelerated. The facial skin changes colour, usually it reddens, the eyes flash, the eyebrows knot together, the voice becomes loud, harsh, shrill or discordant. There is also a desire to 'strike out' verbally or physically. The hostile gesture of the clenched fist is ubiquitous, the derisory V sign, words of abuse or obscenity all indicate rage or hostility. Horace[13] described wild anger as Ira furor brevis est, this means 'a brief madness'.

Many years ago when I was a young doctor I had to visit a Professor of Medicine in the hospital where I worked. I had forgotten to do something or other and had not realised its importance. Clearly I was in the wrong and I went politely to apologise. He looked up and appeared to be perfectly normal but as I spoke I noticed that his face had begun to redden, his eyes became bloodshot and his voice gradually got louder until it had a singularly strange wailing note which turned into a kind of howl. He appeared to swell up before my eyes and raged at me as if I had committed the most heinous crime. I was so stunned by this apparition of extreme wrath that I became curious to see how far it would go. My differentiated feeling prevailed, and prevented me from falling into a possession. If that had occurred God knows what might have happened. He (the Professor) may very well have struck me. I had the distinct impression that he would quite simply explode, and I was afraid that he might strike out or fall down. I have never before or since witnessed such a manifestation of rage. At first he was quite calm, but it seems I engendered for reasons unknown a negative emotion. Perhaps I touched an unconscious complex. As he became aware possible of his rapidly beating heart he realised he was angry and became furious.

I did learn a profound lesson which I have remembered. One can never prognosticate when someone will be seized by such a possession. After this episode I always avoided him whenever possible. My crime was very slight, I had forgotten to fill in a form.

A less alarming but simular incident occurred during a medical conference. The speaker, a physician of immense stature, was questioned whilst on the podium by a fellow countryman, also a physician of equal standing, concerning a point of contention. The question was unexpected, and threw the speaker momentarily off balance. At once he paled, hesitated, faltered in his immediate response but gained his equilibrium and replied satisfactorily. All would have been well, but the questioner re-posed the question in a different way. Immediately the speaker reddened, a deep flush spread over his domed forehead, highlighted by the arc lights above. It was then that his face began to swell, his cheeks puffed out and achieved immense size as he held his breath. It was a purely animalistic response and unforgettable. He had assumed the appearance of a prairie dog which puffs out the cheeks to scare off an enemy. It was clear that the men knew each other, and undoubtedly were bitter enemies. Each was a shadow of the other carrying the appropriate hook for projections. These reactions so described always cover to a greater or lesser extent unconscious shadow problems which usually lie at the base of much animosity and enmity. Intense reactions so engendered usually involve unrecognised inferiorities of functions, of the parties concerned.

These changes described are visible and physical in nature. However there are invisible changes which are not discerned by the observer (or even by the subject). When internal organs are affected organic changes may ensue, producing symptoms and signs. These when they become perceptible may play a distinctly separate part in the process, apparently unrelated to the emotion of anger.

As already mentioned any one organ (or more) may be involved. In particular gastro-intestinal disturbances are usually evident in any emotional upset with anger playing a not inconsiderable rôle in a great many disturbances.

The gastro-intestinal tract starts at the vermilion border of the lips and ends at the junction of the anal mucosa and the outer skin. This organ is as already indicated, commonly, frequently and profoundly afflicted by the emotion of anger. Manifestations occur in the shape of all manners of disturbances, such as aphthous ulcers of the tongue, difficulties in swallowing, sore throats (sometimes associated with a spritiual problem on account of its connection with the respiratory tract), indigestion, abdominal upsets such as nausea, vomiting and diarrhoea, appendicitis, colitis, haemorrhoids, diverticulitis, spastic colon or the presently fashionable irritable bowel syndrome. All have an emotional background and the affect is usually anger, ranging from dull brooding resentment to overt rage.

Some examples may illustrate this point.

A man developed a severe painful spasm of the oesophagus.[14] It used to start at any time of the day or night, and usually lasted for about a quarter of an hour. It was very painful, and sometimes he was unable to get his breath. Nothing relieved the pain and he had to wait until the spasm passed.

He had been investigated and assured that there was no physical disorder of the organ. It came to light that the pain had started some years earlier when his wife of many years decided to visit her parents in another country. As far as his wife was concerned his creature comforts had always played a secondary rôle to those of his father and mother-in-law. Gradually the wife began to visit them more frequently as they aged and became more dependent upon her.

The pain in the throat gradually became more and more severe. The time arrived eventually when his wife began to speak of a permanent home with her parents. Since the patient had always permitted his wife to have her own way this new decision became at once an anathema for him as he did not wish to accompany her abroad. At last he sought medical help, and soon learned that this condition was a form of Globus hystericus, where a lump appears in the throat due to spasm of the oesophageal muscles. He simply could not as it were, swallow his wife's high-handed inconsiderate behaviour. Instead of swallowing his rage he had to act in some way in order to survive, and his physical symptom was the pointer towards his release.

The victim was a moral coward unable to express emotion which was quite justified in this particular circumstance. In each case the affect which should have been suffered and dealt with consciously was banished only to reappear in the somatic reaction as an unbearable physical problem. Au fond, it appears that anger induces a sensation of shame which acts to block unacceptable shadow impulses. It appears that at all costs the glittering pristine persona must not be dulled, hence the banishment of the emotion. This is a sin which everyone commits at some time or other in life.

Finally a woman had had a pain in the right hand side of the abdomen for twenty-five years. She was seen by innumerable physicians but a valid diagnosis was never reached. A number of profered, indeed probable diagnoses were made but in spite of constant therapy she suffered excruciating pain.

A cure came when she was questioned about the onset of the pain in the past and gradually it came to light. Although she and her husband had tried to produce children they had failed. A boy was adopted, and for a while all was satisfactory until the woman developed pain in the abdomen The baby was difficult, he was the child of an unmarried mother and little else was known of his background. He developed into an unruly boy, an uncontrollable teenager, a youth given to mis-demeanours and petty offences and a young man who committed murder. Indeed he was serving life a sentence, at the time his adoptive mother found the abdominal pain so unbearable.

This woman refused to face the fact of an inner monumental rage against her situation and her adopted son. She lived a desperate lie by insisting that he was only wicked because he had never had a real chance in life. She simply did not see that she and her husband had given this young man as good a home as was humanly possible, and that instead of blaming herself she was to understand the reality of the nature of her adopted son who was a brutal killer. This fact had to be faced squarely and ingested. After a long time she had the courage to admit that she had never faced her own psychic distress, and had never admitted that she disliked her son, indeed hated and feared him.

The gastro-intestinal system like the organ of the skin is a barometer mirroring faultless changes in emotional disturbances.

When anger is seen from the psychic side it is seen to be a mental disturbance, a displeasure, a discomfiture of a painful kind. It arises from opposition, hurt, or harm received operating like a reflex act, that is an immediate active response or reaction without any deliberation or recognition of the unacceptable or affecting fact which caused it. (i.e. activation of a feeling toned complex.)

What induces anger is something that has to be got rid of. This is of prime importance. Moreover if the real cause of the offence is not readily approachable the anger is vented on a person or a thing which is within reach such as a tool, a book or a vase. The pent up energy must find discharge somehow or an explosion is inevitable. Anger since instinctive, does not wait for reason though it may be brought under the control of reason. It is aroused in us by that which opposes us, thwarts us, by what we object to, or what offends or pains us. In other words that which we resent.

Like all passions, anger lacks in moderation, transgresses limits and defies proportion. When it acts like the wind it exercises a useful function but when it becomes a whirlwind it may do serious harm. After the anger comes depression and then exhaustion.

THE ANGER OF THE GODS

From earliest times the emotion of anger and fire have been closely associated. In Finnish-Ugric myth fire holds pride of place. It is a friend which warms the house and cooks the food, but if it is angered by misuse it jumps out of the fireplace and burns up the house and also the village. Fire because pure cannot endure defilement. The ancient belief amongst the Northern European tribes is that the mighty god Donar, the Thunderer, was the giver of fire. Donar-Thor is the Loud-Sounder, the Thunder God was the earliest aspect of this deity. The cosmic thunder-lightning storm has equivalence on the microcosmic scale as a sudden violent rage or eruption of fury. It is as if one is possessed by a god.

Suppose one feels angry and realises it, at that moment one becomes aware of the pounding heart. It is as if the drumming of the heart is a kind of muted thunder, and the lightning flash is the realisation of one's own anger. Then one is completely aware of the fire, it is like a sudden conflagration, in which one may be severely burned or indeed may succumb. The aftermath, the sequelae has the coldness and desolation of ashes, as cheerless and sad as the embers of a spent fire. One might also use the same description for a love affair that has faded and died. It is the same with spent anger, one may well ask when the storm is over, where was the passion and where was the fire?

'Donar the mighty' is named in a charm against epilepsy in a twelfth century manuscript. Epileptics are characterised by the possession of unpredictable and furious tempers. Jung teaches that it is always as well to bear in mind, with the problem of very angry children given to temper tantrums and rage, that there may be latent epilepsy.

Once when I was in medical training on duty in a hospital, at about 2 a.m., always the worst time in large cities, I was alone with a nurse. A man was brought in unconscious. He had suffered several fits after imbibing a great deal of alcohol. His breathing was stertorous, and the police who brought him to hospital said that he was known to them and was usually violent. I decided therefore to strap him to the couch with leather straps in order to prevent him from injuring himself by falling on the hard tiled floor. It was a precaution that saved my life and that of the single policeman who accompanied him. Whilst I was writing up the notes at the desk I heard a loud roar of rage, as I turned I saw the patient grinding the tongue clamp, which had secured his tongue to prevent him from swallowing it. In seconds the metal clamp was in pieces, then I realised that he was trying to break the leather straps. This alerted the policeman, a young man probably of my age but rather slight in build, the nurse had fled. He stepped forward to investigate and at that precise moment the first leather strap, (there were two) which was two inches wide snapped. I picked up the telephone and dialled the emergency police. Then the second strap went, and the patient grabbed the policeman by the throat and began to strangle him. I seized the man's arms but was thrown to the floor, this however allowed the policeman to escape the patient's clutches for a moment and to breathe. Then he was again seized by the throat, and overpowered. I still remember the terror of that night. I thought the policeman would die. Fortunately the police station responded with alacrity and the police arrived before the patient turned his attention to me, also the fleeing nurse came back with a night porter and a hospital sister. The policeman was unconscious for a long period, and it was three days before he recovered completely, but he did make a full recovery.

That taught me 'violence in extremis' and the rage contained in epilepsy. The epileptic attack is always terrifying since the victim is shaken exactly like a puppet in the hands of a giant. Since ancient times epilepsy has always been called the divine or sacred disease.

A man came to see me with a skin disease of the face and a depression. His face portrayed a severe Acne Rosacea, a dermatitic manifestation of repressed resentment or rage. During analysis it emerged that he was epileptic. It had begun quite suddenly when he was 56 years old. I asked him when the epilepsy had started. Surprisingly he knew the date and the time. He told me that it was at the funeral of his daughter. She was 30 years old and as the coffin was lowered into the grave, the patient suffered his first epileptic attack. He had been investigated afterwards, and the diagnosis of epilepsy had been made because of the physical signs and the descriptions of a great many witnesses, the mourners at the funeral. He was told that there were no real changes in the brain waves in his Electro-encephalogram, but he was epileptic. However he continued to suffer from the condition, and in order to protect him from the effects of the violent attacks he was given medication which was highly beneficial, and kept the epilepsy under control.

I decided to ask him about his daughter. He told me that he had loved her dearly. She was a very nice person and had made a good career for herself, then she married and had two children. She became pregnant for the third time and somehow in some way she was neglected during the course of the parturition, and a hurried Caesarian section operation was performed at the hospital, during which tragically the mother and baby both lost their lives. The father believed that gross negligence had occurred, and that his daughter and her child had been murdered. However he had been reassured by the medical authorities that the deaths were quite unavoidable, and he therefore accepted this view.

At the moment that his daughter and her child were returned to the earth, the inner rage most probably reached a tumultuous climax and exploded in an epileptic fit. It was as if he had been touched by the Mjöllnir, the Hammer of Donar-Thor. So indeed it was a divine anger. The hammer of Thor was a sacred symbol and it was used in consecrations and blessings as well as to slay giants and enemies, and *it never failed him* and always returned to him. This indicates that the rage belongs to the god. Thunder and lightning always preceded its stroke. (Flint weapons found in the earth are believed to be thunderbolts.)

Odin was the great god of Norse mythology. His worship was widespread throughout the whole of Northern Europe, including England from the 5th century at the time of the Saxon invasion.

Odin, or Wotan as god of the Teutonic race was a god of warriors, a war god.[15] He was also like Hermes, an inventor of the arts and the god of travellers. Naturally he was a great wanderer and was not only the god of the dead but also the leader of the dead.

The name Wotan is very interesting and has been connected with the root 'wod', a word found in the Old Teutonic word 'wōdo' which means mad, furious or frenzy. The Indo-Germanic word wâ which means 'to blow' connects with Wotan being a wind god or a spirit, to do with the wanderings of the wind, and movement of the air. The spirits were supposed to wander with the wind making Wotan not simply the god of the dead but also the Spirit of the dead. German legend knows the wind as the wild huntsman in lustful pursuit of the maiden. Wotan gallops along in the storm after the wind bride (Frigg) who is fleeing before him.

The 'Wudes Heer' was the Furious Host, the leader of which would be in dialect Wode, Wude, Wute. Wudes Heer means the host of Wotan, Wotan's Host.

Wotan reputedly wore a long blue coat and a large broad hat. He had a long grey beard, and one eye since the other had been sacrificed for wisdom from Mimir. He rode upon his black horse called Sleipnir together with his hounds, and his followers some of whom were souls.

Wotan was the god of poetic inspiration and also the god of rage. The Furious Host always presaged evil and was often a precursor of a battle.

In his splendid article on Wotan, Jung[16] explains how it came about that the German nation became possessed by Wotan. This god had disappeared when his oaks fell and apparently fell into a deep sleep in the Kyffhauser mountain, but 'he reappeared when the Christian god proved too weak to save Christendom from fratricidal slaughter'.[17] Jung explains that as an Ergreifen of men, that is one who grips or seizes, Wotan transformed the German state into Ergriffener (the one who was seized). He adds 'a mind still childish thinks of the gods as metaphysical entities existing in their own right, or else regards them as playful or superstitious inventions. From either point of view the parallel between Wotan redivivus and the social, political and psychic storm which shook Germany might have at least the value of a parable'.[18]

The storm which seized Germany was described by Jung as a 'furor teutonicus'. He explained that the essence of the fury was the 'possession' of one man, Adolf Hitler, who was able to infect the whole nation.[19] This is the great danger of psychic possession, and why primitive peoples were mortally afraid of it. It leads to collective madness as is its natural wont.

Wotan was, Jung believed the truest expression and unsurpassed personification of a fundamental quality that is particularly characteristic of the Germans. When he wrote his paper just prior to the onset of the Second World War, Germany was at that time caught as it were in 'the eye of the cyclone'.

Jung[20] wrote these profound words, 'It is above all the Germans who have an opportunity to look into their own hearts, and to learn what those perils of the soul were from which Christianity tried to rescue mankind. Germany is a land of spiritual catastrophes, where nature never makes more than a pretence of peace with world ruling reason. The disturber of the peace is a wind that blows into Europe from Asia's vastness, sweeping in on a wide front from Thrace to the Baltic, scattering the nations before it like dry leaves, or inspiring thoughts that shake the world to its foundations. It is an elemental Dionysus breaking into the Apollonian order. The rouser of this tempest is named Wotan, and we can learn a good deal about him from the political confusion, and spiritual upheaval he has caused throughout history. For a more exact investigation of his character however we must go back to the age of myths which did not explain everything in terms of man and his limited capacities, but sought the deeper cause in the psyche and its autonomous powers. Man's earliest intuitions personified these powers as gods, and described them in the myths with great care and circumstantiality according to their various characters. This could be done the more readily on account of the firmly established primordial types or images which are innate in the unconscious of many race, and exercise a direct influence upon them. Because the behaviour of a race takes on its specific character from its underlying images we can speak of an archetype 'Wotan'. As an autonomous psychic factor Wotan produces effects on the collective life of a people and thereby reveals his own nature.'

He is the rouser of the tempest, and the Germans were powerless to resist when seized by this raging storm. Wotan as the god of the beserkers, the god of frenzy or furious rage embodies the instinctual emotional aspect of the unconscious. But at the same time he permits the manifestations of the intuitive and inspiring side of the unconscious, for it should not be forgotten Wotan read and understood the runes, and so he can interpret fate. After the War, it seemed he disappeared as suddenly as he came.

It is essential that we try to understand these autonomous psychic factors and be aware of the insidious development of collective movements in our own day, some three quarters of a century since Germany was gripped by the archetype of Wotan. Such movements are singularly seductive with their curiously beguiling prophetic promises which inspire hundreds of thousands of people. 'All human control comes to an end when the individual is caught in a mass movement. Then the archetypes begin to function, as happens also in the lives of individuals when they are confronted with situations that cannot be dealt with in any of the familiar ways.'[21]

This was what happened to my epileptic patient when he was swept into an emotional storm as his daughter's body was lowered into the grave. As Jung said 'It has always been terrible to fall into the hands of a living god.'[22]

It may seem that I dwell too long on events that happened a long time ago. But if we begin slowly to gaze around us, to really see the changes which are taking place in modern society, to become aware of a new form of archetypal rage and madness; the anger, the frenzy of the strikers, the militants, the nationalists, the terrorists, all caught in mass movements for apparently a diversity of causes. It may be ostensibly religious as with the Irish Sinn Fein, overtly religious as with the Islamic movements or questions of nationalistic power in the Baltic and certain erst Russian states.

In England the populace has been subjected to innumerable strikes and to a whole year of frenzy engendered by the miners, and led by possessed Marxists during which murder was committed and injuries were rife. This was a mass movement. In 1967 the students rebelled in France, led by a rabble rouser. In all of these uprisings there may or may not be justification, but they are all examples of collective movements in which psychic possession has occurred. The individuals without control are swept along in the fury of the torrent willy-nilly. These mass movements are characterised by brute force and violent aggressivity, frequently insensate rage, and are defeated always in the end. But not until great damage has been wrought, as in the case of the Soviets and the Eastern bloc countries, many decades were to pass.

Today we can hear the rage, the aggressivity in the way people address each other and the language which is used. The so called four letter words which are words of obscenity encompass enormous hostility and repressed anger. The thunderous sound of modern music with the constant repeated drum beat, and the concomitant lightning flashes of the neon lights of discotheques and rock band concerts encompass ideas of storm and storm lightning.

Rage is visible in the graffiti, the curse of modern cities, the spoilation of land, river, the sea even, and all the great cities. It is the disdain of collective consciousness for the world of nature order and discipline. We are enamoured by the rational intellect and the power of the machine. We are no longer aware of the dark instinctual irrational forces which have begun to act autonomously, and to sweep us away into rage and aggression.

As this most terrible of centuries draws to its close, one may describe it as the time that a dormant archetype became re-awakened. Wotan the god of rage reappeared in Europe and the most advanced and cultivated Christian countries were thrown into genocide, mass murder, global wars, privation and spiritual dereliction. The Christian church stands powerless before the magnitude of such evil.

The rise of the scientific rational intelligence, in the eighteenth century promoted its severance with its instinctual roots and this provided a basis for the denial of God. Mass movements began to appear in which men sought to replace the spiritual loss by a sense of human bondage under the patriarchal slave states. The individual became simply a number, and was lost into the maelstrom of the collective, without definition. Suddenly the state was all, with its bureaucracy, secrecy and corruption. But there were too few individuals to cry 'wolf'! and those who did were disposed of quickly.

So it is with all mass movements be they of whatever nature or aim, the individual is lost and no longer exists, he must run with the herd as a unit hither, thither and yonder. His direction is not his own but that of the state, and the tragedy is that he believes it is his own. Spiritually he is no longer alive, for his soul is lost to the collective. This is the present day plight of modern man.

It seems that Wotan has disappeared again, but has he? Immense changes are taking place, but euphoria is not to be indulged. Such times are fraught with danger when 'peoples are in the hands of a living god'.

The awesome nature of these changes can be perceived in the collectivism of state control which is again prevalent, but of a different pattern. All the separate European nations are being submerged into a giant conglomerate based of materialism. Other continents have fallen victim to the contagion of this new mass control.

The submerged anger of countless millions of faceless individuals in Europe and the Asiatic continent erupted into a monumental unconscious storm of frenzy and rage in the earlier part of the century, climaxing in two global wars, to be followed by a succession of others. Now at the present time it is visible in the perceptible rage of smaller groups, such as is seen in the various associations of terrorists who roam without home or boundary, intent only to torture, wound, maim and kill. Human life has no value anymore, and murder is rife, the victim is not considered to be important, only the punishment of the criminals is given consideration. An individual person is set at naught. Obedience is to the leader (be it a Khomeni or similar, a Sinn Fein leader, a Ghadaffi, or any 'ism' chieftain). Therefore, au fond, the allegiance is to an idealist concept which has gripped the mind of the leader.

The unconscious rage has rendered itself visible in modern language, behaviour, art, literature and music. The aggression and hostility is expressed towards 'the other', be it a question of colour, race, sexuality, religion, politics or simply the material world itself. Behind is the portentous problem of the darkening of man's ego awareness and deepening of the unconsciousness of Self.

At the same time, there is an increase in personal unawareness of one's own shadow which is found projected upon 'the other'. The duty of the Christian church in the past was to remind individuals of their sins, and wickedness. In the outer world one finds the enemy who in reality is an aspect of one's unknown dark self. In order to repress him so that unconsciousness must be retained it is necessary to fight him to the death in the outer world. This is the insoluble problem set before mankind today. Insoluble since the cure cannot be found in the external world, but in the inner one, where hubris prevents us from seeking it. It is understandable why the Church Fathers came to consider rage to be a mortal sin.

Yet perhaps it is in just this raging fire where illumination lies.

Every person who undertakes a study of Jung's work, or who undertakes analysis is seeking an increase of consciousness in some form or other for that is the myth of mankind today, the myth of consciousness. Each individual person requires a different level of consciousness or an individual solution for his life.[23]

Barbara Hannah[24] writes that 'Jung was never tempted to despair, for he knew that there was a light in each individual life, even 'a sunlit island'[25] where the opposites are harmoniously united (as they are in light and shade wherever the outer sun shines) at the centre of the life of every individual, and of the world however lost it appears to be in misunderstanding, unconsciousness and strife. How many people can open their eyes wide enough to become aware of this? It seems as if the future of the world depends on the answer to this question.'

THE ARCHETYPE OF FIRE

It will have become clear that emotion and in particular an affect, which affects one such as anger, may be represented or more explicitly symbolised by fire.

So many words used to describe an angry state or anger itself have the connotation of fire. One speaks of a raging temper, a fiery nature, a burning resentment or a boiling fury. All theses and more reveal the association. A sudden blaze of anger is exactly like a fire, and moreover when caught in a rage heat is felt. A sweating occurs exactly as if before or in a fire or immersed in a hot bath. In order to understand emotions the meaning inherent in the symbol is the clue. As far as possible, penetration into all aspects of the symbol must be undertaken.

Fire with its brightness, illumination and warmth is an integral part of human life. In the western world it was always regarded as an element whereas in China it was never considered so. Chinese thought believed that fire was a phenomenon in its own right. It is both purifying and destructive (as in anger) and because of its inherent nature has occupied the minds of men for countless aeons.

The word inflammation from the Latin inflammationem means the action of inflaming or setting on fire, with the associative condition of being in flames. In somatic pathology it is characterised by heat, redness, swelling and pain. Inflammation in all living tissues occurs when they are attacked by antagonistic forces. It should result in regeneration because that is the goal towards which the body strives. Regeneration is the healing of damaged tissue so that it again presents the same form which pre-pre-existed the injury. This is the reaction of the body to all injury or disease. Because of its closely allied connection with psychic anger, it hints at the meaning of anger itself. It is a pointer to a condition where there is antagonism, something is wrong and must be put right. Anger is an inflammation of the psyche.

The image of fire is found universally in myth. The image of fire and the fiery world is well documented by Eliade.[26] The smiths of the circumpolar regional Siberian and North American Indian tribes were all great medicine men and spiritual rulers because they could handle fire, use it, conserve it, produce it all without injury to their persons. They were entitled 'Master of the Fire.' They could perform all manner of tricks or fine acts with fire. They could burn a man to ashes in the embers of the fire and a few minutes later he would be seen taking part in a dance a great distance away. They could swallow live coals, touch red hot iron, or walk on fire. Mastery over fire implied that the master had acquired 'inner heat'. Mystical or inner heat was creative resulting in a kind of magical power which creates. Fire and mystical heat were connected with the ecstatic state indicating that the shaman had entered the realm of the spirit world. Enfolded in all these ideas is the meaning of creation and production by means of fire.

Fire played an interesting rôle in the mediaeval epoch in the Phlogiston theory. This substance was defined as a principle of inflammability supposed to exist in combustible bodies. It was understood to be present in all things, as an invisible and hidden heat, also to be a principle of life. Jung[27] explains that Phlogiston was 'a certain quality of the unconscious which imparts the warmth of life'. It is therefore an inner phenomenon which may be experienced directly during an emotional condition such as an irruption of an irritable thought, an outburst of anger or a blaze of furious rage. The ancients perceived it as the fiery substance of Phlogiston incorporated in outer objects. It was not related by them to their own emotional being, it was a projection upon the external world.

Fire played an immense rôle in Alchemy, a subject which was brought into Jung's life following an important dream, and which he was to study for many years. It was this work which substantiated his concepts concerning the collective unconscious.

The fire was always kept alight in alchemy, all alchemists had to keep the athanor (the stove) burning, so that the goal of the opus could be achieved. This was ostensibly to produce the elixir of life, the Alexipharmacon which neutralised poison and cured the mortal ills of the body.

Jung[28] said that fire 'in itself is a uniter of opposites, and is a very ancient image of God', Christ[29] in the extracanoniacal saying 'Who is near me is near to the fire, He that is far from me is far from the Kingdom.' Jung explains[30] that 'the inmost nature of Christ is fire, the everlasting fire which is the goal of alchemy'.

The meaning contained in the symbol of fire reaches from the very lowest depths of the most heinous passions inherent in the Luciferian fires, to the highest possible purity of the fire of the spirit in its purest divine essence. At the same time its meaning is enfolded in the vast extremes of human wrath from the sulky irritable child, the sullen adolescent to the resentments, anger, rages, frenzies and fury of adults, and the rancourous bitterness of old age. In social congress these emotional disturbances are unacceptable, and are usually hidden suppressed or repressed.

When rage in whatever form is present it appears very often that behind it is the Self whose goal is to bring the subject to an awareness of his inferiorities, his failings or criminal tendencies, by rendering 'visible' or illuminating as it were these unconscious contents. If inner affect or rage can be contemplated and perceived in this light, it usually recedes and falls away with an increase consciousness.

If it is not accepted it may be acted out in a blind fury, a tempestuous

[handwritten margin note top left: NOUN UNCONSCIOUSLY BLOCKING]

[handwritten margin note top right: VOLUNTARILY BLOCKING DELIBERATELY FORGETTING]

quarrel, a fight or even a murder. Or it may again be suppressed or repressed. Any bodily system may then become involved and portray the inner unconscious rage.

As has been observed the gastro-intestinal system is often involved in instances of unexpressed rage, so are other organs, in particular the renal and musculo-skeletal systems, but the organ par excellence is that of the skin. This organ as the primitive mind has always known, acts as a reflector of the soul, and it is the mirror of the psyche.

Numberless maladies which afflict the skin have an emotional background, and by learning to 'read' the skin disease as a mirror image of the state of the soul, the underlying psychic imbalance may be brought to consciousness without much difficulty in a majority of cases.

I SHADOW EFFECTS PORTRAYING MUSCULO-SYSTEM DISORDERS.

One sees this in disorders of the musculo-skeletal system. Often a great deal of hostility is concealed in the disorder.

Many years ago a woman told me that some forty years earlier when she was a young woman of thirty-five years old she had been stricken with an acute severe, and crippling generalised rheumatoid arthritis. All her joints were flexed, and it was thought she would never walk again as in those days the treatment of such a condition was expensive, and deficient of a cure.

She was a religious person, and she prayed that she would be cured for the sake of her children. She made a promise that she would give thanks for the rest of her life if she recovered. A few months later she was able to go to church unaided, but still very lame. In church it suddenly came to her that God was angry with her because her husband had been unfaithful prior to the onset of her malady, and she had not forgiven him. In the church that day she knew that she herself was furiously angry with the husband, although she had not realised it consciously. She had described herself as 'hurt'.

From that day she recovered and in two or three years she had virtually returned to normal health. As almost an octogenarian she was both sprightly in body, quick in mind and was still with the erstwhile unfaithful husband. The attack could be described as a reaction to rage.

A similar case of rheumatoid arthritis did not have such a satisfactory solution. A young girl of good family, whilst at finishing school went abroad and fell in love with a Spanish fisherman of no education or culture. She ran away to live with him and found that he was a loutish brute who ill-treated her, and almost killed her.

She had no money and was forced to live in a rocky cave, with only the company of the village priest who came at night with food. She developed sever arthritis of the rheumatoid type. The priest contacted her family and she was brought home to die within weeks. Prior to her death, I asked her if she was angry with the Spaniard, she looked at me and said 'No I cannot be angry, it would be un-Christian, because I loved him.'

Another example was a young man of twenty-two years who was unmarried and had only one sister of whom he was very fond. The rheumatoid arthritis which had crippled him was of a particularly severe type. The whole of his body was affected, and the appearance of his body was suggestive of being caught in a strait-jacket. Likewise his heart was affected by the disease process and he died before he was twenty-three years of age.

He told me that the disease had started nine years previously when he was thirteen years of age. At the time I had the privilege of looking after this young man. I was only recently qualified as a doctor and I remember taking great pains with the case history. One day I asked him how the disease had started. This is a question of the utmost importance in any case history. In the question how and when did the disease start, usually one finds the answer to the whole problem.

He told me that the disease started when he and his sister who was some years younger were placed in an orphanage. He enlarged and told me that he had gone there when his parents died. I assumed that he felt some anger because they had died and left him, and I wondered if this emotion had been repressed.

However some days later, he requested that I go to see him. As I stood at the bedside he said 'I think you ought to know that my father killed my mother when I was thirteen years old. I came home from school and found my mother's body, and when I went into the kitchen I found my father had hanged himself.'

I realised at that moment that my assumption regarding the unconscious presence of anger in the subject was correct, in that it was responsible for the crippling and devastating illness.

In such circumstances one can visualise the immense anger of an adolescent boy against the father who had deprived him of his mother and of the father himself. He and his sister as orphans were destitute, and in their dereliction at the mercy of the state. They were in fact deprived of any right to appeal as he put it, 'to an unjust God'. In the end he was deprived of life.

II. SHADOW EFFECTS PORTRAYED IN THE RENAL SYSTEM

A woman had a severe father complex. She had loved and hated him, she was his beloved daughter and he was her adored father, most of the time.

Her mother had died when she was thirteen years old, and she had helped to bring up the three younger children.

When she was about twenty-five or so her father thought of marrying again but the patient became so angry she fell into a decline. To save her life the father relinquished his plan to marry, and the father and daughter lived on in an uneasy partnership until the father died.

The woman who had made a success of her professional life had a good job, she liked to travel, to socialise and please herself. She then found a husband, and expecting a life of unending happiness they settled down together.

But she soon found out that her husband was a home-loving person, and did not wish to travel or socialise. She had met her unconscious introverted shadow in which resided a strongly opinionated animus. However the husband did not permit arguments and she found that she could no longer express herself as regards the anger engendered by the husband's positive, reasonable, (but in her view unfeeling) point of view. 'A stalemate was reached', is how she described the situation.

Some years after the marriage she developed a malignant tumour of the kidney which was removed, and from which she recovered completely.

The problem of her anger however was unresolved and she began to express herself in an equally destructive way, she began to vent it upon friends and family.

'Stalemate' is an unusual word. It means standstill. Its use is chiefly in the game of chess. It occurs 'when a position in which the player whose turn it is to move has no alternative move open to him, but has not his king in check'.[31]

'Stale' as an adjective means tasteless, vapid, musty or trite. The verb 'to stale' means to discharge urine as cattle or horses. The noun is the urine of cattle or horses.

In dreams the discharge of urine is to express one's innermost nature. This woman was quite unable to discharge her innermost anger which appertained to the rigid stance of the animosity of the father complex, reactivated by the personality of the new marriage partner seemingly.

SHADOW EFFECTS PORTRAYED IN
DISORDERS OF THE SKIN

I propose now to present case material from dermatological patients to dilineate the aforementioned point in order to illustrate the meaning of unconscious anger in individual cases. It is an endeavour to reveal how the archetype of fire which is one of the two dominant archetypes in skin disorder, the other being of course that of the serpent, is activated in these cases. It brings first recognition of a skin disorder, and at the same time is indicative of psychic imbalance, then secondly the means of a cure for the sufferer.

Fire as an enlightener or illuminator signifies emotion. It is only through emotional interest or excitement that there is illumination and clarification of a psychic content. Emotion as we have observed is the carrier of consciousness. The entire disease process represents a symbolic fire-making process, and the goal is consciousness and re-vivification, but alas not usually achieved without suffering and its hidden partner, insight.

In all cases of skin disorder where an inflammatory process is observed, the fire archetype has been activated.[32]

It brings via the skin disease its activated presence by way of heat, warmth, swelling, pain and reactive reflex actions in an endeavour to guide the victim to a higher level of consciousness where psychic difficulties are recognised.

The same of course occurs in other organs but are not usually visible to the naked eye. Furthermore in my experience it seems that when a 'skin problem' arises it is easier for consciousness to grasp the nature of the psychic problem than it is when deeper organs, kidneys, lungs and heart are involved.

As has been observed the rôle of anger in cases of skin disease is of supreme importance. But as in all things the question of degree is often decisive in the actual disease process itself, be it eczema, psoriasis or one of the blistering disorders. When the rage is deeply repressed as was observed in the case of the woman with lupus erythematosus, it is usually many years before the problem can be dealt with in consciousness. Sometimes the unexpressed rage may be so violent, producing a skin disease of such morbid intensity that the patient may die.

A young man of seventeen years became gravely ill.[33] It was believed that he had developed Small Pox (Syn. Variola Major) by his doctor since his body was covered in blisters. He was feverish and in a state of grave toxicity. The actual dermatological diagnosis was a severe form of a disorder named Dermatitis Herpetiformis.

Briefly the story was this. The young man had just taken his University examinations and whilst waiting for the results he had gone to celebrate Mid-Summer's Eve with a group of friends. The idea was to climb a nearby mountain renowned for huge bonfire parties on the summit in order to welcome Mid-Summer's day each year.

He returned for breakfast the following morning having spent the night on the mountain to be greeted by his wrathful mother. He was unable to give her any kind of explanation because she was so caught up in her furious anger. Three days later he awoke and found that his body was totally covered in blisters.

When I met him he was very ill and remained so for some three or four months. One day much later I was able to discuss the sequence of events which had led to his illness, and he told me that although his mother was a good woman she restricted him and he was not able to love her.

Eventually he recovered, went to the University and then left to live in another country.

The boy's mother was ambitious for her children, and she was held to be possessed of many virtues by her family and friends. She never raised her voice in public and on the occasions when I met her I saw no evidence of emotional display, not even at the onset of her son's illness when I had to inform her that there was a very real possibility that he might die. Undoubtedly as we have learned she had a furious temper, and she gave an impression of coldness and distance that was singularly repelling. Clearly she was dissociated from he inner instinctual world and the realm of feeling. Her unconscious mind, the animus had a thrusting bullying over-riding masculine force and this is what her son had too face.

The illness of this young man was no less than an initiation into consciousness of his mother's darkness, and it was this awareness which enabled him to become in the fullest sense of the word, a man. His masculine qualities of courage and resilience together with obedience, learned with pain through the years with his mother enabled him to pursue the goal of health and survival. This recognition of his mother's mean spiritedness was his release from her power.

The principle factor in this strange story was the setting of the prologue to the drama, the mountain, and the time Mid-Summer's Eve. These great fire festivals celebrated for thousands of years were at base a pledge to the god or the spirit of the fire in its creative aspect, whilst at the same time a seeking to annul or neutralise the destructive effects.

When the young man returned from these rites of initiation he had to confront the archaic image of the archetype of the mother in its negative form. It was this aspect that he had to realise in his serious illness which as stated was a rite d'entrée into manhood.

The long illness and in particular the peculiar blistering aspect is evocative of someone 'burned in a fire' as indeed it was for this patient. The fire was a conflagration of the unconscious mutual anger of the mother and son, and from which the son not only sacrificed his childish dependence but gained his life.

REFERENCES

1 Jung, C. G., Collected Works, Vol. XVIII para 46 n. 14.
2 Ibid.
3 Ibid.
4 Ibid.
5 Ibid.
6 Maguire, A., Skin Disease, A Message from the Soul, Free Association Books, 2004.
7 Definition of Intuition and Sensation functions: Two of the four psychic functions. Both irrational. Intuition informs of possibilities inherent in the present whereas sensation is the contrast function which perceives immediate reality through the physical senses.

8   Jung, C. G., Collected Works, Vol. 2 para 1036 Psychophysical Investigations with the Galvanometer and Pneumograph in Normal and Insane Individuals.
9   Maguire, A., op. cit.
10 Budge Wallis, The Book of the Dead, Routledge & Kegan Paul, London, 1960. The Judgment: The Scene of the Weighing of the Heart of the Dead.
11 Ibid., Chapter 125.
12 Watterson, Barbara, The Gods of Ancient Egypt, Batsford, 1984.
13 Horace, Epistle I ii 62.
14 Definition: Oesophagus: the gullet or food pipe.
15 Jung, C. G., op. cit. Vol X para 371 ff.
16 Jung, C. G., Collected Works, Vol X Wotan (First published as Wotan, March 1936, Neue Schweizer Rundschau (Zürich).
17 Ibid., para 384.
18 Ibid., para 387.
19 Ibid., para 388.
20 Ibid., para 391.
21 Ibid, para 398.
22 Ibid.
23 Hannah, B., Jung His Life and Work, p. 186, Putnam, 1976.
24 Ibid.
25 Jung, C. G., Memories Dreams and Reflections, p. 198, Collins and Routledge & Kegan Paul, London, 1963.
26 Eliade, Mircea, Shamanism, Arakana, 1964.
27 Jung, C. G., Alchemy Lecture Course Vol II para 124.
28 Op. cit. Vol I para 82.
29 The Apocryphal New Testament, p. 35, Trans M. R. James, Oxford University Press.
30 Jung, C. G., op. cit.,Vol I para 94, Notes on Lectures at the E. T. H. Zürich, November 1940 Edition, 1960.
31 Shorter Oxford English Dictionary, Oxford.
32 Maguire, A, op. cit.
33 Ibid.

3

THE DEADLY SIN OF
JEALOUSY

Jealousy is ubiquitous and is found at every age from the child in the cradle until the tomb closes. One may therefore deduce that it is both universal and rampant. Rarely however is it ever discussed except perhaps in the superficial on going chatter of children, young girls and adolescents, where it is frequently an overt phenomenon. One hears it discussed in analysis but perhaps less so in religious counselling. It is of course freely admitted that jealousy is a problem, but although it is seen with alacrity and clearly in others, it is unusual for it to be perceived clearly in one's own character, and is rarely acknowledged in oneself. It is usually denied if the subject is broached, and a strange disinclination to discuss it arises. It is often suppressed or repressed, and is almost always unconscious.

Sokoloff[1] in giving a pertinent and fully documented example of jealousy stated that the most devastating of all the criticism levelled against Richard Wagner was made by Nietzsche in his book 'Nietzsche Against Wagner.' It is the most savagely severe of any criticism against the musician. What makes this so interesting is that Nietzsche in his maiden lecture at the University of Basle, at the age of 25 years spoke of the relationship between music and tragedy, a relationship which was well known to the Greeks. He went on to explain that there was only one living man who fully understood the described relationship, the man was Richard Wagner, the German composer. His great genius was extolled by the speaker whose lecture was warmly received.

On the strength of the lecture the story goes, Nietzsche was invited to visit Wagner at his home at Triebschen near Lucerne. When he arrived at the lonely villa at the foot of Mt. Pilatus he was received by Cosima von Bulow, the daughter of Franz Liszt, who was himself an exact contemporary of

Wagner. Cosima von Bulow was living with Wagner at the time, apparently she greeted Nietzsche very warmly on his arrival, and Nietzsche fell in love with her at once. So began a love, pregnant with deep-rooted jealousy.

This love lasted for twenty-five years and Nietzsche loved no other. It was a love never reciprocated, never returned and Cosima married Wagner. As the years passed the love Nietzsche bore for this woman whom he rarely saw remained intact and unchanging.

Before the mental illness which was to dominate his last years took possession of him, he used to say, 'Where is my wife Cosima?' She never was his wife or lover, except in his imagination. But side by side with this devastating platonic love there grew an overwhelming hatred for the husband, a man he had formerly admired to the point of idolatry.

This hatred was culminated in the writing of the book. Never anywhere in his vast writings does Nietzsche mention his jealousy of the musician. He was however pathologically jealous and the jealousy was murderous in its intent. The book was written to 'kill' Wagner. In Nietzsche the jealousy of his shadow personality was totally unconscious.

In analysis when jealousy is uncovered the prime aim must be to help the analysand become conscious of the jealousy he has towards another, or point out the envious eye, both of which run like hidden uderground streams in the vast unknown caverns of the unconscious psyche. Needless to say when jealousy is unconscious dire effects upon external relationships are rife, and may be cruelly destructive even annihilating, both for the object of the jealousy and the subject's personality itself.

Everyone has or will be jealous at sometime, be it past, present or future. The jealousy may be against parents, siblings, one's spouse, children or friends. Sometimes the jealousy is directed against another who is thought to be more beautiful, more successful or more intelligent. Many are jealous of those who are better educated, richer or born into higher social strata. Some women are jealous of younger women, and older women may be jealous of their children's friends or lovers.

For jealousy to be recognised, one has to face shame. There is probably no other emotion so shaming as jealousy. There is in it an aspect which is despicable, something akin to ignominy, menacing or perhaps harmful and dangerous to the structure of personality. It is an emotion which can split the personality and produce a dissociation. Jealousy can truly be a dangerous emotion, and should always be taken seriously.

Strangely as has been said it is a subject rarely under discussion particularly if it is one's own jealousy. If one studies hundreds of psycho-analytical writings in the course of research one finds comparatively little in the way of a deep exploration of the problem.

One often hears an admission made concerning jealousy which occurred in the past, few individuals appear ready to confess present jealousy, and even when it is admitted there always seems to be a qualifying statement as if a certain justification is necessary before the actual confession is laid bare. This leads one to perceive that jealousy is like a fire in its exposure. During the sequence of events in a house-fire, when the doors and windows as it were are opened, the ensuing conflagration may totally destroy the house. There is a similar potential danger of destruction in jealousy for the personality of the subject. The essential aim of jealousy is to bring down the other, the object of one's jealousy. The idea behind it is to destroy or reduce the other to the point of annihilation. Its essence then is to kill, and that is why unconscious jealousy when unacknowledged by ego-consciousness is so destructive for the subject. It is the central core of schadenfreude, malicious glee at another's humbling, humiliation or downfall.

Not only is it one of the most common of human emotions, but it is often disguised. In one's metier as an analyst, it has to be sought out and exposed to the light. Sometimes this is exceedingly difficult and time consuming because proof must be found in order to pin point and inform the analysand with proof as to where the jealousy lies. It frequently presents itself in bizarre ways, and is deeply concealed behind admiration or love. For years it may seem to be absent in a relationship only to explode unexpectedly with savagery, destruction, and perhaps death.

Jealousy is a phenomenon which must be viewed gravely and every endeavour made to expose it to ego-consciousness. Awareness of its presence is vital for everyone concerned because it is present in every human being, and will affect one at some time during their life. One must know if one is jealous.

ETYMOLOGY OF THE WORD JEALOUSY

The noun 'jealousy' means the quality of being jealous, to be jealous indicates that one is uneasy through fear of, or on account of preference given to another. It also has the meaning of being suspicious in love, apprehensive of rivalry, anxiously fearful, or careful whereby there is a solicitude for others. (This is a very important point, which is central to the deception of the deceiver.)

The actual word 'jealous' is derived from the Middle English word 'Gelus' which in turn stems from the Old French Gelos, the modern French is jalousie, 'jalouse' being the feminine adjective, and 'jaloux' the masculine. The French word jalousie has a double meaning. It is identical with jealousy, and it is also used to denote a blind or shutter made of slats of wood which slope in such a way as to admit air, and only a certain amount of light. When someone is jealous he cannot see clearly. For this reason a thick ribbed and non-transparent glass was called jealous glass.

Gelos is derived from the medieval Latin 'Zelosus' and the late Latin word 'Zelus' or Zelotypia which has a negative aspect. The Greek word

Σλλοζ = zeal or jealousy and it means excessive love.

In the English language since 1661, this word has meant an implication of vehemence, wrath, desire or devotion. Vehemence itself implies ardour, violence, force, impetuosity or fury. From the start it has been clear that there is something excessive about jealously. It is commonly intertwined in meaning with devotion, desire or wrath. The quality of vehemence should not be cast aside in recalling the true meaning of jealousy, one may think of jealous desire, jealous anger or jealous devotion. It could just as easily be said devotedly jealous or furiously jealous. The qualifying word again implies vehemence.

There is also the slightly older meaning (since 1555) that to be jealous is to be ardently amorous, fond or lustful. There is also the meaning of vigilance in guarding something or someone suspiciously watchful. One sees this in the animal world when an animal seeks to protect its food. Such words vigilance and watchful appertain to the eye. In all these aspects there is the background meaning of something excessive, something primitive not civilised.

Finally there is the fact that when one is suspiciously vigilant to prevent something from being expressed or understood one may be accused of jealousy. Vigilance in scrutiny can also be described as jealous, a jealous watchful nature. This brings up the further meaning of suspicion or apprehension of evil.

Jealousy is also connected with rivalry, and therefore indicates an implicit fear of the 'other'. It is not by any means a simple phenomenon it is a deep emotion whose roots descend into its primitive origins in the deep layers of the collective unconscious psyche.

Envy and jealousy are often confused. Perhaps it might be helpful to examine 'Envy' at this juncture.

ENVY

In general terms it is a noun used to describe pain or discontent excited by another's superiority or success, it also implies malice towards the object of envy. One feels envy 'towards' or 'on account of', one begrudges another.

Envy stems from the medieval word 'envie' which is derived from the French 'invidus' and the Latin 'invidia'. Both words being related to the Latin 'invidere' which means 'to look at or look upon in a bad sense'.

Francis Bacon[2] in his essay on 'Envy' wrote the following:

'There be none of the affections which have been noted to fascinate or bewitch but love and envy; they both have vehement wishes, they frame themselves readily into imaginations and suggestions, and they come easily into the eye especially upon the presence of the objects which are the points that conduce to fascination if any such there be. We see likewise the scripture calleth envy an evil eye.

Of all the affections it is the most importunate and continual, therefore it is well said 'Invidia fastus dies non agit,' that it is ever working upon some or other. It is also the vilest affection and the most depraved for which cause it is the proper attribute of the Devil; Who is called the most envious man that soweth tares amongst the wheat by night.'

Envy means ill will, malice and enmity, and has done so since 1707. Prior to that date it meant odium in the English language or unpopularity. The meanings of ill will, harm and mischief, together with mortification occasioned by the contemplation of anothers superior advantages are combined in such a way that one is able to speak of an object of envy. With this must certainly be found emulation and a longing with enthusiastic desire for another's advantages. It is just here that confusion with jealousy may arise.

The wish to emulate in order to be the same as the apparent superior other is instigated by an envy incidentally unconscious which lies behind the mask of adoration or admiration. The reason for the envy is the unrecognised pain and discontent with oneself. Envy in its covert positive side is very often an instigator of change in the life of an individual, but not always with consciousness of the sequence of events, and not always for good.

To summarise it means that to be envious one feels envy at the supposedly advantageous state of the other, or one regards with discomfort another's possessions of some real or imagined superior nature. One wishes oneself at the level of another or to be possessed of that which the other has by virtue of birth, acquisition or merit.

The envious one feels a grudge or begrudges another, and is malicious.

It is one's duty to know when one is jealous. If one is not conscious of being jealous, and the conscious mind is unsullied by doubt the dark demon lives on in satanic majesty behind one's adaptation to the humdrum life of everyday events. The unconscious jealousy slowly undermines the object of our jealousy, and its aim is to produce harm or even cause death. By doing so the subject's own life is then in peril.

The consciousness of the presence of envy or jealousy does not erase these emotions, but at least consciousness prevents the shadow from cleaving to it with such passion.

THE NATURE OF JEALOUSY

It appears that envy concerns that which one has not, but would like to have, whereas jealousy concerns that which one has, but which one does not wish to lose.

Psychologically it is not always easy to perceive the difference. Jealousy is not a subject open to discussion in all circumstances. It is usually hidden or partially concealed. It is never quite legitimate because it depicts private possessiveness of a singularly disagreeable nature.

Why is there so much shame attached to this emotion, and why the necessity for concealment from oneself?

In a psychological study of jealousy Sokoloff[3] said, 'Neither anger nor fear produce shame quite like that attached to jealousy, nor do they respectively evoke such protest.' It seems that the integrity of the jealous subject is menaced by this emotion more than any other.

Jealousy is an enigma, the least known of all human passions, and as stated the least discussed. The danger attached is always a serious one because of the concealment and denial, and the affects on both the subject and the object.

All relationships are complex and nothing is as it seems, particularly in the realm of partners and lovers. It seems superficially that jealousy is simply a possessiveness or vanity, a will to power or simply egocentricity.

It is undoubtedly a common and widely held belief that jealousy is easily understood since 'one knows what jealousy is'! Yet this is an opinion, for jealousy is indeed difficult to define. It is basically bound up with envy and excessive love.

Sokoloff asks 'Is jealousy a part of love?' and states that the French are very jealous by nature and believes 'that jealousy follows love as a shadow follows man'. He also quotes Montaigne who believed that the source of jealousy was sex. Molière who thought 'only the one who loves without ardour is not jealous', La Rochefoucauld on the other hand blamed self love and vanity as the underlying factors. Proust[4] writes that 'Jealousy is one of those intermittent maladies, the cause of which is capricious, imperative, always identical in the same patient, sometimes entirely different in another.' He implies that jealousy as an illness produces a sick patient.

He continues, 'Rare indeed is the jealous man whose jealousy does not allow certain concessions. One will consent to infidelity provided that he is told of it, another provided that it is concealed from him. They appear to be equally absurd since if the latter is more literally deceived inasmuch as the truth is not disclosed to him, the other demands in truth, the food, the extension, the renewal of his sufferings.' He expands, 'What is more, these two parallel manias of jealousy extend often beyond words, whether they implore or reject confidence . . . ' Furthermore 'however skilfully jealousy is concealed by him who suffers from it, it is at once detected by her who has inspired it and who when the time comes is no less skilful . . .' 'Jealously it seems is endless, for even if the beloved object by dying can no longer provoke it by her actions, it so happens that posthumous memories of later origin in any event take shape suddenly in our minds as though they were events also, memories which until now we have never properly explored, which had seemed to us unimportant, and to which our own meditation upon them becomes sufficient without external action to give a new and terrible meaning . . .'

Enlarging further Proust[5] continues, 'Jealousy is moreover a demon that cannot be exorcised, but always returns to assume fresh incarnation. Even if we could succeed in exterminating them all in keeping forever her whom we love, the Spiritual Evil would then adopt another form, more pathetic still, despair at having obtained fidelity by forces, despair at not being loved.'

This description brings to consciousness an extension of the definition of jealousy, but does not include the exact selfishness of malevolence which is inherent, the secret aim of which is to bring down, reduce, harm or destroy the object who does not love us, or does not love us enough.

Sokoloff[6] includes Descartes' definition of jealousy 'as a kind of fear, related to a desire to preserve a possession'.

In the plant world, one may see how one plant will overtake or even overthrow its neighbour to get to the sunlight. In animal litters the same phenomenon with reference to nourishment is observed.

Undoubtedly inherent in nature, the supremacy of the will to survive must be associated with what in human terms is described as a jealous disposition. It is an inherent pre-disposition which is age-old to seek the means to survive, be it of whatever nature. It is in this area where confusion with what is humanly described as envy, enters the picture.

Sometime ago I was greatly alarmed whilst sitting in the kitchen of my house to hear a deep sustained and ferocious growling sound issuing from my cat. She had been curled up purring contentedly a moment before. She left her cushion at once, went to the window and continued to exhibit her displeasure. On the other side of the window the head of a man appeared, it was my gardener who was in the process of repairing a path. His approach had not been heard by me, but my cat was extremely concerned. He had invaded her territory of which she was the jealous guardian, with knowledge of every nook and cranny, all its inhabitants on, above, and below the surface. The instant and tremendous change from the contented purring to the terrifying deep-voiced growl was very striking. It brought rapidly to my consciousness the thin layer of domesticity which covered her wild nature. By her growling she established to all and sundry (myself in this instance) her grave displeasure at the intrusion of a human being. He had put 'his foot' in her place. I was at once reminded of a Mayan guide in Mexico who told me that it was unlikely to find a true Mexican Indian who had been bitten by a rattlesnake, because an Indian would know where to put his foot and would not therefore tread upon the house of his brother, (that is, the rattlesnake) guarded jealously by its occupant. The gardener was quite unconscious of my cat's incurred displeasure, and of the fact that the garden was her territory!

Again one finds the same phenomenon in the relationship between the animal world and the human species. Many years ago a friend of my mother's brought her new baby to be admired. She put the child in a chair which was usually occupied by my mother's cat, a gloriously dignified golden Persian. At the very moment that the child was placed in the chair the cat walked into the room. He gazed at the child, dropped his ears flat, and began to stalk it across the room exactly as he would a bird or a mouse. The cat gaze was hypnotic, indeed it hypnotised me until his body began to tremble as he gave out a fierce and frightening growl. It was only instant human reflex intervention which saved the child from serious harm. The cat was normally very placid, but the child was occupying his rightful place.

In the aforementioned cases the feline jealousy concerned endangered territories.

With respect to jealousy in the canine realm it appears to derive from loss of human affection or relatedness.

A friend of mine had a fine Chow Chow. He was renowned for his great independence, but he truly adored his master, who lived near to me. One day and God knows why he did it, the latter brought home a young male Chow Chow as a companion for the older dog. They seemed at first to get on. I for one did not care for the newcomer, I thought he had a singular malevolent expression and appeared to resent the old dog's presence particularly when the master greeted the old dog first. Within a little while, Chang, the older Chow began to scratch himself, and soon developed eczema. He was taken to the veterinary surgeon who gave him the usual medication, but without avail. Eventually he was brought to me. I told his master that I felt he was unhappy with the new dog, but he (a true rationalist) refused to believe it. However a strange thing occurred, I found that on my return home in the evenings Chang would be waiting at my gate. He would come into the house and stay until I telephoned his master to come and fetch him. The penny at last dropped, and the master got rid of the young dog. Chang's eczema cleared, and he stopped calling upon me in the evenings.

However we remained on extremely friendly terms until his death some years later. Here was a case of jealousy between two dogs for their master's affection. The older dog suffered the most, and it was the development of a psychogenic eczema which did in fact bring the whole incident to consciousness and thereby the resolution of the conflict.

Chows are very proud dogs, extremely independent and live in a particularly self-contained manner. A friend of mine[7] had a beautiful Chow Chow called Hassan, who roamed the streets of central London independently at the turn of the century when she was a young girl, and when there was less traffic than today. However if she met him in Piccadilly or Regent Street early in the morning he did not acknowledge her. But on arrival home at breakfast he became his usual friendly self. He guarded his privacy in the streets of central London jealously. All of these canine jealous reactions are atavistic.

One should however never underestimate jealousy particularly in the animal world. I read some years ago of a tragic incident. A woman owned a bulldog which was very much attached to her, and followed her every move. The dog did however show signs of jealousy every time someone tried to touch or embrace her. He was quite jealous of her husband. Then the woman had a little girl, and it appeared that the dog became neglected. The woman played with the child in front of the dog and paid him no attention. One day the little girl attempted to stroke the dog in her mother's presence. The dog leapt at her throat, and before the mother was able to free the child from the dog's grip death occurred. This tragic story illustrates a not uncommon example of jealous dogs who object violently to others who seemingly take affection away from them. It also indicates that in such cases it behoves the human being to be conscious of the emotional life of their pets.

In the human world, and in particular the family environment, the same rules apply. So often parents dismiss out of hand any suggestion that their offspring are jealous amongst themselves or show signs of it towards the parents.

A woman had a small son who had a minor skin eczema. At the time he was seventeen months old. In the same room at the time of examination a baby girl was sleeping in her cot. She was one month old and he was at great pains to explain that it was his baby sister. The solicitude was excessive, there was something desperate about it. I asked the mother if he was jealous of the baby which would have been entirely natural. She would have none of it, her dismissal was instantaneous which led me to wonder if she was concealing something. As I observed the boy he began to climb over chairs and scamper over the sofa knocking everything over. He was quite wild and undisciplined in his behaviour.

After I had looked at his skin his mother left the room for a moment. The boy at once approached the sister's cot, and quite precisely and very delicately pulled the coverlet up over the child's face. Then he looked at me and said quite directly so that I would understand 'All gone!'

He was less than 18 months old, and there was no doubt that he was caught by a powerful emotion and was beside himself. I drew the mother's attention to the situation on her return, but she thought it was amusing. She was quite unaware that her child was gripped by jealousy which accounted for his wild behaviour.

The boy's jealousy in the circumstances was understandable. During the mother's pregnancy with him she developed an infection of the lungs which required long months in hospital prior to his birth. After parturition he was removed, and the first six months of his life was spent in a children's home cared for by strangers. He did not lie in his mother's arms until he was about seven months old. Then less than a year later a sister was born, thus shattering the fragile and recently developed security gleaned from the individual attention of one human being's constant care.

He was then displaced because his sister had become the focus of attention in his mother's life, a mother who because of her illness had been an 'absent mother'. Furthermore one can never know whether there were actual negative feelings directed towards the child by the mother herself during her enforced and lengthy confinement to bed. The mother only knew this child during the in-utero period before he was removed at birth. So in fact the second child the baby girl was the first child to be nursed by her in those critical early months. Undoubtedly she was inexperienced, and this also may have played a part in the development of fear and panic vehemently expressed as I witnessed on the elder child's part.

It was at this point that I became aware of the absence of a basic conscious appreciation of this most violent of elemental passions in the milieu of the family. What I did in fact witness was simply a jealous reaction, and also the beginning of the formation of a jealous complex which came to fruition in the succeeding years.

To be jealous means that one is troubled by the belief, suspicion or fear that the good which one desires to gain or keep for oneself has been or may be diverted towards another.

Perhaps one may be forgiven in reiterating that a jealous individual always carries the potential to harm or murder another.

A small boy of four or five years was found lying by the fireplace in his home. He was unconscious with a depressed fracture of the skull. His sister who was approximately eight years old was reading in the same room. A poker was at the side of the child about two feet away from its usual place. When the girl was questioned she denied any knowledge of the serious accident. However the father did admit that the child was extremely jealous of her brother. This may be classed as an egotistical primitive reaction almost animalistic in nature.

Even in cases where a great effort is made to inform siblings of the arrival of another member into the family circle it does not always lead to prevention of the emotion.

A group of anthropologists made a television film of the Baka tribe in North Cameroun. The team spent several months in a small village in the heart of the rain forest. Apparently Baka parents are exceedingly good to their children and it is the task of the father to explain to the children carefully and slowly about everything which occurs to the them in the daily life of the family. The subjects for explanation include the house, the food, the herbs for cooking, the animals and so forth. The film depicted a father explaining these things to his two year old son.

One must of course bear in mind the film was made by cameramen in the presence of technicians. During the night the mother of the child gave birth to a daughter. The boy was taken to see his newly born sister in the morning as his father had explained the sister's impending arrival. The child could speak, and he uttered a few words. As his face looked down impassively upon that of his newly-born sister the camera caught the intentness of his expression as he scrutinised her. At that moment the interpreter provided the English interpretation of his comment. It was 'Throw it away!'

There is no doubt the expression upon his face conveyed it all. He did not know her, but he held malicious feelings towards the new arrival. She was quite simply 'there' on his mother's knee. That reaction could be described simply as a jealous reaction.

Jealousy is present it seems from the cradle. It belongs to the whole of human kind, and is part of the human condition as well as a phenomenon of the plant and animal worlds.

When jealousy is triggered or focussed it induces a jealous reaction, the echoes of the reality of the instinctual drive may reach back into the darkest aeons of pre-history. It has been described as 'essentially a negative and atavistic reflex'. We are all capable of and do suffer from jealousy of every description from the simple reaction to a profound pathologically jealous state. Most of us inhibit the jealous reaction without difficulty, and provided it remains under control and one is conscious of it then usually no great harm is caused. If the jealousy is not simply a reaction with a rapid resolution but persists actively then one speaks of a jealous feeling or sentiment. A sentiment is not so easy to control even though repressed, since it lives on as an active unconscious content, partly (sometimes wholly) split off from consciousness.

The repression of a jealous sentiment favours the formation of a complex. It perhaps is in order to state that a jealous complex is the most common form of manifestation of overt jealousy. It is the establishment of a jealous complex which leads to obsession.

As an example here is a case which Jung described.[8] A man walking with a friend in the region of a country village became irritated when the church bells began to peel. The friend was surprised because he himself thought that they were harmonious. On questioning his friend he was told that the clergyman of the church wrote bad poetry. The causal complex became apparent for the man who complained of the bells also wrote poetry, and in a recent criticism his work had been compared unfavourably to that of the clergyman. This was jealousy of a more successful rival. The man did not wish to acknowledge his jealousy, and his emotion formed a repressive complex. So because of his unconsciousness of this fact, the complex came out in the irritation, seemingly caused by the church bells.

Clearly jealousy is not only a basic reaction, but also a universally subjective emotion which affects every aspect of human relationships. Age-old and in its most primitive aspect uninfluenced by civilising practices since closely bound up with egocentric drives of the life-urge for survival.

It is here that danger lurks since social factors do not change either its nature or its intensity.

It will depend on specific circumstances as to whether a jealous reaction of the child (or animal) progresses further to a recurring feeling or sentiment and finally to complex formation.

The rôle of consciousness cannot be stressed too strongly and indeed must be regarded as of primary value in dealing with jealousy. However the passionate vehemence inherent in its most primitive essence as an instinctive autonomous drive to kill carries with it compulsion, obsessionalism, violence, sadism and insanity as concomitant possibilities. This is why jealousy has always been regarded by many as the most deadly of mortal sins, and is so feared amongst all primitive peoples.

A CASE OF A JEALOUS MURDER

Jung tells us in his Memories Dreams and Reflections[9] of a case which he had never forgotten.

A lady came to his consulting rooms refusing to give her name, she said it did not matter. She told him she had been a doctor, and he commented that it was apparent that she belonged to the upper levels of society. She came to Jung to confess by telling him that twenty years earlier she had committed a murder out of jealousy. She had poisoned her best friend because she coveted and envied her her husband, and because she wanted to marry him. She had thought that if the murder was not discovered it would not disturb her. In order to marry the husband the simplest and most direct way was to eliminate the friend. She thought that moral considerations were of no importance to her.

The consequences?

After she had killed her friend she did in fact marry the man, but he died soon afterwards at a relatively young age. During the following years a number of strange things happened. The daughter of this marriage endeavoured to distance herself from her mother as soon as she had grown up. She married young and at once vanished from view and then drew farther and farther away until ultimately the mother lost all contact with her.

The lady was a passionate horsewoman, and owned several riding horses of which she was extremely fond. One day she discovered that the horses were beginning to grow nervous under her. Even her favourite shied and threw her. Finally she had to give up riding. Thereafter she clung to her dogs. She owned an unusually beautiful wolfhound to which she was greatly attached. As chance would have it this dog was stricken by paralysis. With that her cup was full, she felt that she was morally done for. She had to confess her crime. And for this purpose she went to Dr. Jung. He tells us: 'She was a murderess, but on top of that she had also murdered herself. For one who commits such a crime destroys his own soul, the murderer has already passed sentence on himself. If someone commits a crime and is caught he suffers judicial punishment. If he has done it secretly without moral consciousness of it and remains undiscovered the punishment can nevertheless be visited upon him as our case shows. It comes out in the end. Sometimes it seems as if even animals and plants know it.'

As far as I know Dr. Jung never saw her again. As a result of the murder the woman was plunged into unbearable loneliness. She had become alienated from animals. And in order to stave off this loneliness Jung tells us she approached him in order to share her knowledge. She had to have someone who was not a murderer to share the secret. She wanted to find a person who could accept her confession without prejudice for by doing so she would achieve once more something resembling a relationship to humanity. (If one carries a secret one is cut off, isolated from the human group.) The person would in Jung's view have to be a doctor rather than a professional confessor. He believed that she would have suspected a priest of listening to her because of his office, that he would not accept the facts for their own sake, but for the purpose of moral judgment. She had seen people and animals turn away from her and had been so struck by this silent verdict that she could not have endured any further condemnation.

Dr. Jung thought that ultimately she would be driven to suicide. He could not imagine how she would have gone on living in that utter loneliness.

In the woman's case it started with envy, and went on to jealousy and finally to murder. The evil eye had been cast at the very outset when she espied her friend's husband, she wanted him and a marriage to him for herself. She got both, but at what cost.

Jealousy is likened to ownership. It is when we exist in a partnership of any kind that we appear to own a person. This is a state of identity, and could be described as a partial state of participation mystique, a term used by Lévy Bruhl.[10] Subjectively the other person then seems to control us, and as Jung explained the wish or need for affection is the key to the relationship. The 'other' then assumes a place of paramount importance in one's life. One must consider the reaction when an intruder enters the domain of the twosome, be it at work, at home or in the bed. At once there is the instinctive rejection.

A young man of about thirty-five years of age was successful in his occupation, and had achieved he believed a relatively relaxed attitude to life. He did not rise easily to anger, and was apparently able to rationalise all uncomfortable emotions.

One day he came for his analytical hour looking rather despondent but assured me that all was well. At the time he was engaged to be married and his fiancée had gone abroad with her employer a young and dynamic man. The whole thing had been discussed prior to her departure, and as my analysand said there was 'No problem'. (A comment which is usually a lie.) The upshot of the matter was that at the end of a fourteen days' absence he had received one brief telephone call from his beloved who told him she was having 'a fabulous time', her very words.

His story was divulged to the accompaniment of a 'hangdog' or despondent expression. He then gave me a dream in which his elder sister was sick. I asked him if he he had anything to tell me about his sister. It is always vital in analysing a dream to obtain associations to the dream figures which appear. He told me at once that his sister had been very jealous of him for his mother's affection because he was his mother's favourite child. In fact the patient was very jealous of his sister.

He does indeed as the dream portrayed have a jealous anima which had become activated by the thoughtless behaviour of his fiancée. When enquiry had been made on previous occasions as to whether he was jealous he had readily denied it. On this occasion he at last admitted it, and moreover had the intention to finish the relationship with the girl and break off the engagement on her return. Here was the element of murder, he had decided to kill the relationship and brutally punish her because secretly he believed that she was his alone, as had been his mother. The fact that she might prefer another was unacceptable to him, and therefore she must be punished.

With regard to jealousy engendered by success Jung[11] had this to say:

'I see you have had some success, it is therefore appropriate to offer my commiserations for they are more in order than congratulations.'

Through the years I myself have discovered there is a great truth contained in this remark. Indubitably success engenders jealousy, and it is very helpful to know it.

Jealousy is not a simple phenomenon and neither is love. When love is rejected, scorned, spurned, displaced, belittled, begrudged, ridiculed or simply withdrawn jealousy enters the arena.

However when jealousy is present there is always the real possibility that love does no longer exist, as indeed may not have been present à priori. Love has a lot to do with kindness, jealousy has nothing whatever to do with it.

To be caught and possessed by this phenomenon is disagreeable and demeaning, but it is its compulsive nature which makes it so difficult to escape from its pervasive grip.

Sigmund Freud[12] saw jealousy primarily as hatred accompanied by wounded self esteem and followed by grief. Anger, sadness and a sense of betrayal are prime effects which lead to isolation because one carries an inner secret. Because of his work on the unconscious through dream analysis Freud was able to delineate the undercurrent of unconscious tensions in familial situations, and demonstrate the intensity of childhood jealousy. He believed that there was a 'normal' jealousy present in everyone which if not overt was repressed. The two other types which he described were neurotic jealousy and pathological. The former he explained as being over-sensitive jealousy based on guilt and projection because it was without foundation. He believed pathological jealousy to be either delusional in nature or paranoid, and due to unconscious projection. In Jungian terms this would be described as projections of the unconscious shadow of the ego personality.

THE SHADOW PERSONALITY

At this point it might be helpful to compare biblical sources referring to envy and jealousy. In Psalm 73: v 3, it is said, 'envy is an evil affection of the heart which makes men grieve and fret at the good and prosperity of others'. In Genesis 30: v. 1, one reads that 'Rachel envied Leah because of her fruitfulness'.

An appalling case was reported some years ago of a childless couple who sought out a pregnant woman in the pretence that the wife was also pregnant. The friendship between the couple and the woman began in a pre-natal clinic of a hospital where the woman was attending for a clinical assessment. When the woman eventually bore her child the childless couple came to see and congratulate her. After her return home they continued to visit her and in the end they killed the woman and stole her child. Thanks to the efficiency and persistence of the police they were traced and the child was returned to its grieving grandparents.

Shadow feelings of inferiority on the part of the envious woman and a satanic lustful envious need to possess a child led to this frightful murder. In all probability the woman was the instigator of the plan to murder and steal the baby, and the husband acquiesced and went along with it. Again in Genesis 37: v. 11, it is stated that 'Joseph was envied by his brethren because his father loved him.' This is again an example of sibling jealousy which is the hinterland of all brotherly animosity and rivalry. Again in Job 5:v.2, one learns 'wrath killeth, and envy slayeth the silly one'.

At base all envy stems from unrecognised inferiorities and the evil or the envious eye one casts upon another which rebounds back to oneself eventually, and the harm which one wishes to visit upon the other is returned to one's own person.

In Proverbs 27: v. 4, there is this cryptic statement, 'But who is able to stand before envy.' One might add the equally terse comment 'Who indeed?'

There are many references to jealousy in the Bible, and mostly they refer to the jealousy of God. For instance Corinthians (2) 11 v. 2. 'For I am jealous over you with Godly jealousy.' Again Kings (i) 19: 10, 'I have been jealous for the Lord of Hosts.' In Joel 2:18 'Then will the Lord be jealous for his land.' Finally in Psalms 79: 5, these ominous words, 'How long Lord shall thy jealousy burn like a flame?' These are examples of divine jealousy.

One sees today in the popular press and in media presentations of the terrifying personality cults which incite and inflame positive and negative passions. However at base there is usually envy or jealousy, and if the cult figure should seemingly commit some misdemeanour, make a mistake, omit a service or should displease the press reporters or media presenters then he (or she) is subjected to the most vile process of destruction. Some fight back perhaps to be ruined by what can only be described as a witch hunt, or they may be forced into mental states which lead eventually to destruction or death. The 'Fourth Estate'[13] can be said to act to a man with collective demonic savagery, and take upon itself the mantle of deity against those who supposedly displease them.

The press and media of the modern world consists of aggregates of individuals with likes, dislikes, inferiorities small and great, unconscious of their passions of envy and jealousy. Where such passions are collective who indeed can stand before such monumental jealousy or envy. How does this come about?

Of course it works indirectly through the shadow. One has only to look at the amazing popularity of such tedious and mundane television series, such as 'Coronation Street' and 'East Enders' on British television. Or on a more materialistic level, but nevertheless equally tedious though more sophisticated is the popular American television programmes to perceive the great rôle of the shadow in all the un-ending conflict situations. Projections flourish in malicious gossip and vituperation, and rather than face one's own defects of envy, jealousy and other passions they are projected and found outside.

The shadow as C. G. Jung has stated frequently in his writings refers to that part of the personality which has been repressed for the sake of the ego-ideal. Since everything unconscious is projected we encounter the shadow in projection. Thus in our view of 'the other' we see our own shadow. As a figure in dreams or fantasies the shadow represents the personal unconscious. It is like a mixture of the personal shapes of our complexes and is the gateway to all deeper transpersonal experiences. Von Franz states,[14] 'Projections of all kinds obscure our view of our fellows thus spoiling our objectivity and chance for real relationship.' As soon as, in our case, envy or jealousy is realised it does not go away but perhaps we may avoid harming the other, and we may then be able to have the opportunity to become objective and see the other's true reality. Von Franz[15] continues, 'It would be easy if one could integrate the shadow into the conscious personality just by an honest attempt to use one's insight. But unfortunately such an attempt does not always succeed.'

The reason for this is that one is always unaware that the drive inside one's shadow is so compassionate and intense that reason may not stand up to it. One knows how difficult it is to overcome feelings of jealousy for another, try as one may it sometimes needs an external event to obstruct and brake the shadow impulses. Von Franz does however stress and explain that often only an external event may stop the shadow impulses and drives, sometimes a heroic decision may, but[16] 'only if the Self supports the individual in the endeavour.'

If we do not become conscious of the shadow it is able to exert its power over us in a projected form which is compulsive and negative. In dreams the shadow appears more often than not as an inferior personality.

However there can also be a positive shadow which appears when we tend to identify with our own negative qualities, and are unaware of our 'good' or better side, thus the positive ones are said to be repressed and stay below in the unconscious. In such cases the human being lives below his or her true level. The ego is compounded of one's inferior qualities and the positive potential remains unintegrated, and one either under values one self or identifies with one's negative side in which case the positive potential becomes the characteristic of the shadow. It is understandable that the shadow is then positive.

A young woman of good intellect dreamed constantly of her older sister who was she believed cleverer, more practical, and in every way superior to herself. When she dreamed that she was in the presence of this sister she always had a feeling of great inferiorities, and felt like a lowly worm. She had identified with her own lesser qualities and felt very negative towards herself. During the course of a long analysis with assiduous attention to dreams, the young woman came to realise that she possessed all these positive qualities of her sister which had been projected, and which had to be integrated into ego awareness. She told me that only then was she able to comprehend that she had been furiously jealous of this sister whom she had professed to admire and love beyond reason.

Von Franz[17] states explicitly, 'There is additional disadvantage in projecting our shadow. If we identify our own shadow with the other, capitalist or communist, part of our personality remains on the opposing side. The result is that we constantly (although involuntarily) do things behind our backs that support this other side, and thus we shall unwittingly help our enemy. If on the contrary we realise the projection, and can discuss matters without fear or hostility, then dealing with the other person sensibly there is a chance for mutual understanding or at least of a truce.'

GENRES OF JEALOUSY

The Divine Aspect of Jealousy

In Hermione on the east coast of Argolis in ancient Greece, there stood on a low hill a temple to Hera who was worshipped there as *parthenos* – virgin, but on a higher hill outside the town there stood the temple of Hera Teleia and Zeus, who it is reputed seduced her in that place. The mountain with this temple dedicated to Hera Teleia had the name of Kokkyx, or Kokkygia which means cuckoo or Mount Cuckoo. It was a name associated only with the peak of the mountain. It displaced according to Kerēnyi,[18] the older name Thronax or Thornax which means footstool, and was based on the older seduction myth of Hera by Zeus. This myth implies the use of the older name meaning the throne footstool, under Hera's feet because it was Hera who was enthroned there. The cuckoo into which Zeus transformed himself needed neither throne nor footstool. Apparently Hera had become separated from the other gods and goddesses, and was caught in a thunderstorm, initiated by Zeus to further the seduction.

Kerēnyi[19] explains the myth in detail:

Whilst Hera sat there on the mountain where her temple was later to be situated she allowed the half-frozen bedraggled cuckoo to alight on her knees, and she covered it with her robe. Then Zeus revealed himself as her suitor. At once Hera had to appeal to the mother because of her ban on marriage between brother and sister. No Athenian bride was allowed to marry a homogastrios, a brother who had the same mother as herself.[20] Such a marriage between them, with Zeus as suitor would have been contrary to the greatest matriarchal incest prohibition. The mother however permitted Hera to trangress this ban on love making between brother and sister, and Hera was permitted to become Zeus's wife. The myth portrays Zeus as the intruder into the matriarchal domain, in which Hera was enthroned as ruler, in much the same manner as the cuckoo slyly lays its eggs in the nests of other birds.

The large intrusive cuckoo fledgling is hatched and fed by the adoptive parent birds, and develops at the expense of their own off-spring who are ousted from the nest. This is symbolic of the growth on an unconscious jealous content at the expense of consciousness which may eventually overpower and destroy it. Such is the nature of jealousy.

The cuckoo as the bird of jealousy came to symbolise the fearful jealousy of Hera the Great Mother Goddess, and indeed Zeus gave her plenty of reason to be jealous with his myriad of infidelities. Although the cuckoo actually symbolises a natural sibling jealousy it also points to the deeper level of forbidden incestuous jealousy.

The moment of the bird's arrival signifies in fact the unconscious fear of deprivation which later gave way to overt jealousy when Zeus invaded the matriarchal realm, and deposed the total supremacy of Hera as divine matriarchal goddess.

THE CUCKOO AS A SYMBOL OF JEALOUSY

This theme of usurpation observed in the Greek myth is also found in Vedic myth where the cuckoo did in fact symbolise the human soul before and after incarnation. The body seemingly served as a strange nest in which the soul deposited itself. This is a profoundly moving belief and imparts a divine quality to the bird.

Everywhere it is hailed as a harbinger of spring, its haunting and clear carrying call heralds the return of the life force of nature. In the circumpolar tribes it is said to be the 'veil of nature' since it reveals the beauty of spring. In India it is the bird of Karma the god of love, and thus it is a bird of love. It is also a rain bird bringing as it does the fertilising spring rains.

Although a much darker image is found in Africa where its call during the hottest hours of the day was said to drive grazing animals mad appears to have accelerated the sexual instinct.[21] This connection with insanity has an association also with Hera who had a notorious power to cause insanity. It is worth remembering that jealousy and madness are not uncommon fellow travellers in the human realm. But it is in Japan that one finds the cuckoo to be a renowned symbol of jealousy.

THE CUCKOO AS A BIRD OF JEALOUSY IN THE HEIAN DYNASTY OF JAPAN

In Japan about one thousand years ago a cult of women writers during the Heian period left a valuable legacy concerning the wealth of ideas surrounding the symbol of the cuckoo as a bird of jealousy in Japanese life and thought.

Buddhism arrived in Japan in the 5th century AD. Before that the indigenous religion of Shinto was all powerful. Slowly the new religion suppressed Shintoism, and as it began to flourish it also commandeered most of the Shinto temples, and annexed the Shinto gods and the spirits of the old religion. The Heian period began in 794 AD and lasted almost four hundred years until 1185 AD. It is sometimes called the Fujiwara Period. The new capital attached to this dynasty was at Heian Kyoto which is present day Kyoto.

The Chinese culture in Japan began to wane as the powerful Fujiwara clan assumed control of a simplified government with the emperors as figureheads. The chief Buddhist sect of the Heian period was the Tendai-sect which was introduced by Saicho who studied in China under the school at Tien T'ai. The Tendai sect's beliefs amount to 'denying reality to a finite conception or 'Thing' taken by itself. But it further urged that reality in the full sense consists of neither in an abstract vacuity nor in a phenomenal actuality alone, but in a synthesis of both'. This is the doctrine of the Middle Path, and is based on the doctrine of the Lotus of the True Law which states that one must conform to life. The debt for life must be paid of course in the phenomenal world. Then afterwards the actual world must be withdrawn since it as an illusion.

In Jungian terms it is said, 'that when a projection is withdrawn reality may then be observed as it is without the illusion caused by such an unconscious projection. By the same token the recognition of the objective reality of the unconscious world gives it credence, and at the same time increases profoundly conscious awareness'.[22] It is of course an essentiality that the importance of this fact is grasped.

95

The Amida Buddha was worshipped by the followers of the Tendai sect, and it was sufficient to call his name as 'Amida' in order to be admitted to Paradise, but only if one was a man. Women were not admitted to the celestial heaven of Amida's Paradise. Thus the overall rational intellectualism of this religion by its omission of the value of the feminine principle produced a lively compensatory reaction in the collective unconscious, which was composed chiefly of the beliefs of the deposed Shinto religion.

From the ensuing maelstrom engendered by the introduction of an intellectual masculine oriented religion which ousted or suppressed an ancient nature worship of the elemental spirits, and a purloining of most of the great Shinto temples, there came a deep rejection and indeed denigration of feminine values. With this however there was an astonishing proliferation of excellent women writers whose work may be classed as outstanding for any period of history. It is to these remarkable women we now possess intimate and detailed knowledge of that period of Japanese history. Amongst them one finds Sarashina, Sei Shonaghon, Kagero (Nikki) and Murasaki. The latter's book was the first great novel and it is an outstanding book. 'The Tale of Genji' is about a great prince of the Japanese court. The theme of this book is above all that of jealousy, all kinds are explored but in particular jealousy of an erotic nature. The book depicts clearly the immense cross currents and underground passions which beset such an insular society compounded by a great many conflicting situations.

It is significant that just before Genji died, and also two thirds through the book, the cuckoo called, and Genji 'the Shining Prince' said that the cuckoo was the 'Headman of the Hill of Death.' The bird as has been seen does have this other worldly or deathly aspect. Genji at the end of his life dies after hearing its call. In fact Genji was overwhelmed by jealousy, and he like all those associated with him died from the effects of jealousy.

The fearful, awesome, and one might say majestic jealousy of the discarded mistress of Genji, the Lady Rokujo, and that of the wicked Empress stepmother the Empress Kokkiden, epitomise feminine jealousy of an archetypal nature directed demonically at Genji. The Empress Kokkiden rejected him since he was the Emperor's child by a beautiful young concubine, and the Lady Rokujo hated Genji because he left her and sought other and younger loves. Jealousy is the absence of love and really only appears when love leaves or has never been present. Hatred often enters quite simply at first as a mild or even intense dislike. At any stage this may be whipped into a frenzy if a situation presents itself where the subject fears harmful effects or loss.

Jealousy is always underhand, insidious and frequently devilish. As has been observed it seeks to pull down, damage or destroy the object to whom it is directed. It is the negation of life for nothing constructive can take place where jealousy abides.

The Lady Rokujo was possessed by a demonically jealous shadow. She had as an older woman been flattered by the attentions of the youthful, witty exquisitely charming brave and young Prince. But when Genji left her she followed in ghost form and killed his young mistress Yugao (the Moonflower in the midst of a romantic tryst. The scene of the latter's death is quite horrifying. Again and later Genji's wife the Lady Aoi (Hollyhock) died in equally terrifying circumstances in which the ghost of the Lady Rokujo enters the body of a small hypnotised boy, and eventually kills Aoi. Finally in similar manner Genji's second wife died, lastly Genji himself as so described. The evil spirit of Rokujo hovers throughout all these hauntings. The book depicts the destructive nature of overt and unconscious jealousy in the circumstances of marriage versus concubinage in the court circles.

Jung[23] says: 'Possession means to be gripped, seized. If the inner reality is not sufficiently real and one does not realise that the inner figures are absolute then one is in great danger of possession which inevitably leads to inflation.'

Later in another letter Jung[24] has this to say, 'There are experiences which show that the dead entangle themselves so to speak in the physiology (sympathetic nervous system) of the living. This would probably result in states of possession.'

The jealous possession of Rokujo resulted in the death of the above ladies mentioned, and finally of Genji himself.

In the psychology of the writer herself, the Lady Murasaki, it would represent an unknown aspect of her feminine shadow wherein resided a jealous complex. The collective jealousy which was engendered in the masculine-feminine antagonism would be suppressed in the society of that day by exquisite good manners and aestheticism, and also by the religious beliefs of the Tendai sect of Buddhism. Below the surface the opposition with its inferiorities, fears and jealousy would have free reign. Such a condition of inequalities primarily promotes fear which may lead to overt rejection of the 'other', or acceptance with deep resentment and probable hatred.

Genji as the brilliant and shining prince, enfolded in his masculine being an image of the archetype of the animus the spirit of the masculine unconscious of the feminine psyche. Its splendour appearing as an unconscious compensatory figure to the lowliness in which the feminine was held in outer reality. The spirit, or the animus is the true psychopompos which uncovered and brought the feminine jealous eroticism into the foreground of consciousness. The feminine principle belongs to both sexes, it is not the prerogative simply of the female sex. The consciousness of a woman has a feminine nature, and is often symbolised by the moon whereas her unconscious is masculine, and vice versa in men. The anima is the carrier of the feminine principle in a man. When women are held in low esteem by men it is worth while remembering that the man holds his anima which carries his unconscious feminine side also in low esteem. One sees perfectly clearly that in spite of everything Genji continued by his various acts to further jealousy.

97

The hope of every woman of the Heian dynasty was to secure the affection of a man who however many concubines or mistresses he might possess would by sure to protect her in a polygamous society. Such was Prince Genji. It was not because of his beauty, his sensitivity or his talents that he emerges in Murasaki's novel as the ideal male, but the fact that once he had given his support to a woman he never withdrew it though he may well have lost all interest in her as a mistress concubine, or 'petite-amie'.

One reason why jealousy was regarded with such distaste was that it forced the vindictive spirit of the jealous person to work supernatural revenge both before and after death. This was believed universally in Japan at that time. It is not quite so far fetched as it would seem. One has only to witness the acrimony, the resentments and the wrangling which takes place in law suits involving divorce settlements, and family wills with all the bitter quarrelling which mushrooms after the death or deaths of family members. Inter sibling rivalry, not apparent previously to the allocation of lands, properties or monies suddenly becomes apparent revealing unconscious antagonism of varying degrees. In such cases the jealousy which is encountered is usually of the most savage murderous nature, brought forth by deep unconscious brooding rage of long duration.

The degree of malign power that was attributed to jealousy is suggested by the fact that the only example of 'a living ghost' in the tale is the spirit of the Lady Rokujo, whose jealousy arose to a murderous frenzy without her being aware of the fact.

This is the salient point.

Jealousy is at its most dangerous when it is completely unconscious in the subject. The Japanese Taiho code stipulated jealousy as one of the seven permissable grounds for divorce.

Morris[25] states 'the book reflects the anxiety and the fears engendered by polygamy but none so dramatic as jealousy. Unquestioningly, although they accepted the permissive sexual customs of the day, they were afflicted with jealousy in all its forms both men and women. Because of their immobility and inability to act the women suffered most'. Morris continued:[26] 'Deep rooted tradition inhibited the Japanese women from expressing jealousy, but the very taboo may have made them experience it all the more poignantly.'

Among the Heian aristocracy there is every indication that they suffered the pangs in full measure. Morris describes how their practical dependence on men, their natural desire for their exclusive possession of a husband or lover, (a desire no less real for being totally impracticable) their fear of losing him to another woman all this made it hard to bear the uncertainties of the polygamous system and produced a tension that resulted in hysteria and sometimes madness.

In Murasaki's time jealousy was regarded quite properly as a spiritual evil, and looked upon with harsh disapproval. The awareness between jealousy and madness was evident in those days. Unquestionably pathological jealousy does lead to a splitting of the personality and insanity.

In modern life one does not sense the same degree of disapproval since jealousy is not viewed with the same seriousness, in spite of the fact that in the Christian church the Church Fathers made it a deadly or mortal sin. There is alas a deep unconsciousness or self awareness both collectively and in the individual of this grave aspect of evil with its devastating and truly dire effects.

Behind such reluctance to face jealousy in oneself, or even in another is the nature of the intention on the part of the jealous subject. The aim, or the 'sting' of jealousy is to pull down, harm, injure, maim or kill the object. The impulse is therefore the first step towards the crime of murder, the most grave of all sins. Caught up in the grip of this possession by the emotion of the jealous shadow, be it jealous complex or content, conscious awareness is at once diminished. The accompanying loss of self worth, inferiorities, hate, shame and sometimes one's sense of self preservation are lost to consciousness. All that exists is the intense wish to harm the other. Such an intention at base is also directed against oneself, the jealous one, the subject. Finally the subject is wounded to the same degree as the victim. He who contemplates murder contemplates his own murder, he who commits murder murders his own soul and thereby loses his life. It is essential in studying the nature of jealousy to understand why it is regarded as a mortal sin.

DIVINE JEALOUSY DIRECTED
AGAINST MANKIND

For more than three thousand years the gods of Sumer were worshipped by Sumerians and Semites alike, and the religious ideas promoted by the Sumerians played an extraordinary part in the public and private life of the Mesopotamians; their institutions, literature and all their activities were based on it. 'In no other antique society did religion occupy such a prominent position because in no other antique society did man feel himself to be utterly dependent upon the will of the gods.'[27] Sumerian life was focussed round the temples, and was established upon a theocratic basis giving it a solid durability. In theory the land never ceased to belong to the gods, and the mighty monarchs of Assyria were but the humble servants of the gods.

The equivalent high god to the Greek Zeus in Babylonian mythology was Anu a sky-god whose name meant 'High' or Heaven'. From Anu it seems that the water-god Enki (latterly called Ea) 'God of the house of the waters' was descended. He as creator of mankind received the title Nudimmud, 'creator of the form of man'.[28]

Each of the gods of the pantheon was assigned an activity or a specific task. Anu was in charge of the sky, whilst Ea all the waters of the earth.

Humbler deities were in charge of the plough, the flint or the pickaxe. The Sumerians believed that every element, or each category of objects possessed its own dynamism, its own will, and it was these forces immanent in nature which the gods embodied.

'These gods like the Greek gods had the physical appearance and all the qualities and defects of human beings, they were both intelligent and could run out of ideas, they were decent but also had evil thoughts and performed evil acts. They were subject to love, hate, anger, jealousy and other human passions, they got drunk, quarrelled and fought. They suffered and some died, in other words they went to the underworld. It seems that they the gods, represented the best and the worst of human nature on a super-human scale.'[29]

Jealousy of the gods against man and the intervention of the water-god on their behalf reveals itself repeatedly in Sumero-Babylonian mythology, and also in Hebrew mythology. A poem known in Assyrian as Ala Isitu, the city they hated[30] shows this. 'In the beginning when men had become numerous the gods of Heaven (the Igigi) hated them. It was the gods of the nether sea (Ea and his pantheon) who wished to organise them into an ordered society.'

Although undoubtedly Ea was consistently thought to be the patron and saviour of mankind, according to a theological school at Eridu it is believed however that mankind lost eternal life through the jealousy of Ea. This is suggested in the Adapa legend.

According to Roux,[31] Ea (or Enki-Ea) possessed all the qualities of the life giving fluid, his name as has been observed means House (or Temple) of the Waters. Ea possessed purifying and fertilising properties, he was liquid, had limpidity and ubiquity and was the tutelary god of Eridu. Like water he possessed deceiving mobility and treacherous charm. He was also the god of wisdom and intelligence, and was sometimes referred to as the 'broad-eared one who knows all that has a name'. As initiator, Great Teacher and patron of magicians he was regarded as the Great Superintendent who having organised the world oversaw its functioning.

THE LEGEND OF ADAPA[32]

Ea created Adapa as 'the model of men'. He was a priest of Eridu and his task was to supply his master with food. One day as he was fishing on the great sea, the south wind suddenly blew with such violence that his boat capsized and he himself was nearly drowned. In his anger Adapa uttered a curse whereby the wings of the south wind, the big demon bird, were broken and for a long time 'the south wind blew not upon land'.

When the great god Anu heard what had happened to this important wind which brought the rain he was angry and sent for Adapa. Ea came to Adapa's aid, and told him that upon arrival at Anu's gate in heaven he would meet the two vegetation gods, Dumuzi and Ningishzida (whom Adapa had it seems indirectly 'killed' by suppressing the south wind) but if he clad himself in mourning and showed signs of grief and contrition the two gods would be appeased; they would 'smile' and even speak to Anu in Adapa's favour. Anu would then no longer treat Adapa as a criminal, but as a guest; he would, after oriental fashion offer him food, water, clothes to put on and oil with which to anoint himself. The last two Adapa could accept, but Ea warned him as follows:

> When they offer thee bread of death
> thou shalt not eat it. When they offer
> thee water of death,
> thou shalt not drink it . . .
> This advice that I have given thee,
> neglect not; the words
> that I have spoken to thee, hold fast.

Everything happened as Ea predicted, but Anu touched by the fact no doubt of Adapa's sincere confession offered him instead of food and drink of death, 'the bread and water of life'. Adapa obedient to Ea, followed his advice, and refused the gifts that would have rendered him immortal. Whereupon Anu dismissed him with these simple words, 'Take him away and return him to earth.' Adapa lost his immortality, and with him mankind because of blind obedience. But what of Ea – the all wise, the great initiator. It seems he was jealous of mankind's proposed and desired immortality, and one sees the dual nature of the god in this.

One evening I had occasion to meet quite by chance the mother of a patient of mine who had had a huge success in life because of a remarkable career. I took it upon myself to congratulate the mother upon her off-spring's success. The mother looked at me quite coldly and said 'I would never have chosen such a metier!'

Parents are often, but usually unconscious of it, dangerously jealous of their children.

The Babylonian-Sumerian gods also provided for the ills of mankind which came about through mortality, by the introduction of a goddess who was named Gula. She was the patroness of medicine who cured diseases and prolonged life, a goddess of childbirth, a protector and a defender of homes, the dog was always associated with her, and was her companion. Gula became as it were the antidote for the jealousy of Ea. Gula who is the planet Aquarius is often called the great physician. Gula as the upholder of protective care, a divine healer whose symbol represented unceasing watch-fulness and perception of all dark contents in the underworld, was indu-bitably the appropriate antidote against the possessive demon of jealousy which seized Ea (and other gods) bestowing mortality upon man, and with

101

it the innumerable ills of the lot of mankind.

Psychologically in cases of pathological jealousy only the support of the Self, the greater personality can mitigate the intense and passionate drive in the shadow of the personality of the individual.

At this point it might be helpful to regard for a while the myth which appears in an ancient Hebrew document, and which has influenced the beliefs and conduct of mankind more than any other legend in the last two thousand years. The legend is told in the third chapter of Genesis in the account of creation as given in that document. 'Yāw Elohim planted a garden in Eden towards the east. In this garden he placed a 'man', Adam, (afterwards used as a proper name 'Adam') and all the trees good for food, and the 'tree of life'. There was also a 'tree of knowledge of good and evil'. Adam was forbidden to eat the fruit of this tree, in other words his happiness rested upon his remaining entirely unaware of evil, for 'good' has no meaning before evil exists.'

In Babylonian/Sumerian mythology,[33] Anu planned to keep man in ignorance of the secrets of Heaven and Earth, and when he found that Adapa (man) had learned them from Ea the water god he had no alternative but to give him the bread and water of life.

Yāw had the same intention for Adam who became a gardener in Eden. Yāw caused a deep sleep to fall on Adam and took one of his ribs closed up the flesh and from it made a woman. They, the man and woman were naked and yet had no sense of shame, for shame must spring from the knowledge of evil. Into the garden of paradise came the serpent. In Sumeria the snake represented the fertility of the earth, and was especially connected with Ningishzida and Tammuz.[34] 'The introduction of the serpent probably arises from and rests upon the same motif, the jealousy of God who since all-knowing knew that man was immortal, tempted him to his doom. Yāw had told Adam that in the day when he should eat of the 'tree of knowledge' he would die.'[35] Indeed by eating of the tree of knowledge man did come to know death,[36] the apple of the tree signifies this. 'You shall be as gods knowing good and evil.'[37] When one confronts one's own evil it may be an experience akin to death, but like death itself it always points beyond the simply personal meaning of experience.

The shadow, as Jung so frequently explains, when it is realised consciously becomes the means of rebirth and renewal in a human life. The shadow is the means whereby one first sees the unconscious part of one's personality, and through the shadow one may come to realise one's own individual nature. Jung said that the shadow is the only route to the unconscious and to one's own reality. Only by realising this part of oneself can one proceed to the source from which it arises and then also understand the basis on which it rests. Thus the shadow represents the first step towards meeting the Self, the greater personality.

The serpent discovered from the woman that Yāw had permitted them to eat the fruit of all the trees which He had caused to grow for them, but had forbidden them to eat of the tree 'in the midst of the garden' lest they die. The serpent replied that on the contrary, by eating from it they would discover the secrets of God, and knowing good and evil they would be like Him.

There you have it, the serpent as the dark (unconscious) demonic or divine, jealousy insinuates to them that which is against them, it furthers the negative aspects, disobedience, lust for power with subsequent indeed concomitant inflation. Already there is envy and jealous resentment inherent in the couple against God.

The woman took and ate the apple and gave it to her husband who also ate. Straightaway their nakedness was revealed and they concealed it with garments and fig leaves. They were ashamed of their disobedient act against the divine.

Yaw discovered that they had eaten from the tree of knowledge. Adam then told Yaw that the woman had given him the fruit. The woman told of her temptation by the serpent, and then the serpent was cursed by Yaw (who had put the serpent there in the first place).

No progress is made in analysis until the shadow is adequately confronted and to confront does not merely mean to realise and talk about it. It means that one must see oneself as one really is instead of as one thinks one is. If one really tries to see one's true reality, perceive and experience one's own darkness then one usually arrives at the problem of jealousy. As an analyst I always feel very uncomfortable when analysands in the early stages of analysis tell me so innocently that they are never jealous.

For we are all jealous, it is part of the human (and divine) condition. But it is our life's task to really know our dark aspects, and bring these deep hidden and therefore destructive passions to consciousness.

Jealousy is a will to power as has been observed in these examples where the archetypal nature of this emotion has been explored. In the unconscious all instincts, negative and positive, and all drives of whatever nature lie together. Thus jealousy may be combined as a jealous fury, or a zealous devotion. In consciousness it must be discerned and recognised for what it really is, this takes persistent effort, constant attention to one's thoughts, feelings and reactions, and ceaseless observation of one's own behaviour. It is of course much easier by far to let one's attention wander, and permit one's jealousy to continue its own serpentine unhindered way. However this is not the way to reach one's individual being. One often hears of certain persons to whom everything appears easy, and riches flow towards them like streams of quicksilver and creative gifts abound. Perhaps once again a further example of divine jealousy may permit one to recall how dangerous it is to be so well-endowed with gifts.

There is a famous story of a Greek of Samos,[38] one Polycrates whose continued prosperity excited the anxiety of his friend Amasis who wrote to him thus:

'It is pleasant to hear of the good fortune of a friend and ally. But the excess of thy prosperity does not please me because I know how jealous the deity is! As for me, I would choose my affairs and those of my friends should something be fortunate, and sometimes stumble rather than be fortunate in everything. For I cannot remember that I ever heard of a man who was fortunate in everything, who did not in the end finish in utter ruin. Be advised therefore by me in view of your good fortune do this. Think what it is you value most and the loss of which would grieve you, and cast it away so that it may never be seen again amongst man. If after that your good fortune does not alternate with misfortune repeat the remedy which you have from me.'

It is well known that Polycrates cast a valuable ring into the sea but by the most extraordinary good fortune it turned up again in the belly of a fish. This so convinced Amasis that his friend's ruin was inevitable that he sent a herald to Samos to renounce his friendship and dissolve all obligations of hospitality between them, 'lest if any great and dreadful calamity befell Polycrates he might himself be grieved for him as a friend'. Polycrates' luck was in fact god-given. When Amasis suggested that he propitiate the gods he did so at once, and obediently cast his most valuable ring into the sea. Such a ring would represent union as well as treasure. For the ring to be picked up by a fish and returned to Polycrates himself signifies that the gods had accepted his gift, but because the ring belonged to him and had been(in Jungian terms) a gift to Polycrates from the Self, it was forever his, and could not be lost to him. Seemingly there was no evidence of divine displeasure incurred by Polycrates' wealth accrued with concomitant humility. Undoubtedly Amasis's zealous solicitude for his friend overlies a truly but unconscious jealous nature. When once again Polycrates had the good luck to receive the ring back Amasis could not bear it, and decided that it was better to rupture the friendship than have to bear any further grief. It is not difficult to surmise that it was the present grief for his own jealous shadow which was unbearable.

It would seem that if a man is attended by unbroken honour or success he must restore the balance by a voluntary sacrifice of some portion of his happy lot in order to honour the god's largesse.

When Amasis wrote to his friend and said that 'he knew how jealous the deity was', it would seem that his unconscious jealous shadow had been projected upon the deity. It was Amasis himself who secretly wished to see his friend brought low.

It is as well however to remember that it has often been said and certainly by Aeschylus in the Agamemnon that it is the sin of hubris (arrogant pride) which attracts the jealousy of the gods. The moment when one believes that one's luck, one's wealth, one' good fortune is entirely due to one's own prowess ego-consciousness is at once seized by hubris, and one's next step is fraught with danger.

In the ancient Chinese book of Changes, the I ching, the Hexagramm of the ting (No. 50) has a line in the second place and I quote, It is

'There is food in the ting
My comrades are envious
But they cannot harm me.
Good Fortune'

The ting is the cooking pot, and like the kitchen and the organ of the stomach in the animal body, all represent places where a transformation may occur. The food is placed in the pot, the fire lighted and the food is transformed and prepared for digestion and assimilation. When one throws this hexagramm it signifies the possibility of transformation and a change of attitude in one's life.

Jung had this to say concerning the meaning of this particular line in the hexagramm. He explains[39] 'Since a share in something great always arouses envy the chorus of the envious is part of the picture. The envious want to rob the I Ching of its great possession, that is they seek to rob it of meaning or destroy its meaning. But their enmity is in vain. Its richness of meaning is assured, that is it is convinced of its positive achievements which no one can take away.'

I have observed many times during analysis that an analysand is sometimes surrounded in dreams by persons of a jealous nature. It seems that friends and relatives sense the inner world through the analysand's work and they become envious. They seek to rob or destroy the analysand's newly found contact with the inner world. This is one of the reasons why it is so unwise to discuss dreams and their interpretation with others outside the analysis. The envious eye is indeed full of bale.

Today in the modern world of business, medical and scientific investigation into the problem of spying is one of great significance. Whenever a new development appears someone will to endeavour to steal it, or appropriate it as his own.

THE EVIL EYE

The problem of jealousy and envy is instigated by the perception of an object by the sensation of sight through the medium of the eye. It is ubiquitous.

Throughout the Mediterranean basin the near and middle East in particular the phenomenon of the evil eye is universal.

This is the name given to the eye of the envious one, the one who is jealous or malicious. It is the belief that such a being has the power to cast a spell, strike dead, turn to stone or cause an injury upon those persons or animals to which its gaze is directed.

A woman doctor of Polish origin was captured by the Russians just after the commencement of the 2nd World War. She was sent to a camp in

Siberia where she remained for 5 years. It was an atrocious and hellish place, and the sojourn there scarred her psychologically for the rest of her life. One day she saw a man kill another for one grain of rice which had remained to be eaten on the man's tin plate. Just as the victim was about to pick it up with his fingers to convey it to his mouth his neighbour whose eye had been fixed on the solitary grain of rice picked up a tin mug and with a single blow killed him. This is a particular and singular example of individual murderous envy.

The doctor said that in those camps she witnessed barbarism of unbelievable primitivity. In those circumstances men (and women) reverted to wild lawless instinctualism which characterises power driven unconscious motivational forces.

One sees the seeds of this in childhood and adolescence. As civilising influences succeed it disappears from view but does not vanish, it is ready to emerge when situations in the outer world are conducive. This lawless instinctualism is at the base of collective picket lines, uprisings, rebellions and in individual situations of barbarous behaviour in the savagery of domestic quarrels and inter-familial relationships which may lead both in the collective and in the personal situation to frenzy, madness and murder. The following example illustrates this point.

Towards the end of the Second World War, whilst I was a medical student it was my privilege to be taught by one of the most foremost of all forensic specialists, a physician who brought the science of criminal medicine to the forefront in legal trials involving serious crimes.

One day in the classroom he appeared carrying a canvas bag which he placed upon the desk in front of him. After a while he opened the bag and extracted a human head which had been severed at the post mortem examination. He held it in his hands and asked us (his class) to step forward and look. It was the head of a young and handsome blond man! We were requested not to speak of this case. Since it is now many decades since the murder I feel that I may relate this strange story. The impact upon the class was electrifying. There is something extraordinarily shocking at the sight of a severed head.

We were then shown the track of a bullet as it coursed through the skin of the left side of the face; the tract was bloodless, and it was so because of the manner in which the victim had died after being shot. A witness to the murder said that the shots rang out in quick succession as one, two, three with 'a second between each of the three'. The first bullet penetrated a shoulder, the second penetrated the aortic artery in the chest, and the third ran through the skin of the face from chin to temple as the body fell backwards. Between shot number two and shot number three all the blood in the body disappeared. The head had been brought to demonstrate a scientific fact that in one second the body can be exsanguinated to a degree sufficient for the course of the third bullet to be bloodless if the aortic artery is punctured.

Is it not surprising that after all these years I remember the events clearly? The reason is that as a young girl I sustained a very severe emotional shock at the sight of that cadavre's head. Because of the intense emotion I still recall every detail (I can even picture today the blond eyelashes of that long since, dead young man.) Those who are against physical punishment such as retention in school, caning and so forth for children in the practice of modern education, it would be well advised to study some of those older views whereby a child who received a punishment did not forget the lesson to be learned. One learns well when emotions are excited. Why had the man been shot?

Apparently he was an embassy attaché in the diplomatic service, and he had had a love affair with the wife of a senior official.

One day whilst the latter was searching for something in the conjugal bedroom his eye alighted on some of his wife's letters tied up in blue ribbon at the back of a drawer. They were addressed to his wife, and were in the handwriting of the victim. The officer in question took his gun, and went at once to the embassy arriving there within a few minutes. In a short time apparently he encountered the victim, and taking aim he fired the shots without preamble. The shooting had occurred the day before I witnessed the head of the victim. The murderer was not brought to trial since it was a time of war, and diplomatic immunity was claimed. In Europe at that time (and perhaps even so today) it was regarded as 'un crime passionnel'. The officer had been cuckolded, and was overwhelmed in a fit of fury, one might say jealous rage.

The moment the crime was conceived was the instant that the husband's eye alighted on the victim's name in the letters addressed to his wife. One may be permitted to wonder if the finding of the letters was an accident. The moment the eye perceived them it became an evil eye in its most portentous aspect.

Jung[40] states 'that the primitive peoples fear and dread the sharply focussed stare in the eye of the European which seems to them like an evil eye. From archiac ages nature was always the receptacle of the spirit, but today for the first time we live in a nature which is empty, void of spirit, the gods have deserted it. The act of enlightenment which overtook the European two centuries ago destroyed the spirits of nature, but not the psychic factors which correspond to them, such as lack of the critical faculty, suggestibility, fear or panic, prejudice and superstition. All of which qualities make possession possible'. As Jung continues 'although nature is depsychised the psychic conditions which breed demons are as actively at work as ever. The demons have not gone away by no means, they have assumed another form and they have become unconscious psychic forces'. As Jung points out 'the process of re-absorption went hand in hand with an increasing inflation of the ego which has become more pronounced and more evident since the 16th century. Instead of spooks haunting the old attics and ruins they began to flit about in the heads of apparently normal Europeans. Tyrannical, obsessive, intoxicating ideas and delusions were abroad and people began to believe the most absurd things just as the possessed do'.

This possession is present everywhere, and like a vast mushrooming cloud has come to envelop both our century and our world. We have seen the end of an epoch as the Great War destroyed all the old values of 1914. Germany was seized by a possession which led to the Second World War as has been observed. Russia has been caught in the most awesome enslavement since 1917 and like a virus this enslavement has penetrated the entire world in a greater or lesser degree. An envious lustful eye was aimed or focussed upon world domination. Karl Marx himself urged this, seeking to possess and indoctrinate all those beings who by their opposing nature or simply having the wish to continue a different way of life caused by pain to that envious eye.[40]

In a survey conducted by Mowat[41] at Broadmoor Prison for the criminally insane half of the male patients examined and four of the female patients had an irrational belief in infidelity. Indeed he describes that of the sixty two criminals convicted of jealousy murders, examined in the survey, only fifteen did not appear to be caught in a delusional pattern involving infidelity.

It is always worth remembering[42] 'that a deluded person may be so competent intellectually in all respects outside their delusion that nobody suspects what they are saying about their partners in untrue'.

This is sometimes a very difficult problem in analysis. It is for the analyst to detect if the jealous complex lies in the personal shadow personality, or issues from deeper layers.

A woman apparently of impeccable character came because she allegedly had the most immense problems with her young daughter towards whom she professed a great affection. It became clear that in truth she was pathologically jealous of this adolescent girl.

The treatment brought to light several hidden years in the life of the woman at the time of her own puberty. During this time she had led a path of descending depravity. It was difficult at first to relate the fact of this ostensibly respectable middle aged matron with the wicked girl of her past, who although hidden still lived a dynamic life in the psyche. From time to time this dynamism erupted into her present life with periods of infidelity and serious theft.

Clarification came through a dream in which she was in a hospital bed as a young girl, lying together with an unknown man. He was old, ugly, deformed, dangerous and a murderer. After this dream I never saw her again, but the dream and the way she told it to me gave me concern for a long time. It also explained why her young daughter could not tolerate her mother. She undoubtedly sensed the presence of the unconscious murderer symbolised in the dream by an image of archetypal evil. In all probability she sensed that her mother was a criminal.

Morbid jealousy appears to be more dangerous than most mental illnesses. Sommers in his book of sexual jealousy states that 'searches of the records for cases with irrational and extreme jealousy as a major symptom give a rate of about 2 to 5% of the clinical population'. But in the criminally insane those who commit crimes of violence under the influence of irrational jealousy the proportion is higher. Mowat[43] found a rate of 12% to 15% in his report on English murderers or attempted murderers at Broadmoor Prison (England), that is three or four tome higher than the rate among clinic and hospital patients.

Those who are pathologically jealous exhibit hostility, antagonism and violence, without it seems at the time a presence of moral conscience as to the nature of their reactions. This state of abnormal jealousy depicts a partial or total possession of ego consciousness by sadistic brutal and barbaric unconscious impulses, or its disintegration and descent of the personality into psychosis.

PATHOLOGICAL JEALOUSY

Pathological Jealousy or the presence of obsessive compulsive complexes is described as abnormal jealousy. Severely jealous people frequently reduce those around them to despair and even to states of disorientation. Sometimes it is difficult to know who is the actual victim. When delusions of infidelity develop there is always au fond, a very real danger of murder.

THE KREUTZER SONATA

One of the most valuable literary works upon the subject of pathological jealousy is the Kreutzer Sonata by Tolstoy,[44] the Russian nineteenth century writer. Tolstoy also wrote of jealousy and suicide in his novel 'Anna Karenina.' In the Kreutzer Sonata the portrayal in the terrifying account of jealousy depicts how in leads to murder.

Prior to his marriage Tolstoy had led a profoundly dissolute life as a gambler and seducer. Then he met and later married his wife Sonya. Whilst affianced and just a week before their marriage, Tolstoy gave his eighteen year old bride-to-be his diary to read. He had it seemed recorded all his activities, his many conquests and his destructive gambling over a period of many years.

In the diaries he was quite explicit about his sexual activity with all manner of women, gypsies, prostitutes, women of Sonya's mother's circle and last but by no means least, his own serfs.

The great estates in those days were each a world in themselves and were ruled by strict laws of hierachy. Of course all levels of society were accepted but the noblemen were expected to marry into their own class. Undoubtedly the members of such a class would be aware of the problem of illegitimacy when it arose, and although probably not accepted by the wife she would have been brought up to understand the situation at least. One finds this problem in most households of European society of the time. However Tolstoy chose as his wife a lady of a lower stratum, the daughter of a doctor.

He was it seems immensely drawn to Sonya who was one of three sisters. The elder sister had been anxious to secure Tolstoy as her husband, but the younger sister succeeded. Apparently prior to the beginning of the courtship Sonya had herself written a story in which she describes one of her own admirers, and in which she also revealed that although she was attracted to Tolstoy she did not find him physically appealing. She left this story in a place where Tolstoy found it and read it. Perhaps this was a punishment on Sonya's part for Tolstoy's having à priori favoured her sister. The fact of his apparent unattractiveness caused pain to Tolstoy who decided in the end that his love would conquer Sonya's ambivalence towards him.

Already the seeds of jealousy may have been sown in the relationship. First it had been present on Sonya's part because her elder sister had been wooed by Tolstoy, but this appears to have receded. Then there was the question of the deposed elder sister's possible jealousy which would be compounded of both sibling jealousy, and that of the spurned woman.

It seems that Sonya punished Tolstoy because of her jealousy of his former lovers, and by permitting him to learn that she found him physically unattractive. One wonders how much love was present in this union since so much unconsciousness as to the other's feelings abounded.

The outcome was that the diaries provided Sonya with knowledge of Axinia a peasant woman, one of his serfs with whom Tolstoy had had a sexual liaison, and who had borne Tolstoy's illegitimate son who was four years old at the time of Sonya's marriage to Tolstoy.

In the short term after reading the diaries, and before her wedding Sonya was in 'a state of seething horror and disgust' as she explains in her own diaries.

But this state was nothing compared to that which occurred some weeks after her wedding when quite unexpectedly she entered the house and came face to face with a strong peasant woman on her hands and knees scrubbing the floors. This was the serf Axinia. The impact made upon Sonya as the mistress of the house and the serf when they encountered each other was virtually indescribable. Within moments of the realisation as to the identity of this woman, Sonya was out of the house and running. For hours afterwards whilst the whole household searched for her she had hidden along with her dog under a pile of old clothes in an out-house on the estate.

110

She was hysterical for weeks. The actual phrase in the diary which had sent her into delirium was that used by Tolstoy concerning the liaison with Axinia. It was 'Never so much in love.' Sonya was hysterical and beside herself in a fever of jealous rage. Later she was to write that she would liked to have killed him, and then remarry another man exactly like him; presumably without a previous sexual life. She was jealous of his past, his hitherto erotic life which she could never share with him. She wrote, and it is significant, 'He doesn't understand that his past is a whole world of a thousand different emotions which will never belong to me, just as his spent youth, heavens knows where, or what, and which will never be my property.' Here quite clearly is the overwhelming possessiveness and a kind of longing producing a distinct isolation. There is no recognition nor gratitude for Tolstoy, the man as he is, and for what he had been which had produced him as her husband. Her words reveal an unresolved unconscious will to power which had gripped her.

Women rarely forgive men their infidelities before or after marriage. It is wise to meditate long and hard before deciding whether to indulge in soul baring concerning previous love affairs, or indeed present ones. One can never be sure how much jealous rage is repressed or suppressed in a personality.

The brutality of Tolstoy's disclosures for whatever reason depicts his cold and brutal shadow. In the immediate situation prior to the marriage, he exhibited little sensitivity.

The marriage was hardly equable, it rocked from passion to rejection, attraction to repulsion. Ambivalence was ever present. Tolstoy's jealousy was fired later in the marriage by an intense, but seemingly platonic friendship of Sonya for a well known pianist, and composer Tanayev. It is very interesting that this friendship had been foreshadowed by Tolstoy many years before when he wrote his superb book, 'The Kreutzer Sonata.'

In this story an intellectual man, Pozdnisheff, had just been acquitted of murder. The story unfolds as he recounts the story on a train as it flashes through the night across the wide expanse of Russia. Prior to his marriage which had taken place several years earlier, he had been a voluptuary, (like Tolstoy himself), and had led a dissolute life.

When he married he found the marriage to be seared with passion, although it seemed it was a loveless one, (like Tolstoy's own). The children arrived, and totally occupied the wife's attention. There came a day however when she became overwhelmed by her constant fussing and fretting about the children's welfare, so much so that her doctor advised her to abstain from further childbearing. These advices afforded her great pleasure. At once she blossomed and returned to her former coquettish, bewitching, elegant and soignée self. At this point she went out into society, took up music, and became a particularly skilled pianist.

One day a former friend of Pozdnisheff arrived, a famous violinist en route from Paris. His name was Trukhatchevsky.

He was known to be by reputation a ladies' man, yet in spite of this insight into the character of his friend, Pozdnisheff introduced him into his home and to his wife. Clearly his shadow had a hand here, and arranged the situation which was to act against his wife and himself.

The ensuing friendship between the wife and the musician culminated in a soirée in the couple's house. Afterwards the violinist was to leave for abroad. The very next day Pozdnisheff left his house for the country where he was to undertake his routine magisterial duties.

On arrival in the country the following day he received a letter from the wife with the usual ordinary and mundane matters of home life. But the last line revealed that Trukhatchevsky had called at the house with some music, but she added that she had not permitted him to stay.

Imagine the situation, Pozdnisheff knows that a certain situation had developed between the musician and his wife, indeed he had arranged it. He also knew, that apparently the day before they had bade goodbye to the musician prior to his trip abroad. Undoubtedly à priori the matter of the absent host's duties on the morrow in the country would also be discussed; one wonders just why did the wife give the information in the letter that Trukhatchevsky had returned the following day, and that she had not permitted him to stay. This appears to be intentional, an intent to punish her husband, this reveals a primitive animosity, a desire to wound him.

At once Pozdnisheff was seized with a furor of jealousy. He decided to leave the country at once, and return to his home. He took a carriage and travelled thirty miles to the railway station, fuming and fretting at the driver, the horse and the vehicle. There followed an eight hour train journey back to Moscow. The description of the ride and the delayed railway journey is superb. The tension mounts, and one lives with the fury of the husband as he describes his return into the house after midnight to find his wife and the musician together, having supper. The effect upon the reader is breathtaking as Tolstoy's superb writing brings the story to a conclusion.

Pozdnisheff had removed his shoes on entering the house, unsheathed his dagger, and as soon as he saw the couple he lunged at Trukhatchevsky who escaped his grasp and fled the house. His wife had interceded, Pozdnisheff grasped her, threw her to the floor, but she held on so he struck her in the side with the dagger. Then he left her, he had lost his opponent, and he went to his room and apparently fell into a stupor and dreamed that the act of wounding his wife had occurred. Upon awakening he felt that all had been a dream, but he discovered that the house was filled with people and he learned that his wife was alive. Reluctantly he went to see her, and she told him that he had succeeded in killing her, but he would never get the children. Then she died.

The book is a masterpiece. It describes the dynamis which precedes the act of murder, and the torment endured by the jealous subject which reaches a climax when the knife enters the wife's body. The husband was in fact also the victim because he was compelled by a superior force, for jealousy is such in its obsessive form. Ego-consciousness is devoured, and only the demonic compulsion to bring down, harm or kill exists. A compulsion requires to be assuaged by a physical act of some kind. Pozdnisheff's soul had fled and the engulfing complex over-rode his conscious being to commit the act of a madman.

Pozdnisheff said at the end that it was only when he saw his wife's dead face in the coffin that he understood what he had done, and that he had killed her with the dagger. Then and only then did the realisation of the act become conscious, and the possession was over, he was released.

In all probability the story explains a great deal of the unconscious background of the Tolstoy household which cannot be ignored. It is possible to conjecture that Tolstoy, by examining the nature of his own and his wife's jealous possessiveness over many years, together with the emergence of the book, may have averted an actual act of murder in his own situation. As mentioned the fact of the loveless marriage, the jealous but seductive wife, the husband with the lecherous shadow, the overwhelming protestations of love eternal as found in the book are reflected in totalis in the Tolstoy's own marriage. They were caught in an inextricable tangle. Each carried the others projection, and the two human figures were shadowed by a seductive anima, and a lecherous animus.

The passion, the anger, the jealousy it appears were not resolved either in the book or the real life situation of the Tolstoys, for Eros was absent, and one finds no evidence of a psychic relatedness to each other.

If the woman is unsure of her husband's love, or if love is absent or he cannot or does not express feelings for her she becomes resentful at his apparent rejection. Her feelings are wounded, and she becomes aware of an inferiority somewhere. It is at this point that her inferior function, usually and commonly in a woman either her thinking or sensation function is activated. Then the animus may enter the picture, and she begins to develop thoughts as to how she should or must behave. She then becomes much angrier than before and aware that perhaps she ought to punish him. She is caught by an opinionated animus, and love vanishes. It is then that she begins to sense her isolation and hatred enters her conscious life.

Sonya Tolstoy had the evidence of her husband's former relationship with the serf actually under her feet, quite literally with the fruit of their union, the child of Axinia and Tolstoy. One can only wonder at the husband's insensitivity, not just to the wife, but also to the feelings of the serf herself. Perhaps one is perfectly justified in suspecting at base that Tolstoy's over-riding vanity concerning his sexual prowess with women was the cause. The touchiness of the jealous anima is always immediate when a man's sexual vigour is in any way denigrated by his wife's actual or suspected interest in another man.

113

Taking into account the marriage of the Tolstoy's, the story in the Kreutzer Sonata, and that of Anna Karenina, (said to be the greatest novel ever written) it is clear that an exceedingly jealous anima lived in the shadow world of Tolstoy himself. This highly intellectual and brilliantly erudite human being undoubtedly had a shadow enchanted by the primitive and barbarous underworld as evidenced by his gambling licentiousness, and activities in the gypsy world. The ferocious jealousy of Pozdnisheff (also formerly a libertine prior to marriage) leads one to suspect that an inner figure in his shadow psyche was of a jealous feminine nature which had gripped consciousness and overwhelmed it: only to be released when he consciously realised his wife was dead. He had as it were killed his own inner anima and as such by then was dead himself.

Often in marriage it is taken for granted that each loves the other, but one cannot be negligent with love for such carelessness leads inevitably to death of this emotion.

Tolsoy's Kreutzer Sonata brings into clear focus the immensely destructive potential which is latent in marital jealousy.

The force of a morbidly jealous nature should not be undervalued. The prime task is for the subject to recognise its presence, and be aware of its innate danger. Good will and a moral sense are requisite, but in its most pathological form one may hope for support from the Self, or the Grace of God to achieve a resolution.

RESUMÉ

As has been seen there are degrees of jealousy, but in the severe forms there is vehemence which engulfs consciousness as was seen in the case of the woman who came to see Jung after she had murdered her friend in the past, the husband in the Embassy who killed his wife's lover – and the figures from Tolstoy's imagination.

It has become clear that jealousy, a combination of resentment, fear, rage and hatred points to a void in the realm of love. The aim of jealousy is to harm, reduce, maim or kill the object.

Like a contagion it comes to possess consciousness, and the sense of reality is weakened. In former years the emotions were believed to have a substance like a cloud or a gas which could invade an atmosphere or a room. They were invisible but were believed to have a tangible presence, as one today may say that evil has a tangible presence. One does not see it, but one feels it.

As we have seen in our discourse with children in the nursery, there is the one who wanted to conceal his object of jealousy, and the other who wanted to reject it. Jealousy of a lover, a spouse or a friend is like a sudden stab of emotion which chills the heart, and brings painful recognition of our dark side. It is then we wish that the other is gone to hell, damnation, perdition or heaven. Sometimes a deep longing pervades one for a reversal to the status quo or a wish that it had never happened. At base however is the murderous wish which should be consciously realised with a moral sense still intact. A man should know, and also a woman that to sever a marriage or a friendship in a brutal way is an act of murder directed towards the 'other'.

A modern woman sacrificed her career in order to further that of her husband. She passed through a difficult period of twenty years in a humdrum job to provide financial support for him. She returned home from her work to find her children waiting to tell her that their father was leaving. Indeed he had packed his bags and ordered the taxi to take him away. He had found another woman who was about to have his child. The wife learned of the liaison for the first time on the step of her front door as he stepped into the waiting taxi-cab to leave her for ever.

She never forgave him, nor did she divorce him. She remained a bitter jealous woman until her tragic death years later which released her husband to marry.

In order to dispel the brooding monsters of darkness in the unconscious, the solar light of consciousness is the prerequisite if a mental equilibrium is to be sustained. The presence of one's shadow personality and its emotional storms has to be consciously realised as a reality.

REFERENCES

1 Sokoloff, Boris M. D., Jealousy, A Psychological Study, p. 11, Carroll & Nicholson Ltd., 1948.
2 Bacon, Francis (22.1.1561 – 1626), Lord Verulam, Essay No. IX Envy, Esays & Counsels Civil & Moral, 1597.
3 Sokoloff, ibid.
4 Proust, Marcl, The Captives, Chatto, London, 1957.
5 Ibid.
6 Sokoloff, ibid., p. 17.
7 Personal Communication from Miss Barbara Hannah, Jungian Analytical Psychologist.
8 Sokoloff, ibid., p. 31.
9 Jung, C. G., Memories Dreams and Reflections, Collins and Routledge & Kegan Paul, London, 1963.
10 Lévy Bruhl, How Natives Think, Participation mystique is a term used for a peculiar kind of psychological connection with objects and consists in the fact that the subject cannot clearly distinguish himself from the object, but is bound to it by a direct relationship which amounts to a partial identity.
11 Miss B. Hannah – private communication to the author.
12 Jones, Ernest, 1930, Jealousy, Chapter 16, 1948, Papers on Psychoanalysis, 5th ed., London, Reprints 325–340.

SEVEN DEADLY SINS

13 The Fourth Estate is the Press.
14 Jung, C. G., Man and His Symbols, Von Franz, M. L., Pt. 3, p. 172, London, 1964.
15 Ibid.
16 Ibid.
17 Ibid.
18 Kerényi, C., Zeus and Hera, Archetypal Image of Father, Husband & Wife, p. 122 ff, Routledge & Kegan Paul, 1975.
19 Ibid.
20 Ibid.
21 Servier, J., Les Portes de L'Année, Paris, 1962.
22 Jung, C. G., Psychological Types, p.582, Routledge & Kegan Paul, 1964. Projection: This signifies the transveying of a subjective process into an object. Introjection: was defined by Ferenczi as the opposite of projection namely as an indrawing of the object within the subjective circle of interest . . .
23 Jung, C. G., Letters: Vol. I p. 246.
24 Ibid., p. 258.
25 Morris, Ivan, The World of the Shining Prince, Oxford University Press, 1964.
26 Ibid.
27 Roux, Georges, Ancient Iraq, Chapter 6, Penguin, 1980, 2nd. ed., (Note) (3) H & A Frankfort, J. A. Wilson Th. Jacobsen, W. A. Irwin, The Intellectual Adventure of Ancient Man, Chicago, 1946. Published under the title, Before Philosophy by Penguin Books, 1951.
28 The Mythology of All Races, v. 5 p. 92. New York, Cooper Square Publishers Inc., 1964.
29 Ibid.
30 Ibid.
31 Roux, Georges, op. cit.
32 Op. cit. Chapter 7 (n. 4) Recent Translation of the Adapa Legend by A. Heidel, pp. 147–153 & E. A. Speiser, Anet pp. 101–103.
33 The Mythology of All Races, Vol. 5, New York, Cooper Square Publishers Inc., 1964.
34 Ibid.
35 Ibid.
36 Old Testament, Book of Genesis 3:19.
37 Old Testament, Book of Genesis 3:5.
38 Encyclopaedia of Religion and Ethics V viii p. 27a Herod III 40 ff.
39 Jung, C. G., Collected Works, Vol. II para 980. Ibid. Note 8. For ex: The invidi (the envious) are a constantly recurring image in the old Latin books on Alchemy especially in the Turba philosophorum (11th and 12th century).
40 This paragraph was written before the fall of the Berlin Wallk, and the collapse of Communism in the Soviet Union, but the aim still exists, and persists, but now has different names.
41 Jung, C. G., Collected Works, Vol X para 431.
42 Van Sommers, Peter, Jealousy (Chapter 8) Penguin 1988, (n Mowat, R. B., 1966, Morbid Jealousy and Murder, London, Tavistock).
43 Ibid.
44 Ibid.
45 Tolstoy, Leo, The Kreutzer Sonata, Oxford University Press, 1940.

116

4

THE DEADLY SIN OF
SLOTH

Many years ago whilst undergoing training to become a dermatologist I spent a great deal of time at the Zoo in London, and also in the small Zoo used for research purposes in the medical school where I worked. The latter consisted of a small but interesting menagerie of animals.

Part of the learning process in the understanding of the organ of the skin was to become involved in research into the nature of animal skin. It was during this period of my life that I became deeply interested in the animal world, an interest which has engrossed me, and seized my attention over the years. In order to be able to understand the human psyche it is essential to endeavour to comprehend the animal world, for the roots of our psyche rest in that realm. If one keeps a domestic pet such as a warm blooded animal like a cat, or a dog, one soon becomes aware how very easy it is to identify and enter into a participation mystique with it.

In the hospital menagerie there were about five or six arboreal tropical American mammals, belonging to the order Edentata, sloths. The sloth is completely arboreal living among the branches of trees, hanging beneath them back downwards, and clinging with the hook like organs to which the terminations of their limbs are reduced. When obliged to descend to the ground which they rarely if ever do voluntarily, they crawl along a level surface with considerable difficulty. Though generally slow and inactive they can on occasion travel with considerable rapidity along the branches. Sloths are nocturnal, silent, solitary animals, and produce but one young at birth, and they show an almost reptilian tenacity to life.

Each morning when I had the opportunity between patients I used to race up about eight flights of stairs and seek the peace, tranquillity and sanity of the animal world.

117

The sloths fascinated me. There they were hanging upside down on their perches which simulated trees, and their limbs would move with truly extraordinary slowness. They would gaze blankly at me, their strange little faces peering from under a heavy brow. Their limbs moved constantly, but because of the slowness almost imperceptibly. One limb would slowly weave over the head of its owner, and another limb after a long pause would perform a similar movement. Sometimes they would simply stare without the flicker of an eyelid for what seemed like hours. They exuded 'non-movement', they were singularly and peculiarly inert. They were not inactive, though torpid in appearance, they seemed curiously unaroused, and certainly they were contained in an air of apathy. That is why the name sloth has been applied to this group of animals.

The girl who looked after them was about twenty-five years old. She was quick and adept, and inclined to impatience with them. She used to feed the animals at about 10 a.m. with raw carrots. Naturally since they were by nature nocturnal, at that time in the morning they were sleepy, and already preparing for the day's rest. It was a most interesting sight to observe these creatures hanging upside down, and very slowly and langourously eating a carrot whilst gazing straight at one. I used to look deeply into their mournful sad eyes, and wonder what they saw, heard, felt and thought.

One morning whilst I watched this rare performance the girl who cared for them pushed a carrot through the bars of the cage of a male sloth, in rather a peremptory fashion. The sloth refused to grasp it, so with her finger instead of a stick, which she was required to use in such circumstances, she gave him a prod. Instantly and like lightning he turned and bit her finger. Now this was exceedingly dangerous because there is always the possibility of serious infection with bites from wild animals. Many infections are potentially fatal. Fortunately she received prompt and high quality therapy and she made a splendid recovery in a few days.

In my observations of these creatures I was astonished at the speed of movement, and the precision of the bite. It taught me a lesson which I never forgot, although normally the sloth is indeed practically inert and very sluggish in movement he can when required move with the speed of a lightning flash. The young lady miscalculated her charge, and neither she nor I realised at that time that the very nature of the sloth must contain the opposites.

The deep exploration into the darkness of the human soul continues with an examination of the sin of accidie.

The almost obsolete word 'Accidie'[1] was once current as the name of a quality related on one side to sloth, which superceded it in some lists of the principal vices. The correct Latin is 'acedia'.

Accidie was the besetting sin of the monk. It sent him to sleep in his cell or drove him out of it. The same vices attack everyone, but not all in the same fashion.

In its Latin derivation, the Greek origin being forgotten, accidie was variously derived from 'acidum' which means 'sour', and also 'accidere' to come upon, as an 'accident' or 'access'. Whence the medieval Latin corruption 'accidie' and O.F. and English 'acci-de, or accidie'. With the restoration of the Greek learning the Latin again became 'accedia'. Whatever errors of etymology may have altered the form of the word the medieval conception of the sin remained fundamentally unchanged, the state of 'don't care', a torpor and indifference to good, a dull melancholy, paralysis of a healthy interest in life and work, in God and man. Melancholy or tristitia is sometimes substituted for accidie or sloth.

There is a sense in which all sins are spiritual and psychical, but some are more purely mental, while others are more immediately carnal or fleshly.

At first it may not be obvious why sloth is regarded with such gravity. It is described as a thankless distaste for life, an irritation arising from a lack of bodily tone, or a general feeling of apathy. Why should such a state be regarded as a fault, so grave as to finally separate the subject so afflicted from God? It becomes clear however, that even more than a coarse excess or an outbreak of passion, it may be the result of a deep seared selfishness, which is at base a sullen rebellion against, and an alienation from God. It is generally an unconscious sin, insidious and pernicious, and extremely dangerous for the health of the soul.

In the Old Testament,[2] 'A slothful man hideth his hand in his bosom, and will not so much as bring it to his mouth again.'

'I went by the field of the slothful
and by the vineyard of the man
void of understanding and lo, it was
all grown over with thorns, and
nettles had covered the face
thereof, and the stone wall thereof
was broken down.'[3]

In both these there is a deep unwillingness it seems to undertake the basic requirements of life, to provide food and drink for the body, and to tend the land to produce the food and wine. This occurs when people are afflicted with torpor for whatever reason. It is first a state signified by a descent into deep unconsciousness. Other examples of the slothful man in the Old Testament are, 'The slothful man saith, there is a lion in the way, a lion in the streets.'[4] Thus an excuse is always provided to avoid taking action at all costs. 'He also that is slothful in his work is brother to him that is a great waster.'[5] Finally, 'Not slothful in business, fervent in spirit serving the Lord.'[6] A thousand years ago a book was written in Japan by one of the celebrated Heian women writers. In her old age she remained in her family home, her husband had died, and the family had left her.

In a sad and mournful state she sent a poem to a nun from whom she had not heard for a long time. She wrote:

'Wildly the sagebrush grows

outside this house where no one comes to call,
And my tears well up like the drops of dew
upon those leaves.'
The nun replied:
'Your sagebrush and your dew
belong to worldly houses.
Think how overgrown the thickets
are, in the cell of one who
finally renounced the world.'[7]

An overgrown sagebrush (Yomogi) was a standard symbol for lonely desolation and was particularly associated with the silent decaying houses of women who were no longer visited by men. It depicts melancholia, with concomitant unwillingness to take action, even for upkeep of house and garden. This as suggested signifies a fall into unconsciousness and loss of self worth.

ACCIDIE THROUGHOUT HISTORY

Now let us explore some of the thoughts about accidie from various scholars throughout the span of centuries.

As long ago as the first century the Shepherd of Hermas was to speak of it. But in the fourth century there lived a writer called John Cassian whose long life covered the second half of the fourth century, and the first half of the fifth century. I think because of his time-moment and also his writings that he should be placed first, although the Poimen came before.

He was in fact trained during his early years in a monastery in Bethlehem, and later was to spend a long time among the hermits of Thebaid before he turned to his great work in the far West, which was to plant the monasticism of the East in the West.

He was to found two communities at Marseilles in France, and to write in all some twelve books.

The tenth book of his De Coenobiotum Institutis is entitled 'De Spiritu Acedae' and in the first chapter he gives a review of the subject.[8] He says that Acedia may be called a weariness or distress of heart, it is akin to sadness; the homeless and solitary hermits, those who live in the desert are especially assailed by it, and monks find it most troublesome about twelve o'clock; so that some of the aged have held it to be 'the sickness that destroyeth in the noonday' or the 'daemonium meridianum' of the 91st Psalm, the 5th and 6th verses of which are as follows:[9]

'Thou shalt not be afraid for the
terror by night; nor for the arrow that
flieth by day;
Nor for the pestilence that walketh

in darkness; nor for the destruction
that wasteth at noonday.'

In Greek mythology the hour of noon was held to be sacred to the God
Pan, who then rests after the chase. It has always been known as the hour
of enchantment or the hour of bewitchment. Pan represented Nature in the
form of a half god-half man figure. His horns symbolised the rays of the
sun and also the aggressivity of the forces contained in Aries, the ram of
spring-time. The hairy aspect of the lower limbs represented the energic
force of the vegetation, the power of growth of the grass, the shrubs, that
is the lower forces of vegetative nature, or the instincts of the animal world.
It should be recalled that Pan was also the companion of Cybele the great
goddess. He played a flute of reeds, a reed pipe in fact whose notes could
enslave those who heard it.

An analysand of mine once dreamed that it was noon, the sun was high
in the sky, and she saw her shadow on the ground. She thought that the
configuration of the shadow was very beautiful, and her shadow-body had
a perfect outline. In other words the dream portrayed a beautiful and hitherto unknown shadow. Suddenly she heard an exquisite sound, three long
notes which trilled into each other in a melodious and beautiful call like
that of a bird. In the dream she knew she had heard the pipes of Pan. She
was extraordinarily enthused when she awoke, and said she felt delirious
with joy.

This beautiful dream depicted something quite extraordinary. She was a
woman of excellent intellect, caught, entrapped almost, in the world of
academia. She came to me because she had really come to an impasse in her
life. Her fiancée to whom she had just become engaged, a good man by all
accounts had begun to bore her, and the question was should she marry
him. I intuited at once that in reality she had no intention of doing so, but
consciously she appeared to want marriage, a home and children. She had
hardly ever dreamed in her life, so she told me, when suddenly after the
death of a parent she had the most vivid and disturbing dreams. That was
apparently the real reason why she came to me.

The Pan dream marked a turning point in her analysis for I realised that
she was that rare being who was living as it were below her potential, she
had 'a beautiful shadow', as Dr. Jung would say, she was a woman 'whose
shadow was almost pure gold'.

Outwardly she was rather difficult, unpleasant and frequently disagreeable. But she herself was unaware of the unusual inner spiritual potential,
all she knew was that she had a bad effect on people. She had been possessed by the destructive effect of the noon-day, she who had worked hard
for high rewards in the outer world had not turned inwards to her soul, and
she appeared to have lost contact with it. She was inert like matter in this
regard, Pan had called her and she had been caught in the torpor and
drowsy sleep of noon-day. Then in the dream she heard his music, and she

knew what had enchanted her, she had to learn that it was an archaic pagan nature god who had seduced her. She was in her thirties when she entered into analysis, and I do believe that by doing so she saved her life, indeed she certainly rescued her soul. Had she married that particular man she would have died of boredom. Fortunately that was not to be her fate. I asked what 'noon-time' meant to her. She was very surprised and said that as a small girl she was seized quite often by an unaccountable sadness when she was alone in the garden or in the woods at noon. This was particularly so when the sun was bright, high and very hot. She explained on such days she always wanted to cry before lunch, for no reason that she knew. The archetype was already at work and she was touched by something exceedingly ancient, pagan and very potent. The sadness was a pointer to her spiritual inertia and for something she had lost.

In the 91st Psalm, 'the sickness that destroyeth at the noon day' is of course the sin of sloth or accidie. The noon day is when the sun, the solar power is most intense. Figuratively speaking it is the zenith of life. It is the time when ego-consciousness is required to turn inwards to the inner world, in the preparation for the death of the body, and the liberation of the soul.

Cassian[10] describes a monk who suffers from this condition in the second chapter of his book. It is an excellent treatise of the malady.

'When the monk is beset by it he detests the place where he is and loathes his cell; he has a poor and scornful opinion of his brethren near and far, and thinks that they are neglectful and unspiritual. It makes him sluggish and inert for every task, and he cannot sit still nor give his mind to reading. He thinks despondently how little progress he has made where he is, how little good he gains or does – he who might so well direct and help others, and while where he is has nobody to teach and nobody to edify. He dwells much on the excellence of other and distant monasteries. He thinks how profitable and healthy life is there, how delightful the brethren are, and how spiritually they talk. On the contrary where he is all seems harsh and untoward, there is no refreshment for his soul to be got from his brethren, and none for his body from the thankless land.'

It continues: 'At last he thinks he cannot be saved if he stays where he is, and then about eleven or twelve o'clock he feels tired as if he had walked miles, and hungry as if he had fasted for two or three days. He goes out, looks this way and that and sighs to think that there is no one coming to visit him. He saunters to and fro and wonders why the sun is setting so slowly, and so with his mind full of stupid bewilderment and shameful gloom he grows slack and void of spiritual energy, and thinks that nothing will do him any good, save to go and call on somebody, or else to betake himself to the solace of sleep.'

'Whereupon his malady suggests to him that there are certain persons whom he clearly ought to visit, certain kind enquiries that he ought to make, a religious lady upon whom he ought to call and to whom he may be able to render some service, and that it will be far better to do this than sit profitless in his cell.'

A student who was suffering from a mild melancholia once came for therapy because she had taken a dislike to everything at the university where she was preparing her final thesis. She hated to sit down and write, she preferred to telephone friends, go out for coffee, buy clothes, do anything in fact except prepare the thesis.

Clinically she was diagnosed as a depressive, in spite of medication she did not improve. She found that her colleagues bored her, 'they were all dull', and she explained that they had nothing of interest to say.

Here was a sever case of sloth, it had developed because her tutor whom she adored had gone abroad. She had developed a great rage against him of which she was quite unconscious. The rage was masked by the slothful-melancholia. She was rendered impotent by her condition, and found herself powerless to act one way or another. The recognition of her anger was brought about by the means of a dream in which she saw a volcano burst into flames. When she began to perceive her fury, the depression began to lighten, and then slowly she was able to set to work as she became conscious of her unconscious emotionality. Quite simply her depression was the result of loss of energy, which was caught in the rage engendered by her tutor's absence. Because the rage was not recognised, it acted like an inner magnet, and drew her psychic energy into a vortex.

The monk whose words are quoted lived some 1600 years ago, yet he could very well have described the situation of the modern student as the sin of sloth, or in his terms ' accidia'.

In a preceding book Cassian[11] speaks of sadness or melancholy which today would be described as depression. The severance of sadness from accidie was deliberately and severely censored by Thomas Aquinas, and certainly the sullen gloom which Cassian describes in his ninth book forms a congenial and integral part in the complex trouble which accidie generally portrays, whilst it is clearly present in the picture of the 'acciduous' monk just described.

By accepting the delineation of sadness(Tristitia) the conception of 'Accidie' may be completed. For the sadness of which Cassian speaks is the gloom of those who ought not to be sad, who wilfully allow a morbid sombreness to envelop them like a cloak. It is a mood which severs man from thoughts of God, or as it is described in Jungian terms, he is no longer in tune with his inner instinctual world, the world of the Self. He permits himself the exquisite luxury of being singularly unkind to all those around him, his peers, friends and family.

Cassian wrote,[12] 'Sometimes without any provoking cause we are suddenly depressed by so great a sorrowfulness that we cannot greet with courtesy the coming of those who are near and dear, and all they say in conversation however appropriate we think of it as annoying and unnecessary.'

Gregory the Great,[13] who tabulated the sins said that 'Those who are sad after this fashion have anger already close to them, and from sadness such as this comes forth malaise, grudging faint-heartedness, despair and torpor as to that which in commuted, and the straying of the mind after that which if forbidden.'

Depression one of the commonest of ills to beset modern man is in most cases a pointer to unconscious anger which has not been resolved in conflict. Sometimes however depression may precede the advent of a creative work.

In the seventh century A.D. John Climacus, or Saint John of the Ladder, took his second name from a book which he wrote entitled, 'Ladder in Paradise.' An English translation was published in 1959 under the name of 'The Ladder of Divine Ascent.' He was famed as a holy man throughout Palestine and Arabia, and spent sixty years in the ascetic life, eventually to become the Abbot of the Monastery on Mount Sinai at the age of 75 years.

He writes of the besetting sin of the monk and does so vividly. He describes it as 'an offshoot of excessive talkativeness, slackness of the soul, remissions of the mind and contempt for the holy exercise and a hatred of one's profession, it extols the blessedness of worldly life, and speaks against God as merciless and unloving. It makes singing languid, prayer feeble and service stubborn. So peculiarly does it tell upon the voice that when there is a psalmody it remains unnoticed. But when the psalms are being sung it causes the victim to interrupt the verse in an untimely yawn'.

Saint John does in fact then personify the sin of accedie, as a woman by describing the cell of the Anchoret in her eyes, how she laughs to herself and goes to settle down close by him. She then suggests all kinds of reasons to the anchoret why he may well leave his prayers and the cell and go out.

It is a perfectly vivid picture of a secular moody disgruntled anima figure, who is seeking to get the monk out of the cell and into the world. One may be permitted to conjecture that this brilliant portrayal of the feminine nature of a man could only be possible if John Climacus had fought hard and long with the wily and disruptive intentions of his own inner feminine nature.

Although these words are now almost fifteen hundred years old, they are still relevant today. An example which proves the point is from the enclosed life of a modern woman. A relatively young nun who had in outer life been the head buyer of a prestigious fashion store had developed lesions on the backs of the hands, which had a similar appearance to Christ's stigmata.

During the course of her investigation it became clear she was exceedingly difficult in the community, and took a perverse liking to injure by small means the goodwill of the other much older nuns. She would go early in the morning to the convent garden and destroy all the flower heads, or cut off the water supply to the vegetables grown for the convent's food supply. She told tales, refused prayers, fell asleep during the hours she should be awake, and was awake when she ought to have been sleeping.

She had undoubtedly a destructive animus which overcame her, and perpetrated bad feeling amongst the other nuns, and between the nun herself and the community. Moreover the lesions on the hands were artefacts which she used to demonstrate to the Mother-Superior her Christ-like devotedness to the Order, and suffering which was engendered by the 'bad' nuns' animosity towards her person. Cassian and John Climacus both would most certainly have described her as a sinner, caught in 'accidie'.

It was the state of mind of a nun who had chosen the wrong vocation, which had taken her away from the world. Exactly the same state as the monks who so long ago suffered from the sin of accidie.

THE PARSON'S TALE[14]

Chaucer writing in the 13th century had this to say: 'After the sin of envy and ire how will I speak of the sin of accidie; For envy blindeth the heart of man and ire troubleth a man, and accidie maketh him heavy, thoughtful and wrawful. Envy and ire maketh bitterness in heart, which bitterness is mother (mooder) of accidie and bynymeth (taketh away from) him the love of all goodness. Then is accidie, the anguish of troubled heart, and St. Augustine saith it is lack of (anoy) goodness and joy of harm. Certainly this is a damnable sin, for it doeth wrong to Jesus Christ, in as much as 'it bynymeth (taketh away) the service that men ought to do to Christ with all diligence' as saith Solomon.'

But accidie dooeth no such diligence. He dooeth all things with anoy (lack of) and with wrawness (slackness) and excusacioun, and with ydelness and unlust for while the book saith 'Accursed be he that dooeth the service of God negligently.' This passage demonstrates again the close connection between anger and accidie. 'Wrawness' is a species of anger, it means half-peevish, half-morose and wholly bitter.

Dante[15] sets this condition in the black slime of the River Styx. It is however to be noted that Dante set Accidie as the central evil of the seven deadly sins.

It has become clear from these various descriptions of sloth, that formerly accidie was well recognised in the religious life, and proved to be dangerous for the soul of those afflicted. One of the central problems was the disinclination to accept the ordered discipline of the monastery, or the convent, and to participate in the adoration of God through prayer. There was at base an alienation or rebellion against God, and that was the reason why accidie was regarded as the deadliest of the sins.

Sloth today is not generally considered to be the same as depression, the mournful aspect has been severed. Yet very often inherent in idleness, inertia and sluggardly ways one finds depression and its co-partner 'wrawfulness' or resentment, if not actually the fury of anger.

The desolation or the blight laid upon the life of an individual who finds himself in a state of inertia, languourous slothfulness or a frank depression, corresponds to the land when the frost has cast its glacial spell over all life.

The symbol for this desolation which has slowly evolved through the centuries, and which has now become associated with sloth is the symbol of the boar which at first glance is sometimes difficult to reconcile with the overt picture. Only when one permits one self to perceive the inner dynamism which attracts psychic energy, as would a magnet, does one realise the unseen but nevertheless raging central fire of fury behind melancholia.

THE BOAR AS SYMBOL OF SLOTH

The symbolism of the boar has an archaic origin, and is found throughout the greater part of the Indo-European world. The tradition of the boar is Hyperborean which simply means it issues from the land of the Hyperboreans, which Heraclitis thought was the extreme North, from whence came Boreas the North Wind. Hyperborean means beyond the North Wind.

This land gave rise to dreams and memories of childhood, and the Golden Age. Apollo lived there as a youth, and his mother Leto was born there. Every nineteen years Apollo went back because it was his refuge against the vengeance of Zeus. Olen the founder of the oracle at Delphi was a Hyperborean, and likewise it is said that Pythagoras was an incarnation of a Hyperborean. So the boar's lineage is closely entangled with the age when beings who were wise all-knowing were often endowed with magical powers.

When a boar or wild boar, or perhaps a warthog appears in dreams we are dealing with a primordial image which is age-old.

The boar represents a spiritual authority. It has a strong rapport with the solitary existence in the forest with the druid in the Celtic tradition, and the brahman in seclusion. It has the unique ability to sniff out, unearth and dig out the truffle, that subterranean mushroom or fungus of mysterious origin believed according to ancient legends to be due to lightning. It is in fact anciently believed to be the fruit of the lightning flash as it penetrates into the ground. It is a kind of union between the dynamis of the spirit and the passivity of the earth. The truffle has a particular flavour, and a singular perfume.

It develops in the roots of oak trees which are sacred in most cultures. It was thought to be a direct gift from the gods and became a symbol of hidden revelation in a flash of lightning or like the rain itself, and ordained by deity. The succulence and the taste of the truffle therefore does not result from human culture, it is a sacred gift. It is this which the boar seeks and finds making of him a terrestial diviner.

In Ancient Greece and also in Gaul the boar was hunted, and in the boar hunt sometimes one met death. The hunt is an image of a spiritual chase or a tracking of a spiritual quality by the temporal.

There is associated with the image a sensuality, a vulgarity and a coarseness together with hunting courage, impetuosity and also spirituality. The boar renders service at the time of the Spring sowing of crops by clearing the soil of weeds so that the earth is ready to receive the seeds. The boar has come to signify new growth by way of this service, but at the time of the harvest when it routs and destroys the corn then it comes to represent decay and death. The boar's flesh was eaten by man, ostensibly to receive courage, (it is a courageous beast) and also strength.

Its other side, the side related to death and decay, is typified by the month of October when the boar-hunting season begins, and lasts until February 2nd in the church calendar, the Feast of Candlemas. The season of hunting ushers in the autumn the dying vegetation and the decay. It is clear why the boar is representative of idleness, sloth and inertia, and is of course a symbol of the decaying nature or the dereliction of depressive states in human illness.

As autumn advances finally death supervenes, and the whole earth goes into a stasis of inertness. Nothing moves, the storm demons lash the land and drive the animals to seek shelter. The grass dies, the trees are broken and injured then the frost comes, the world is seized in a vice-like grip. That is winter. As a ravisher of crops, a slayer of life, the boar has come to signify the absence of the sun, the withdrawal of light, warmth and life. Apollo and the Egyptian Set took upon themselves the guise of a boar. The animal is also sacred to Hermes, Ares and Artemis.

One cannot speak of the boar without reference to Celtic and Norse myth. The Celts worshipped animals or their anthropomorphic representations, the horse, the swine, the stag, bear and serpent. The word for 'boar' does not differ greatly from that for 'bear'. The Zend for boar is 'hu' and the Cornish for sow was 'baneu' which meant 'The good hu.' The Old English word 'Hog' meant the mighty one, as 'Hu' and the Celtic-Welsh word for boar was 'Twrch' which is almost the same as torch meaning a blazing light. The Welsh for boar is 'moch', and the Gaulish was 'moccus' that is, om – ok – us which means the 'Sun' or the 'Great Light.' Moccus was the Gaulish term for Mercury, and Moccus was the Celtic god of swine, and indeed as already mentioned Hermes' animal was the boar. The French word for wild boar is interesting 'sanglier'. Before 1298 it was 'sengler' derived from the Latin singularis which means solitary because the boar was 'the male who lives alone' in ancient tradition.

The wild boar of Gulban belongs to the Celtic Irish hero tradition. Gulban means green, and he was huge, invincible and of a great strength. The great Irish hero Diarmid was under a 'geasa' (oath) never to hunt boar because his father had killed the son of Roc in the síd of Oengus. The latter was the god of love and of spring-time, and his harp was the wind. Roc had transformed the dead body of his son into a boar, in some variations of the myth the boar was Gulban. It was decreed by Roc that the boar would have the same length of life as Diarmid whom Oengus had adjured never to hunt.

Diarmid was tricked by his mother's brother Fionn into hunting the creature, and the great hunt took place with Diarmid resolving to kill 'the old fierce magic boar'. Gulban also signified the storm demon. It was killed and Diarmid was the victor. However just at the moment of the death of the boar, Diarmid stepped over it, and one of its bristles entered his heel and made a fatal wound which took Diarmid's life. Diarmid was the foster son of Oengus, and was irresistible to women because he had a love spot on his forehead. The enmity between Fionn and Diarmid represents the struggle of the sun with the moon for supremacy in the sky. The boar as storm darkness and death indicates the impending darkness and disappearance of the moon, which as Diarmid the hero must submit eventually to defeat in death.

In the Celtic world, a boar without bristles(that is without the sun's rays) is the last darkness of the world, and the destruction of the sun at nightfall. Inherent in this idea is the brute force of nature. The black boar represents decay, destruction and winter with inertia, a superb symbol for sloth or depression.

Finally in Norse mythology Gullinbursti which means 'golden bristles' drove Frey's chariot. He was a magnificent boar (like Gulban) and symbolised a field of golden ripe corn swaying in the wind. The moment of maturation of perfect ripeness inevitably marks the beginning of the slow decline into loss of vibrancy, inertia and death. Again the boar suggests the dark decline.

In Christian tradition, particularly in France the boar signified sin. He was charged with being the steed of gluttony, anger and intemperance because of his impetuous and insular behaviour. But he was also attributed to Melancholicus and the Earth. This because of the innate inert quality of earth as matter.

THE MAN WHO DREAMED OF A WILD BOAR

A male analysand of about fifty years of age came because he had a difficulty in his life.

He was charming, intelligent and anxious to learn about himself. Thinking was his superior function, and he had a marked extraverted attitude. He was consistently late for his appointment but he always gave a valid excuse. He never apologised, but charmingly offered the reason for his delay. He was a family man and had a successful working life.

From his dreams it became clear that there was a constant background of darkness, everything was shadowy, and the dream figures were always depressed, sad or grieving. He told me that in reality he had lost all the friends of his youth. They had simply disappeared. He added that it was because he never had time for anything. There is an old maxim 'A slothful man never has time.' I told him of this, and together we explored the various aspects of his life. In every area there was a stultification, he has given up his voyages which he had enjoyed, his visits to his parental home were in jeopardy, and he never went to the theatre because 'there was no time'.

Each hour with me was directed to the gloomy life situation and the sombre mournful dreams. Yet he never complained about the marriage, it was clear that his children were important to him. Gradually I realised that he brought with him an air of dejection which also began to affect me.

The immediate problem of the marriage was secondary to a mother complex. It was as if he was bewitched, and suffered from a curious inertia in his ability to deal with it.

He had married a woman not unlike his mother in that she was practical, but disinclined to show her feelings. Slowly, but imperceptibly over the years it seemed he had lost a certain sparkle, a 'joie de vivre'.

Although he listened with deep concentration to the interpretation of his dreams, he did no inner work on them, and he did not read about the subject of psyche. He coasted along. There was a profound resistance to absolute commitment to the unconscious. This was the force of the mother complex which caused him to withhold himself from total commitment to the work. It was an unconscious rebellion, seemingly against the analyst as a mother-figure, but au fond he was afraid of the unconscious itself.

Then came a dream which shocked him beyond belief. He was in his house when he heard a noise, he went to investigate and found that a wild boar had entered, and in its rampaging had destroyed an entire room. Suddenly it saw him, and that was the full confrontation. It stopped with its head down ready to charge, but suddenly it backed away. Then he woke up in shock.

The dream made me nervous. When a wild boar attacks it allows itself to be confronted by hunters or attackers, it stands its ground for it is also very brave, and then it backs away. Then it charges, and it can kill several people in an encounter unless of course it is spiked or shot.

I said 'Could you have killed it?' It was a telling question, he did not know. He was stunned by the dream, and in it he had no weapon. He told me that the boar was absolutely real.

During his long years of marriage he had slowly imperceptibly descended like the sinking sun at sunset into an inertia. His emotional life was torpid and in a state of suspension. He was always busy, but had no time for anything. His latent melancholia made him appear apathetic and lethargic, he found it hard to make a decision. This was the winter time, and the wild boar came to image the desolate state of his life, and the immense danger.

The setting sun had removed the illumination, and he was incapable of realising his true plight.

The confrontation with the boar was the shock needed to jolt him into the reality of the unconscious and its objective nature. He demonstrated the sluggard inherent in certain types of mother complex, and in the boar he envisaged his own rage, instinctive and brutal.

EXPLANATION OF THE SYMBOLISM OF THE BOAR IN THE DREAM.

This 'accidie' of the above man was in fact almost the same condition as that of the medieval monks. He was he believed trapped not in a monastery but in a marriage, with the negative feminine of his wife's nature. In reality he was caught by the archetype of the feminine of his own psyche.

Accidie or rather the present sin of sloth is much commoner than is generally realised. Because so many explanations are given regarding the cause of the many disenchantments possible in any alliance between two people the underlying and indeed unrecognised unwillingness to become conscious of one's shadow is overlooked. The inadequacies of the subject are cast aside, and blame apportioned to the other with a childish slothful petulance. Behind this mask is an anger, compounded of fear and inferiorities, which burns in a slow sullen resentment.

It is so much easier to see those faults in others and in the outer world, but which in actuality lie within one's own soul. This is where one fails in virtue, and why sloth is regarded as a mortal sin.

THE WOMAN WHO DREAMED OF A WILD BOAR

A woman in the prime of life suddenly found herself in a state of depression. She sought medical aid which resulted in various treatments, which appeared to be of help. However the depression continued and in the end she was advised to seek psychotherapy.

In her outer life she was successful and her relationships appeared to be in order. She had no idea why she was so 'down' is how she put it. She found everything to be dull and colourless. She had no initiative to undertake new projects, there was no desire either to entertain herself or to be entertained.

She was extremely practical it seemed, and her attitude to life was primarily extraverted although she did declare that she had become withdrawn of recent months prior to her psychotherapy. Her inferior function was intuition. One can never approach this directly, but only indirectly through an auxiliary function, in her case either thinking or feeling. The latter was less well developed than the former. The inferior function is the ever open door to the unconscious, it is the place where the animus in a woman, (or the anima in a man) may enter. Thus he is clothed in the nature of the inferior function. In her case inferior intuition, and she was subjected to a great many negative perceptions of an exceedingly destructive nature, both in relation to her own person and others.

Secretly she always believed that everything would become much worse, and she suspected that disaster would overtake her and her family. She intuited all manner of things which gave her much pain, and coloured both her thought and feeling.

Clearly although this woman was successful with the outer paraphernalia of material wealth somewhere there was a lack of depth in the realm of Eros. I did wonder if she had permitted herself to be swept into a love affair without prior opinions and decisions as to the suitability of its nature, and the social acceptability of the man. This is not uncommon in women who are of a practical cast of mind, and those with undifferentiated feeling are sometimes guilty of this.

It became clear however in the course of the analysis that the problem lay in a deeper aspect of psyche, and her dreams eventually revealed a spiritual problem in which she became conscious that Christianity no longer gave her spiritual support. She had already become aware of a certain malaise when she was young, but instead of thinking about her disquiet she 'bravely' as she described it 'soldiered on'. Secretly she had begun to denigrate most aspects of the religious life as it was enacted by herself.

Then she had the following dream.

She was in her own house, but the floor upon which she was standing was that of the analyst's consulting room. She recognised the vivid colours of the carpet. Through the door from the living room came a young and slender wild boar and in its mouth was a shining red apple. It seemed as if the boar had brought her a gift. Then she awakened.

She had no associations to this dream and was not able to amplify it. She expressed astonishment that the wild boar had been friendly and had brought her a present.

Indeed it had, the apple is the fruit of the tree of knowledge, of good and evil. What a gift! The boar as was noted was the steed of Frey, the Norse god of plenty and his boar was Gullinbursti, Golden Bristle. Also as we observed the steed of gluttony, anger, intemperance and impetuous behaviour. At Frey's festival at the winter solstice the boar was sacrificed to him for the purpose of asking him to be favourable in the New Year to come. The head with an apple in the mouth was carried on a silver or gold platter decorated with rosemary and bay leaves into the banqueting hall. At the same time the boar was also Ottarr as Hildisivini, and was the lover of the goddess Freya who was also his mistress. Freya was the goddess of sensual love, and sometimes of pure love as well as fruitfulness. The early Christians regarded Freya as a witch and banished her to the mountains, her name Freya means 'lady'.

In her dream the analysand said that the boar was 'real' and lean, so the presumption that the winter was over may not be wide of the mark. He brought her a priceless gift. Clearly the dreamer had to participate in the feast by accepting the gift, eating it, and making a sacrifice.

Shortly after this dream she met and fell into a passionate love, and at once left all her former friends. The new lover introduced her to a world she had never known, and for the first time in her life she came fully into life, and realised that she loved deeply. The profound inner changes which had taken place in the introversion occasioned by the long depression were reflected in her outer life. She had to sacrifice a great many of her animus opinions about her religious attitude and her own needs and requirements.

She declared that she had been asleep. She had not of course, but she had been imprisoned in a melancholic inertia and been beset by the sin of sloth. She had to become awake to the needs of her body, the murmuring of her heart, and the yearning of her soul for love.

The coming of the live boar brought with it a vast change. The inertia fell away as soon as it was perceived, and the psychic energy gleaned from the consciousness of the crippling nature of her opinioned Christian animus became available for her life.

The live boar in the dream entered into her consciousness as a preparation for the sacrifice of the sin of accidie which had claimed her. The possession was over, and a new religious attitude was born.

The fact that the boar with the gift entered in the ambiance of the analytical work made a deep impression upon her rational animus, and proved to be a turning point. It was (as is the carpet) her new standpoint.

THE SIN OF SLOTH IN THE DIVINE COMEDY

The Divine Comedy by Dante, is a mine of information concerning the darkness of the human soul, and in particular is a praiseworthy discourse on the deadly sins. After the Inferno, Dante, with the poet Virgil leaves Hell and enters Ante-Purgatory on his way to Purgatory – where the sins are redeemed. The terrace of Accidie is a chaos of helter, skelter, and a rumbustious frenzy of running feet, the antidote for sloth. To one who has accompanied the Pilgrims through the dead air of the Inferno there is something indescribably beautiful in the opening sentences of the II Purgatorio. It is Easter Sunday morning, and Dante has risen with the Lord into 'the new life', after leaving the horror of the great darkness.

The Guardian of Ante-Purgatory was Cato and he bade Virgil take Dante to wash in the dew by the shore of the seaside. This in order to cleanse the stains of Hell. He was to gird himself with one of the rushes which grew in the mud. As soon as it was plucked the reed grew back. This is reminiscent of the theme of the golden bough, the oaken bough covered with mistletoe which Aeneas plucked as a kind of passport to the underworld. As soon as it was plucked it regrew.

In the Christian sense the rush or the reed signifies humility. However, since it is both strange and important as a kind of talisman in the hard quest of redemption of the sins I think it would help to look at the symbolism of the reed, and see what it has meant to those who were not Christian in outlook, and also what does it mean to those other cultures today?

You will recall that the first sinners met were those who were indolent, then there appeared the terraces where those who had sinned by anger, (wrath) pride or jealousy had to pass. The 4th terrace was that of Accidie. The reed symbolically is a sort of protective talisman against sin or evil.

THE SYMBOL OF THE REED

The reed is a symbol of instability and also of fragility as well as flexibility. As I have pointed out it represents the Christian virtue of humility. It is associated with slenderness, weakness and hollowness in the sense of it being a vehicle permitting transit. It is associated with marshlands and music. It has the ancient meaning of being a measuring instrument, and because of its hollow nature and its associations with wet marsh-land and water it has come to be associated with irrigation, drainage and also divination. It therefore controls the flow of, and deals with excess water.

A frequent myth in folklore is the transformation incident whereby a fugitive tosses away a reed which grows into a forest and impedes the pursuers. It has thus the association of magical protection. (Its association with Pan is to be recalled, the God who plucked the reeds and made the first music – the pipes of Pan.) Also in greek mythology it was a hollow reed by which Prometheus brought fire to mankind, also giving rise to associations with lightning as well as life.

In the ancient Celtic world the reed was the tree of the twelfth druidic month from October 29th to November 25th. This is the month of the Boar. In November the reed was ready for cutting, and as the reed was used for thatching roofs it became associated with the final establishment of a house, it also had a spiritual quality since the roof was the part of the house nearest to the sky, and the winds as they blew through the reed thatch whistled, and so the reed permitted the voice of the wind and thus the spirit, to be conveyed to the humankind who resided inside the house.

But a reed shaken by the wind signifies a person who is unstable and moved by any passing influence. A Chinese friend of mine was fourteen when the Japanese invaded Malaya. Each day on his way to school in Kuala Lumpur he cycled past the lamp posts along the road, and upon each was the head of a Malay or Chinese who had resisted the Japanese.

His father admonished him each morning as he left the house – 'be like the reed, bend, do not break'.

In Africa and Indonesian cosmogonic legends the first human pair were made from reeds. The reed also carries the qualities of protector and purifier. After his sojourn in the land of the dead, the Japanese god Izanagi purified himself by burning reeds and then permitting his body to be bathed in the wafted reed smoke. Also in Japan bundles of reeds were tied to doors to guard against evil spirits. In all the great Shinto ceremonies of purification or sanctification the circle (the Chi-no-was) through which the initiate was to pass was formed by bundles of reeds. It was also believed that originally Japan was a vast reed-bed, and that the reed issuing from the primal waters represented in Japanese myth is equivalent to that of the Lotus. In China the reed is the emblem of the phoenix the red bird of the south. Its name is Sheng and it is symbolic of a leader who gathers people together, in much the same manner as music quietens and aggregates a group.

In the Arab world the reed as a musical instrument is ubiquitous. A reed snatched from the reed-bed of the earth and turned into a flute by the Dervishes became the principal instrument of their spiritual concerts, which according to the founder of their sect (Jalad el din Rûmi) sang of the sadness of separation. It became symbolic of the mystic separated from God. The separation was portrayed by the notes and the breaths of the music as it issued from the hollow reed. It signified the mystic's longing to find again eternal life. This symbol of the ardent soul which expresses itself in weeping and singing is found amongst many European and Asian peoples as well as in the Arab world. There is a common tale which says that if a reed grows above the body of a drowned person, the reed accuses the assassin if one makes a flute of it.

So it is the conduit of the voice of truth, the purifying voice of conscience, a very necessary attribute for sinners to deal with their inner evil.

Man is sometimes described as a 'thinking' reed.

When I was writing this part of the chapter, a synchronicity occurred,[16] an analysand of mine brought me a strange dream.

THE DREAM

She was in the water in the sea, and looking deeply into it. The water was as clear as crystal, but she perceived that there were reeds which moved with the current. A man appeared to be standing in the water amongst the reeds. He was upright and swaying rather, she thought he was alive but when she looked directly at his face she saw that he was, she thought, dead. She was not sure. Suddenly he pitched forward in an arc and floated in mid-water with arms outstretched in a jack-knife position in the underwater reeds. Then she knew he was dead. He was a complete stranger and she had never seen him before.

Upon waking she was disturbed by the fact that the man was dead, and she had a feeling of revulsion.

Prior to the dream she had undergone a long analysis in order to explore an obsessional thought which had plagued her for a very long time. It had begun when she had decided to give up her work since she had quite enough money from her invested income. Her work had been arduous, but interesting and creative. When she decided to 'retire' she did nothing except please herself in social activities, chatter, amusements and entertainment. Then a depression intervened and with it a the obsessional thought.

It was difficult to keep her attention because the thought intruded constantly. Eventually after a period of private hell her sufferings began to lessen, she accepted the importance of dreams, and she tried to interpret them herself.

Here was a possessing demon. Her animus produced this thought and she knew that it was untrue, but she was forced to believe it. Prior to her period of leisure her animus had been occupied constantly and was not given time to punish her. She was an extraverted feeling type but her thinking was introverted and the inferior function. The animus as a powerful seducer carried her away to the brink of madness with the compulsive thought.

As she undertook her responsibility for recording her dreams seriously a change became apparent in her personality. She was noticeably calmer, and she spoke less and less of the obsession. Then one evening I wrote up the symbolism of the reed, and the next day she came to see me. She began to sob and weep and declare that she was no better. I felt my attention beginning to wander, and my animus suddenly told me 'What a bore all this is!' The animus when he comes up always wants to fight. I realised that I agreed with him, and that her dissatisfaction was a great bore. So I told her that I felt sure that if she persisted in this mournful and selfish discourse her husband would find her as great a bore as I did. The words fell like droplets of iced-water in the room. I felt deeply sorry to have had to say them, but I knew they were just as well as cruel.

Everything went very quiet, and she gazed directly at me. That night she dreamed of the drowned man in the reed bed. I immediately recalled my work on the reed and I told her the mythology, and she was deeply astonished that she would dream such a thing.

When a person is caught by obsessional thinking or compulsive behaviour there is usually malice, and a considerable degree of evil about. It is clear that an 'assassin' was present in the dreamer's psyche because she had suffered great torture on account of the negative animus.

The next dream a few days later depicted her entry into a building hold-

135

ing the death certificate of an unknown man, she was going to register the death.

As the days followed she suddenly became aware, and was afraid to believe it at first, but the possession had gone.

The accidie or the sloth of her new life had paved the way for an invasion by a destructive content of her psyche which had as it were killed off her positive creative side. The obsessional thought came directly from the central core of the negative pole of the archetype of the animus. The inertia of her new superficial life had permitted the intrusion. Her return to creative thinking in her analytical work was the first step towards her individuation.

My own work, my observations, her work and her dream portrayed the inner transformation amongst the reeds below the surface of the water. The absolute truth of the moment, inner and outer, accomplished the depossession of the demonic thought. This is the meaning innate to the Hexagramm Chung Fu No. 61 – the Inner Truth, in the ancient Chinese Book of Changes – the I Ching.

The reed is associated with earth, water, air and fire. It is a vehicle of wholeness, and in this synchronistic episode played the part of and was indeed an emissary of the Self.

This important symbol is essentially and literally the communion with God, or as we would say the Self the greater personality, and which is the protector and the purifier. Consciousness of one's nature becomes the passport or safeguard to wholeness. One must be aware of one's sins and admit to them before any development in consciousness may take place. Humility is always the essential step.

In the Ante-Purgatory of the Purgatorio in Canto IV of the Divine Comedy indolence is met not quite the same as sloth, but a precursor to it, and also represented by laziness, lingering and a willingness to dawdle.

In the Fourth Canto the first two old friends of Dante are musicians. He meets firstly Casella a singer of love songs, who probably set Dante's poems and songs to music. Casella was fined for loitering in the streets at night in Siena in 1282. To loiter is to move indolently. The second friend was Belacqua a Florentine lute-maker also famed for indolence, he was word saving and laconic of speech, too lazy to be verbose. Music, admirable though it is, is a great seducer of the mind, it soothes and lulls as it enchants and permits a descent into unconsciousness through the pleasures of the ear.

On the fourth terrace, which is devoted to those whose sin is accidie, it is believed by many to be the fourth and most deadly of the mortal sins. It cannot be emphasised strongly enough how much this sin has been condemned by the churchmen throughout the centuries.

As the Pilgrims arrive at the Terrace of Accidie the sun is setting and it is getting dark. Exhaustion overtakes them and they pick up the contagion of lassitude, and they succumb to a sudden cessation of the powers of movement, and fall into inertia.

Thomas Aquinas said that pride is love of one's own excellence, in as much as out of this love springs the inordinate desire of excelling others, which properly belongs to pride. Whereas envy is sadness at another's good because it threatens to eclipse ours. Anger as a mortal sin appears when one desires an unjust vengeance contrary to charity or justice. He also said[17] that in quoting St. Isidore of Seville c 560 A. D. 'that sadness identifies with sloth producing restlessness of the body'.

The souls on the terrace are restless of body, but their minds do not wander. Their wills are resolutely set on one end, redemption, and they run to the goal. This is the opposite of their old weary restless habit of running to and fro. A lazy man is always glad of an excuse to throw down his task and gossip with a passer-by. Aquinas condemns talkativeness as a sign of sloth, and traces it to the wandering of the mind about things forbidden which is one of 'the daughters of Accidie'.

On the fourth terrace there is no conversation. Running without pause until the voice is lost in the distance.

Aquinas[18] had this to say of sloth.

'Sloth is a heaviness and sadness that weighs down the soul, that it has no mind to do anything. It carries with it a disgust of work. It is a torpor of the mind, neglecting to set about good. Such sadness is always evil. Out of this sadness comes rancour and one of the effects of rancour is bitterness and acrimony.'

Possibly no better description could be made and is particularly pertinent for modern society's collective sickness of the soul.

Sloth is a complex sin, and is present in the cowardly shrinking away from and failure of the soul in the presence of high and difficult undertakings.

At the beginning of this century, the Bishop of Oxford[19] in his well known essay on the presence of the sin of accidie – 'Instances in which a great vocation was dismally forfeited through faint heartedness, lack of faith and courage.' One sees this frequently in cases of sportsmen and athletes who show enormous promise, and as their careers reach the zenith they fall or slip, or become ill. From that moment they fade. It denotes a lack of courage combined with a deep desire to avoid failure and of course it is just there that they fail, the will to win strong it may be, but ego is not the master in the house, other unknown factors lie in the hinterland of psyche, shadow factors of great power.

Even Dante tells us that when he set out on his great pilgrimage his heart and flesh fainted and failed. Virgil taunted him and said 'Thy soul attainted with cowardice.' It is just there that lack of courage or cowardice, or faint heartedness must be perceived in oneself, and recognised then accepted.

At the base of accidie is the undervaluation of the gifts God has endowed upon the particular being, and the work bestowed on them also is despised. If one says continually, 'I cannot do it,' 'I am not good enough,' 'I have not studied enough,' or 'I am not clever enough,' it depicts the presence of the shadow who is one's real antagonist. The message is clear, somewhere one despises oneself, and beyond that one may reject oneself in totalis.

In a man, the Anima may impart to him a feeling of unworthiness and cause him to reject his gifts or his prowess. The Animus likewise is very adept at self denigration in a woman, and is quickly able to set her God-given gifts at naught.

Behind in the shadows is the sin of sloth, an inability to turn inwards, to examine these negative thoughts and destructive feelings and to explore the areas from which they emanate.

Sloth as the feeling of 'cannot be bothered' or 'don't care' leads to an attitude which is hidden and constant. It is indifference, a dull melancholic paralysis of a healthy interest in life, in oneself and in one's spirituality. Accidie was and is the central evil of the deadly sins. Sloth is a sin of both the flesh and the spirit. The sins of the spirit, pride, envy and anger are ethically related to sloth, whilst the sins of the flesh, avarice, gluttony and likewise lust have a similar connection to it. Contained in sloth is sullen gloomy resentment, discontent and a sulky moroseness. Its essence is rejection of God, because it secretly rejects life. There is finally a hopeless form of incurable bitterness.

A man lost his right hand and became savage with the sin of accidie. He was caught in excessive pride, which made him uncontrollably envious, and jealous of his former prowess as a musician. If however he was overtaken either in his amorous adventures or his profession he descended at once into a reclusive sulkiness of mood, the common lot of an anima possessed man. This mood gave way to a deep apathy and moroseness. He was also greedy and mean of spirit. He was not physically slothful, but slothful of spirit, he believed God had treated him badly and he did not forgive God. He had a hatred of his Maker and also of the whole of mankind. His bitterness in the end killed him by way of a carcinoma of the stomach. He could not digest his life, and had rejected it together with his God.

The complete disappearance of the word accidie from modern speech has led to the idea that the sin represented by it was a spiritual disease of the cloister. When the aspect of melancholy separated off as a separate psychic entity sloth became apparently a somatic disorder characterised by an indolence of the body – the indolence of the personality seemed no longer to be included.

THE PROBLEM OF SLOTH IN MODERN SOCIETY

Depth psychology has proved to be the means by which a deeper and more comprehensive understanding of the rôles played by feeling-toned complexes and the deeper archetypes, in the evolution of the condition, which is compounded of both spiritual (psychic) and somatic elements. It is generally agreed from this standpoint that the Church Fathers were wise in their condemnation of an unwillingness to take responsibility for one's emotional storms and resentments when this sin as accidie presented itself in those far-off days.

Such individuals living under the Logos inherent in the Christian attitude had lost contact with the natural world, and their own instinctual realm. In neuroses self-knowledge derived from inner work is the answer, and would have combatted this evil in the enclosed orders.

To enter into the rhythm of nature, and work on the land amongst the animals used for food supply of the enclosed orders was excellent therapy, but not possible for all. Those of a rational cast of mind, probably the most in need would be the least willing to humble themselves. The monasteries (and the convents) mirrored in minature the changes which were in potentia and waiting to develop on a vast scale in modern society in the centuries to follow.

Accidie may have disappeared as a word, but the sin remains.

The society of today exhibits the increasing potency of the collective shadow, and the ever deepening unconsciousness of our time. There is no gainsaying, the collective shadow of western mankind has become very dark indeed during the past half century of our era. The darkness is a contagion, and no one is exempt from engulfment. Some small or large crime may catch us. It has become the accepted thing to steal, to lie, to cheat or be an adulterer. If we know that we commit a sin we are blessed, but generally and sadly we are not always aware of that which we do. In analysis these aspects of our personal unconscious become the focus of attention. Indeed one should know one's defects which belong to the personal shadow. But what of mortal sins which destroy the soul?

In the godless society of our day materialism takes pride of place. There is something unutterably stupefying in the fact that a painting can be sold for teens of millions of pounds, and the poor psychotic artist lived and died in penury, whilst others rode on his poor 'ghost' to make money upon a creative talent derived from the Self.

Everywhere we are witness to a strange deformation of the sexual instinct, it has been placed on a pedestal instead of the spirit which it has displaced. In many lives sexuality or the sexual instinct has become the god-head, but sexuality is simply an instinct like many others.

In the thraldom of this magnification of an instinct has flourished all manner of evil, not least of which is murder, and rape (a murder of the soul of a woman) a close second. Drugs with their aphrodisiacal qualities and sensual enhancements engender licentiousness which brings diseases of the body and the psyche.

Every aspect of our lives in now beset with the effects of evil. The churches and the churchmen are powerless because the scientists have told us that there is no God, and in our simplicity, battered by torrents of words from the press and radio, blinded with thousands of visual images from the medium of television, we seem to believe it. The press and the media are composed of men and women usually fairly young, who are moulded by the beliefs and conceptions formulated by the collectivity of the time. In those worlds few individuals risk their employment in order to permit themselves to listen to their own souls; there are fewer still who believe they have a soul at all, or at least that is the impression given.

As Jung[20] said many decades ago 'Mercurius that two-faced god comes as the lumen naturae, the servator and salvator, only to those whose reason strives towards the highest light ever received by man, and who do not trust exclusively to the cognitio vespertina.[21] For those who are unmindful of this light the lumen naturae turns into a perilous ignis fatuus, and the psychopomp (Mercurius) into a diabolical seducer. Lucifer who could have brought light becomes the father of lies, whose voice in our time supported by press and radio revels in orgies of propoganda, and leads untold millions to ruin.'

It does not need a great deal of perception to realise the despair which permeates the collective shadow. Nowhere is exempt. In Europe millions have no work, the volume of inherent sullen anger is unimaginable together with the resentful irritation against those who are not in need. Hundreds of thousands, if not millions of dispossessed migrants without language skills in new countries, are already isolated from their pre-existing culture of whatever nature it may have been. The future in the hands of the children of this rootless society appears precarious since there is a lack of solid foundation. The magnitude of repressed ire, and the sadness together with the fury contained therein is an inconceivable legacy for the days to come.

It is clear accidie is ever present, and sloth as we term it today is the unrecognised but inevitable outcome of current events in contemporary life. The task for each one is to recognise it, admit it and accept it as part of the personal shadow. The first step in the recognition of evil is to brand it as evil. If man is to survive he must awaken and arise from the encumbering sloth.

In short he must try to perceive the pivotal danger of universal loss of soul and contact with the Self as God-image; the Self as the archetype of wholeness and order in the collective unconscious.

REFERENCES

1 Encyclopaedia of Religion & Ethics, Vol. 1, pp. 65–66, Ed. J. Hastings, T & T Clarke, Edinburgh, 1908.
2 Old Testament, Proverbs 19:24.
3 Ibid. 24:31

4 Ibid. 26:13
5 Ibid. 18:9.
6 New Testament, Romans 12:11.
7 As I Crossed a Bridge of Dreams, The Diary of the Lady Sarashina, Penguin Classics, 1971.
8 Cassian, John, (1) De Coenobiotum Institutis, (2) Collationes Patrum in Scythica Eremo Commorantium.
9 Old Testament, 91st Psalm, Versus 5&6.
10 Cassian, John, De Spiritu Acediae, Book X, De Coenobiotum Institutis.
11 Ibid.
12 Cassian, John, Collationes Patrum Collation V Chapter lx.
13 S. G regorii Reg. Past III iiii Moralium liber xxxl.
14 Chaucer, The Canterbury Tales, The Parson's Tale.
15 Prisoners of Hope – An Exposition of Dante's Purgatorio by the Rev. J. S. Carron M.A., Hodder & Stoughton, London, 1906.
16 Definitions of Synchronicity: Synchronicity is described as a meaningful coincidence in time.
17 Aquinas, Thomas, Summa ii–ii q xxxv p. 4.
18 Ibid. ii–ii q xxxv l. 4.
19 Bishop of Oxford, Spirit of Discipline, 1906.
20 Jung, C. G., Collected Works, Vol. 13, para 303.
21 Jung, C. G., Collected Works, Vol. 13, para 301.

5

THE DEADLY SIN OF
LUST

ARMAND JEAN DE RANCÉ

In the 17th century France was renowned for libertinage and licentiousness. Mazarin, a pupil of Richelieu was in an alliance with the Queen (Anne of Austria) who was a born coquette. Together they instigated a court of unsurpassed profligacy. Even the 18th century, also renowned for lewdity never achieved the depths of depravity attained in the 17th century. Through the court moved one of the great beauties of this century, perhaps even of many centuries. Her name was Madame Montbazon, a mistress of the arts of seduction, profligate in the extreme, and a libertine of unparalleled stature.[1]

She had a lover who was much younger than herself. He was Armand Jean de Rancé aged 31 years. He was in fact, and had been since the age of 10 years, the Abbé of the monastery of La Grande Trappe, near Soligny in Normandy. At 13 years of age he had written an essay on the dignity of the soul, many years before he met his beloved. Needless to say, he never went near this desolate place, hidden in the vast forests of the stormy Norman headland, which had been established as a monastery some 500 years earlier in the 12th century. Because of its isolation and neglect it had fallen into a state approaching dereliction.

Armand Jean de Rancé was a singularly handsome man, brilliantly clever, vivacious, sensuous and a ferocious libertine. He became the inamorata of Madame de Montbazon, and could not leave her side. He was fascinated by her, indeed possessed by her, and was with her constantly.

However the coquettish Queen became for one reason or another disenchanted with Madame de Montbazon, they had a quarrel, and the latter was banished from the court to the Touraine in the west of France. Not to

142

be deprived of her presence de Rancé joined her whenever it was possible in order to make her banishment more agreeable. Eventually the Queen permitted the return of the exile.

Unfortunately, or perhaps fortunately, just at the moment of her return to court de Rancé was called away to Paris. However as soon as he was able he returned to be with his lady in Paris.

He found however that the great house in which she lived appeared to be empty. No one was there to admit him, or guide him through the great doors into the interior courtyard. He went to her upper floors finding them all empty. He then entered the private apartments of his mistress. At last he opened the portières of her private bed chamber, and there on a wooden trestle table was a coffin covered by a loose cloth. As his gaze took in the room he saw on a side table the head of a woman, the face of which had been totally mutilated to the point of non-recognition, by smallpox.

In the coffin lay the body of his mistress which had been decapitated so that it would fit into the small coffin. Her head which had been so severely ravaged by the disease was it seemed the witness to the macabre scene.

Imagine the silence of that empty house, the horror of that ghastly sight. It carried an eloquence beyond the power of all words to the very heart of Armand Jean de Rancé as he mutely recognised the face of his loved one.

Shortly afterwards he suffered a hunting accident of great severity, then his patron the Duke of Orleans died. He divested himself of all his possessions, properties and lands except the monastery of La Trappe where he went at once, and over many many years gradually built a fine abbey of the Cistercian Order. An enantiodroma took place and from one day to another he entered the spiritual life, and was to institute the Trappist Order as it was to be known.

In the 18th century Samuel Johnson[2] in his dictionary of the English language described 'lust' as both a noun and a verb.

As a noun he gave it three meanings, carnal desire, any violent or irregular desire, a vigour or an active power. He gave the following meanings to the verb, to desire carnally, to desire vehemently and to 'list'. List is an old English word for lust. It is used in the negative sense today as 'listless'.

With respect to carnal desire, lust also has the meaning of delight or anticipated pleasure. The meaning of lust as a violent irregular desire is illustrated from Exodus. 'I will divide the spoil; my lust shall be satisfied upon them.'[3]

Lust as a certain kind of vigour is implicit in 'Trees will grow greater and bear better fruit if you put salt, lees of wine or blood to the root; the cause may be the increasing of the lust or spirit of the roots.'[4] As a sexual desire in Psalm 63 'Their eyes swell with fatness, and they do even what they lust.'[5] The following illustrates an irregular disposition 'The mixed multitude fell a-lusting and the children of Israel also wept and said, who shall give us flesh to eat?'[6]

These meanings have been held since the 17th century in the English language. In Biblical or theological use the meaning of lust is desire as sinful, or a secondary meaning is sensuous appetite.

Today lust has retained the OE meaning in English of sexual desire or appetite, but it has in modern rhetorical use the meaning of 'Lawless and passionate desire of or for some object.'

To summarise, the meaning of inherent in the verb is to desire, wish or choose excessively and inordinately, whereas the noun has the meaning of pleasure, present or anticipated, delight, appetite, relish or inclination.

Since 1447 the adverb 'libidinous' in English has been used to characterise those given to lust. It means lustful, lecherous and lewd; or it prokes lust. One who persists in habitual licentiousness with regard to the relation of the sexes is said to be a libertine.

Following the practice of Jung, we use the term libido for all forms of psychological energy manifested as interest or desire. The term is not limited specifically to sexual interest as is done by the followers of Freud. An exclusively sexual definition of this concept is one-sided. Appetite and compulsion are the specific features of all impulses and automatisms. (The sexual theory of psychic automatism is an untenable prejudice.)

Jung[7] relates the very wide use of the term libido in the classics with the etymological context and which is helpful in the understanding of the meaning.

Libido or lubido (with liber formerly lubet) means 'it pleases'. Whereas libens or lubens signifies 'gladly' or willingly. The Skr. word lúbhyati has the meaning 'to experience a violent longing', lôbhayati excites longing, lubdha-h means eager, lôbha-h is longing, eagerness; Gothic liufs, OHG. liôb, is love. Also associated with Goth. lubains, hope and OHG. lobôn, loben, lob, have the meaning of praise, glory. O.Bulg. ljubiti, to love, ljuby love; Lith. liáupsinti, to praise.

It is thought that Liber[8] the ancient Italian god of procreation which is connected with liberi (children) would also be related to liber. Libertina the goddess of the dead is supposed to have nothing to do with lubentina or lubentia (an attribute of Venus) which is related to liber.

Jung felt that in a general psychological theory it is impossible to use purely sexual energy: i.e. one specific drive, since psychic energy transformation is not merely a matter of sexual dynamism which is only one particular part of the total psychic field. This does not mean a denial of it, but to put it into perspective along with the drive of hunger, the appetite, for thirst or the urge to victory.

Libido therefore in Jung's psychology signifies the energic standpoint. The Latin meaning of this word has by no means an exclusive sexual connection, but as has been seen, longing, yearning, desiring or urge. Appetite and compulsion are the specific features of all impulses and autonomous possession.

So what has emerged, there is a lust for self aggrandisement, prestige or honour, for victory or material gain, and for sensual appetites of the body. There is lust for another man, woman, child or beast. The latter are described as unnatural together with those lusts to torture, maim or to kill another, as is the lust to turn the violence upon oneself in mutilation and in suicide. There is a hunger, and therefore an appetite for all these things when the 'drive' is turned towards them.

THE VARIOUS TYPES OF LUST

A man in the prime of life came with a physical symptom which had caused him aggravation, it was trifling but persistent, and led to a certain mild anxiety. He became aware of it after he had performed the sexual act with a woman other that his wife of many years.

He was the only son of a powerful, dominating and tyrannical mother. In order to escape her he had married, and in the marriage it seemed, in order to escape again he had fallen into a pattern of lechery, and had become an unconscious Don Juan. He seemed to admire women, he was interested in them, he sought them out, he chased them and he told me he loved women.

He had been in analysis for some years with others before he came to me and so I did not expect him to stay. The idea of escape seemed to dog him constantly. He had indeed left a number of women in his life, by intricate pathways. However he stayed.

The original dream which he brought to me was very strange, very short and completely static. It was as if the dream simply made a statement which was to be accepted as it was. Before he related the dream to me he gazed at me with a curiously compelling intensity, I was reminded of the eyes of a cobra, the gaze was quite unrelated and exceedingly chilling. This was strange as it was at odds with his charm and sparkling wit, which gave the impression of warmth. This was probably why so many women were eas ily seduced by his demeanour and his words. He dreamed that 'he was looking at his own membrum virile, his phallus, and it was in full erection, and was about two feet in length'. He had no associations, and as he gave me the dream he watched me intently just as he did before he related the dream. He assured me that the dream was recent, and since one can make very little of such a dream without amplification or associations, I decided not to analyse it, and told him so. Years later he told me that because I did not analyse it or attempt an analysis of the dream he felt that perhaps it was a kind of secret. In fact I myself had had the thought 'that phallus belongs to the realm of Magna Mater'. He had had the most incredible difficulties with women. The long analysis unearthed his real problem. He had the most immense lust for power, but it was a secret lust, hidden behind an exterior of great charm with erudition accompanying an intense rational-ism where everything had to be explained so that he could overcome it, devour it and digest it. This was the hidden devouring aspect of the divine mother goddess who looked upon the world and its children as the most choice of morsels. The analysand saw the world through these eyes, it was a feast for himself alone.

One could easily perceive the difficulties encountered in the analysis when an exploration of objective psyche began. He had always an imme-diate and child-like wonder for the symbols as they emerged, but suddenly he had to understand them and dissect them, and then they ceased to inter-est him.

His lust was not for women, at base he feared women and had to charm, seduce and overpower them. Then he discarded them and walked away, in that way he had it seemed overcome his fear, until the next woman appeared.

The symptom which beset him after the achievement of sexual satisfac-tion was the manifestation of the reactivation of his unconscious fear. Only in those few moments of orgasm did he secretly believe he had succeeded and was victorious. His was a lust for power and domination which expressed itself in every aspect of his life. The secret contained in the initial dream was in fact nothing to do with sexuality, although he firmly believed it was. Eventually he had to come to the realisation of the innate and intense procreative power of the unconscious psyche for which he was an observer.

Ambition is the desire or the yearning, the voracious lust for power.

LUST FOR POWER

Ambition derived from the Latin, 'ambitio', (the 'going round' of a candi-date for office, canvassing votes) signifies first a desire for a position of power or dignity which leads to eminence. It covers the will to attain, obtain or perform anything regarded by the user of the word as either 'high' or 'difficult'. Almost any desire may become an ambition. (Tradition has it that it is the first sin.)

Many epithets are applied to ambition, the commonest are accursed, blind, base, sublime or even divine. However the majority are pejorative. In general, ambition is regarded with fear and distrust, but sometimes there is a secret ambition in the observer indicating an ambitious shadow who secretly agrees and approves of the ambitious 'other'.

Many years ago I had a patient who always applauded in the most skil-ful way the peccadillos of other patients in the hospital ward. She herself behaved impeccably, but if a subversive element arose or evidence of crim-inality such as impertinence, minor theft or lying against the nurses who cared for the welfare of the invalids, she invariably made judicial comments exhibiting great tolerance towards the wrong-doer. Her shadow was rebellious and criminally inclined, so her secret ambition was a desire to be the same, it was a lust to damage those whom she wished to overpower.

Ambition should always be judged from the inner motive, be it simply vanity, furtherance of a desired end or materialism. In any event the danger to the personality is one-sided and a loss of balance in the face of the compulsion or automatism.

There is such a thing as excessive desire for distinction. This was the problem of the analysand with the severe mother complex. He had to know everything, and he had to know everybody of importance. He searched with diligence and rapacity to secure in his trap-like mind every morsel of information. This made him appear in his own eyes to be unique and therefore distinctive. He lusted for supremacy.

Desire with concomitant arrogant pride are frequently twinned, being bound indissolubly. This was the combination which disturbed the harmony of heaven when Satan demanded God's throne, and as Lucifer he was cast down and fell into the Pit.

My analysand had to learn to deal with the unconscious presence of this primitive lusting shadow which had to rape and violate every object. His shadow was in glaring contradistinction to his suave and urbane persona which he presented to the world.

Many women married to men with such a shadow personality cannot deal with the tyranny of such a lust for domination, and so they retreat into illness, or become shadowy background figures in the lives of successful men with vaulting ambition.

THE LUST FOR APPEASEMENT

Appetite

From desire it is but a step to appetite,[9] a consciousness of want in the bodily organ accompanied by a desire of satisfaction which lasts until the impulse of uneasiness and its pain had been assuaged. Most of the appetites, hunger, thirst and sleep belong to the self preservation of the individual. Sexual desire is referable to the propogation and continuation of the species.

Characteristics of these appetites are that they cause satiety, and injury to the physical being. They belong to the body.

The malaise engendered by the appearance of a want, a need or a desire produces a purposive action to remove it, and the latter brings satisfaction and pleasure, it is appeased.

In the gourmand and the epicure and also with the libertine, the original desire to act comes 'to be the pleasure' which is sought, and not the gratification to assuage the unease.

The pleasure which accompanies sexuality or drinking, and the conscious and deliberate pursuit of the pleasure are no means identical. If desire of the pleasure becomes foremost, and takes precedence over the actual pleasure, the original appetite for food, drink, drugs or sexuality may be supplanted by an abnormal craving. This may be observed in alcoholic or other dependencies, gluttony and lasciviousness, a lust for the given craved object intervenes.

Any artificial craving or abnormal appetite later acquired may intrude. There is no appetite as such but an induced desire (or lust) under the urge of anticipated pleasure. The whole question of addictive cravings, bulimia, anorexia and gluttony are here included.

The anticipated pleasure is the sum of the individual pleasurable experience. It is what the individual has experienced. Compulsive onanism falls into this area.

A woman of a rigid puritanical but hard working family had married young and after her children were born she became a victim of alcoholic dependency. This led her to the dark underworld of sexual deviation. Eventually psychotherapy proved to be invaluable and she emerged with a deep knowledge of her addiction. Consciousness of its nature helped her to live in relative harmony. However at the time of the climacteric her whole life situation changed and she was again thrown into a serious illness. She was once again gripped by disturbing compulsions of a sexual nature.

Dream analysis helped her to comprehend the autonomous animus which for most of her life had dominated her. Then a series of dreams brought to light a new intrusive compulsion, she began to commit a compulsive onanism, and found that her days were punctuated by these sudden compulsive urges to masturbate. It was this phenomenon which was to provide the turning point where she finally understood the meaning of the individuation process. The animus in her case was a lewd and licentious libertine of whom she was mortally afraid.

Her honesty was the key which permitted healing to take place slowly over a long period. This unusual manifestation of lust portrays the meaning behind the urges, the urge to liberation, to alcoholism and then to fornication and self abuse. Behind this pattern there is a clear picture of the search for the spirit, the god within. He in turn led her to the perception of other aspects on unconscious psyche. Aspects which she had found in the outer world to plague the long years of her life, to her cost and to her sorrow. The goal which she sought was the treasure within.

'An affection which is a passion ceases to be a passion as soon as we form a clear and distinct idea of it.'[10]

To summarise appetite simply craves the object, and its means of assuagement or appeasement. Desire of pleasure is a process dependent on experience of pleasure and a craving for that pleasure and where acquired appetites appear the repetitious increase of that pleasure.

In the case of alcoholism and other drug dependencies or libertinism the subject can no longer satisfy his craving by gratification, and the unresolved yearning becomes the master to return again and again. The woman whose plight is described above had an autonomous tyrannical animus whom she was forced to obey, she wished to rebel but she had to obey. That is the autonomous factor psychologically.

The master is an unconscious content embodying the compulsion to act in a certain and singular way. The unknown and unconscious content which is producing the 'urge' perceived in the outer world mirrors the deep unconscious need of the soul itself. The unconscious can only speak to us in symbols, and this is the language which must be learned in order to comprehend this vast and unknown inner world.

It is as well to remember that appetite unduly set upon pleasure always leaves behind a sense of dulled pain. 'But what shall I say of the pleasures of the body? This – that the lust thereof is indeed full of uneasiness (anxietas) but the sating of repentance.'[11]

TAOISM AND LUST

The Chinese Book of Changes – The I Ching is the primary source of all our knowledge of Taoism. It is the Tao-Teh King. It consists of two parts, one concerning Tao and the other concerning Teh.

With regard to desire, wish, yearn, want or to strive this is what evolves from thoughts on the subject. 'The highest good is like water, water is advantageous for all things and it does not strive. It takes the place that all men hate,' i.e: the lowly place.

'He who overcomes men has force, he who overcomes himself is strong.'
'He who knows he has enough is rich.'
'I have three precious things which I count and hold precious. The first is gentleness, the second moderation and the third is not daring to take the first place under heaven.' These virtues propogate an inward state of emptiness that is freedom from desires.

Corresponding to this inner freedom from desires is the outer life of nonaction (Wei-wu-wei), that means the absence of self-determination for particular ends.

CHRISTIANITY LUST AND SEXUALITY

From the 2nd century of our era the stern Tertullian made frequent denunciations against intemperates (voluptates).

The original significance of the Latin word for lust, luxuria, was that it implied an overflow or excess of fertility in crops or fields thence it had the meaning of wantonness and luxury generally.

There was also, but much later in the Middle Ages a connotation of 'uncleanness' concerning lust. From the onset of Christianity a general antagonism set in against all adornment of the body and clothing which was forbidden. Public shows were banned as was lascivious singing, and promiscuous dancing. Likewise sumptuous food and drunkenness were severely restricted and restrained.

Luxuria in the Middle Ages was used to signify 'lust' as an indulgence of the passions not included under adultery fornication and incest. The lascivious desire which stopped short of the overt act of sexual congress was not generally brought under canoniacal censure. The rule of discipline here being that the church judges actions only, and of those actions alone that create scandal! Secret thoughts, lewd feelings, hidden desires were left to spiritual remedies. At the Council of Neocaesarea 314 A.D. it was merely stated that 'any man who desires to sleep with a woman and does not accomplish it has fallen from grace'. There is no mention of penance or a very slight one. If a man meditated uncleanness but checked himself the punishment was light. If a man used wanton words he was punished for seven days, whereas kissing a woman was punished with twenty days. Rape however was treated severely both by civil and also by ecclesiastical law. One of the laws of Constantine imposed the punishment of condemnation to the flames of those who committed rape upon a virgin, and also those who carried off a virgin with her consent, but against her parents' will.

Capital punishment was introduced both for rape and murder, and excommunication of the greater number of offenders of lesser crimes. Likewise unnatural lusts were treated with heavy penalties. Floggings and confinement to monasteries for life were directed against boys who committed unnatural or sexual sins.

The present day fashionable lust to pleasure oneself by seeking one's desire in whatever realm of activity at the expense of others must be considered in the same light as the early Christian fathers viewed it, for it lies truly at the base of evil.

However a fear of leaving the safety of the collective viewpoint to think one's own thoughts, act in an individual way, allow one's feelings to have a place beside one's rational thoughts and stand by one's feelings demands a certain courage.

Eros the principle of relationships appears to be disappearing from society and with it loving kindness. A contagion of saccharine sweetness of sentimentality remains engendered by the underlying coldness of the collective shadow, and which permits wrong doing.

Perhaps a lesson may be learned from the first Christian fathers who had to deal with similar matters, but not by turning the other cheek. If we were to view crime in the way that a physician observes an epidemic or a contagion the first essential is to name the offending microbe or virus. By using the same method it is vital that evil be named, but in order to do so one must learn its nature. The measuring rod is our feeling – only through the feeling function can one evaluate what is acceptable and what is not.

The great symbol for the spirit of divine truth is the beautiful bird the kingfisher. If one observes it, it always directs its gaze to the fish, and then without ever changing its directed gaze it dives with every tiny feather sealed to its body. It is a poem of dynamic energy, it is an arrow to the heart of the fish. That is how our true feeling must be permitted to recognise and view evil, and not be distracted by intellectual opinions, and rational asides.

Lust has a central place in evil, it is the place where the egotistical drive aims to dethrone or possess the Self.

LUST IN THE MIDDLE AGES

In the 25th Canto of the Purgatoria of The Divine Commedy, Dante describes the last of the seven terraces where lust is purged.

There was a wall of fire, and a hot blast of air that shot up from the inner bank of the cliff. Only a narrow path remained where Dante and his companions were forced to walk in a single file.

'I was terrified there was the fire, and there I could fall,' he exclaims.

There is always a very great danger when one is confronted with passion aptly symbolised by the fire and flames where one could so easily fall down.

From the heart of the heat was heard the hymn Summae Deus Clementiae 'God of Supreme Clemency.' This was the hymn of the lustfull which asked God to banish lust and every sinful instinct from their hearts, and to cleanse them in the healing fire. The hymn was traditionally sung in the liturgy at Matins On Saturday. (The modern version now begins Summae Parens Clementiae.) One verse is worth quoting because of its appropriate nature:

> 'Burn with meet fires our veins
> and our sick heart, that having
> put off evil lusts we may keep
> watch with loins girded.'

It is clear that in this poem sexual lust is described, the veins signify the kidneys with strong association to the sexual organs, and the 'heart' is literally 'the liver' the seat of the passions.[12]

Then the sinners cry out, 'Virum non cognosco.' This is the first exemplum of the virtue of chastity – 'I know no man,' taken from the life of the Virgin Mary. The incident occurred when Mary was told by the archangel Gabriel that she would conceive a son. She answered 'How shall this be – I know no man.'[13]

There follows the second exemplum of the virtue of chastity taken from classical myth. In order to preserve her virginity as the virgin-huntress goddess Diana took refuge in the woods. One of her attendants Helice a nymph fell prey to the poison lust of Venus the goddess of love, and was seduced by Jupiter to whom she bore a son, Arcas. Diana dismissed her, and Jupiter's wife (Hera wife of Zeus in Greek myth) turned her into a she-bear. Jupiter took pity and placed her in the sky as the constellation Ursa Major.

These examples signify the antidote as it were for sexual lust, the virtue of chastity. An elderly woman of a Middle European country told me when I was a medical student of her youth. She was very old when I met her as a patient. She was from a good family and well educated, but in her early youth had fallen into promiscuity. She developed syphilis and in those days there was not a certain cure. She endured decades of painful protracted and constant therapy without any knowledge of a possible cure. Every time she developed a symptom she thought the disease had recurred. She never forgave the man who was responsible, but she became chaste so that the disease would not be propogated by her. Eventually she recovered but she said she had 'burned in the fires of hell', only reaching a certain peace in extreme old age. It is a long time since she told me her story, but there was a strange unrelatedness about her. Even as an old woman a singular lack of Eros. This was perhaps why in the first place she had fallen into promiscuity.

On this terrace in Dante's poem are two groups of sinners approaching each other from opposite directions. One group cites the exemplum of the lust of Sodom and Gomorrah, and the other the shameful lust of Pasiphaë. Since no one in either group has acted as a human being should they cry out their shame, (as the animal lust of) 'Pasiphaë'! Each group makes haste to kiss each other briefly and are gone 'as do the ants in their black ranks. They rush to each other, nose each other as if to enquire which way to go, or how their luck had been'.

This is apt, hurried sexual liaisons and brief encounters are as unrelated as the insect world described in Dante's poem. The cities of Sodom and Gomorrah renowned for homoerotic, hetero-sexual and animal lust constitutes one group, whereas Pasiphaë who signifies quintessential animal lust, represents the other group.

Pasiphaë, the daughter of the sun, married Minos Son of Europa and King of Crete. She disgraced herself by her unnatural passion for a bull, who according to some authors she was enabled to gratify with the aid of the artist Daedalus, who made an effigy of a cow in wood and cowhide. This celebrated bull, the instigator of her passion had been given to Minos by Poseidon, to be offered on his sacrificial altar. Minos because of the animal's beauty refused to do the god's bidding, and retained the bull. Poseidon revenged himself by inspiring an unnatural desire for the creature in the person of Pasiphaë, the wife of the monarch.

It is as well to remember that the King disobeyed the god's will by placing the bull in his stables instead of sacrificing it on the god's altar. He lusted for the beauty of the bull, and ownership of its body for his cows.

Taurus or the Bull was the godhead before the Ram, 4000 – 6000 years ago. One senses this on the island of Crete. The presence of the Bull god is ubiquitous there, and particularly in the labyrinthine palace at Knossos. Incidentally in the museum at Heraclion there is a superb sculpted head of a bull, and if one looks closely one sees in the pupil of its right eye the miniscule figure of a woman. It is here in the labyrinth that the monstrous Minotaur was found, the fruit of the union of Pasiphaë and the bull.

The central figure in the cult of Mithras was the bull which played a rôle similar to that of the lamb in Christianity which superceded the Mithraic religion. In Mithraism the bull was the creative power, the great world bull, and was the bull god himself. He represented the world at the beginning of all things. If one can grasp the immense awe in which the mighty god as the bull was held, the full horror of the lust of Pasiphaë becomes apparent, as the reality of the nature of her crime is perceived. The bull's death in the sacrifice in the Mithraic cult represented the demise of a powerful and divine being, and was the immediate cause of rebirth of the initiant. The meaning of the bull sacrifice was the sacrifice of man's bull-like passions, or in human terms his lack of discipline. The blood of the bull represented his life energy, power, fertility and his libido, sacrificed in order to fertilise the earth. It was a kind of blessing for the earth which had given him life in the first instance. As the godhead, the bull represented the image of the divine archetype which is eternal and outside time.

In the Minos-Pasiphaë myth, Poseidon had chosen his bull for the sacrifice, Minos saw it and lusted after it. More correctly one might be permitted to say that his anima, (represented by his wife Pasiphaë) did. Thus the King appropriated by way of the anima's desire the divinity in the form of the divine animal. The King's lust for the animal contained his secret will to be as one with the god, and indicated a disobedience against his subservience to deity. He was punished in the manner of his lust. His wife gratified the bull and was herself gratified, but the fruit of the union – the Minotaur was monstrous, and was confined below in the labyrinth, the unconscious or the underworld. It was neither man nor beast, human or divine.

Some years ago, a physician told me of a man who developed an intractable dermatosis of sever degree. When questioned about the time of onset he could not remember. Eventually, following a persistent line of enquiry the physician discovered that the man had undertaken a fishing trip to a lonely part of the wilderness in his country. Within a few days of his return after the trip the skin disease began. He then told the doctor that he had engaged in an act of sexual congress with a wild duck. The physician declared himself at a loss as how to deal with the man's psychological state. I drew his attention to the fact that the wild duck is a symbol of conjugal fidelity. It was agreed that the depravity of the act signalled a grossly primitive and brutal shadow with an extreme degree of unconsciousness of ego. The conclusion was reached that the hellish fiery nature of the skin disease as his fate was the befitting punishment for the crime. (For indeed it was an act of depravity, and also a grave crime that a human being seek to gratify his lust with a wild defenceless creature.)

The wild duck is also regarded as a messenger from the outer world. In the case of the man, it brought the message hitherto apparently unknown, of his primitive nature which had possessed him.

In the second exemplum of chastity the myth concerns the poison lust of Venus-Aphrodite.

APHRODITE

As the goddess of sensuous and lascivious love she was also revered for her extraordinary beauty. Her cult centred on the Aegean islands and extended from Egypt to the Black Sea. In the great cities of Hellenic life her worship had an important place, she was the goddess of the sea, and patroness of sailors.

Originally she was an oriental nature divinity retaining many of the oriental traits of the great cults of Magna Mater. Bull worship is an earthly cult since astrologically the bull is an earthly sign. Taurus in astrology is the 'domicilium Veneris', the house where Venus-Aphrodite dwells. The bull is very much connected with the cult of the Great Mother circa 2000 – 4000 BC. Aphrodite the Greek name for Venus arises from Aphros, meaning 'foam-born'.

Golden Aphrodite the goddess of love was also the great goddess of fertility in the Orient, and is mentioned in the Old Testament as Queen of Heaven. 'Cypris', a proper name of the goddess points to the island of Cyprus.

Aphrodite often regarded as the 'Greek Goddess of Love' was simply much more than that. Her names are legion. She was at once indistinguishable from the Fates (Moirai).

Perhaps one is on a train or plane, or at a dinner table, when suddenly one meets the love or a potent love of one's life. It may lead to happiness, despair or even tragedy! That is fate! Often that spark in an eye, that expression which the French so aptly call 'le regard' is the impulse of love, or lust, it is vigour, the dynamic arrow of a glance between two people.

The Hindu sages have several ways of classifying the thoughts which they regard as worth learning and handing down. The foremost system is that of the *four aims*. They are Ratma, material possessions, Kama which is the pleasure in love, Dharma, one's religious and moral duties and Moksa which means spiritual release.

Kama is the Hindu god of love, and is a counterpart of the Greek Eros. He carries a flower bow and five flower arrows by which he sends quivering desire to the heart. Kama symbolises desire incarnate, and as such he is therefore the Lord and Master of the earth as well as the lower celestial spheres.

The principal surviving classic of India's Kama teaching is the Kamasutra, its ambiguous reputation for sensuality is misleading, for the subject of love is presented in it on a technical level, like a textbook for lovers and courtesans.

The dominant attitude of the Hindu towards sexuality is austere chaste and extremely restrained in its long tradition. Kama teaching came to correct and ward off frustrations inherent in married life that were the result of marriages of convenience. It came as a balance for the society of frozen emotions, it was not libertine.

In the texts of the Kama Sutra is an exquisitely developed psychology of the heart comparable to the typology and tapestry of human emotions, which came to a full flowering in the portrayal of tragedy in the French theatre of the 17th and 18th centuries.

'Tout le monde sait que l'esprit due christianisme n'agit que pour éteindre les passions, et que l'esprit due théâtre ne travaille qu'à les allumer.'[14]

The Fates are the Moirae. Aphrodite's old name was Moirai and she was said to be 'older than Time'. She governed the world by the 'ius – naturale', the natural law of the maternal clan.[15]

There was also an extremely old and indeed archaic connection with Ares as the demonic spirit of curse and blood by whom she bore Deimos (terror) and Phobos (fear) as well as Harmonia (harmony). In this mythologem one is reminded forcibly of the association of lust with the terror, the fear and the blood in blood fueds, crimes of passion, genocide and war. The children of the union of Aphrodite and Ares should not be forgotten as the progeny of love, its separations and its quarrels together with the acrimony engendered in these states. Such bitterness leads more frequently than one may realise to physical killing by way of murder or annihilation of the soul.

These aspects depict clearly the age old roots of Aphrodite's cult which extend backwards in time, and deeply into the world of Mater Magna. The Great Mother goddesses with their all-embracing 'charitas', maternalism their generosity to all men, and also the inner essential and unutterable coldness of Nature herself.[16] This last is not easy for human consciousness to encapsulate, but it is also part of the Great Mother goddess. It can be seen everywhere in Nature's world, the paw of a domestic cat as with a single blow instantly kills a bird, or a child who tears off the wings of insects, a human adult who tortures or kills an animal, or kills a child in lust.

From all these threads over countless millenia a picture has emerged. It was with an apparent indeed extraordinary precision that an image of the lustful aspect of sensual love became etched upon human awareness. This revelation portrayed its pristine and exquisite beauty, but only hinted at the other darkness which is ever 'in potentia'. Myth has it that the form took shape as the exquisiteness of the divine goddess born from her father's phallus out of the sea, born from the foam as it touched the earth. So she was 'foam-born'.

In itself it is a most extraordinary development, and we owe the refinement of its representation to the genius of the Greek world. The myth as a symbolic representation tells us quite simply that out of the fertilising chaos of the creative womb of the maternal unconscious a separate and distinct form of feminine nature arose. It revealed the beauty of sensual love, but also incorporated the innate potentiality of the darker but recognised aspects of lust. However, parturition from unconsciousness or the revelation was only possible by way of the divine creative principal of the masculine genius. It was a discernment. Aphrodite brings for us an encompassing consciousness of the true reality of sensual sexual love, and the inherent nature of its lustfulness.

Aphrodite is thoroughly Greek. She did become the ancestral mother of the Romans by giving birth to their founding father Aeneas. Also under the name of Venus she became the mother of the Venetii whose capital became that dream-like Queen of the Sea – Venice. Her bird is the dove, of the oriental Astarte, and because like the sparrow with similar sexual proclivity it was therefore declared 'unholy' in Christian circles.

A woman in analysis heard a noise outside in her garden. She went out to investigate and found a dead dove on the doorstep to the garden. She became extremely distressed.

We discussed the matter in depth but she could find no connection in her outer life. She loved her husband, but knew he had no Eros (the principle of psychic relatedness). He was a good man, practical and hard working. He had a brutal shadow which sometimes struck out without warning. He was a rational man, and his superior function was sensation. Although very successful in business life he had little imagination in the realm of feeling.

Shortly after this distressing episode she decided to go to Venice because she loved Italy, and the Italian people. She was a woman from a Northern country, and found the warm lands of the South very congenial to her personality. In Venice one evening, whilst walking back to her hotel where she was staying alone, she encountered a young man. He was masked, and dressed in medieval clothes. In the sudden confrontation he stepped aside, bowed deeply, and greeted her in Italian as 'a beautiful lady'. He then permitted her to pass, and he disappeared. She told me that she stood quite still and wondered who he was, she wondered if she had seen a ghost.

Afterwards, for some reason for which she could not account, she felt very well. The young man had been courteous, and sufficiently sure of himself in his masculinity to pay her as a much older woman a charming compliment. Now this woman was intelligent, a practical housewife, and also a business woman. She was furthermore an excellent mother for her children, and probably a good wife. But she received very little feeling from her husband and it later transpired in the analysis that she had never received any from her mother. On her return from Venice she had a dream in which she perceived clearly the coldness of her mother who in the past had made atrocious and incessant demands. All her life as a child, a young girl, and a young woman she had endeavoured without success to please her mother. A mother who was never content, and who always insisted that her daughter should be constantly available for her needs. Later in the marriage she discovered an exact situation. Although she tried it seemed that she could never receive her husband's unqualified approbation.

She added when discussing this aspect of her life that she 'ached' to please her mother and then her husband. 'Lust' could be inserted instead of 'ache'.

This woman had very little feeling for herself. Somewhere there was a cold detached animosity completely autonomous which had suddenly appeared in her life, and informed or cajoled her to give, to please, or desire the best for others, and to shine as a great giver. She seemed to be happy only when the other smiled or graciously accepted her gifts. Of course in reality this lust to please intimated that she was trying to please a cold unbending distant animus, which it transpired, had ruled the lives of women in her ancestral family for centuries by means of a cold critical detachment.

Suddenly that night in Venice, where she had gone solely to please herself, she did as it were encounter and bravely confront her autonomous animus. In the city of Aphrodite-Venus she had been permitted to meet a ghostly masculine figure masked and centuries old. Whether it was a ghost or a real man matters not. She stood face to face, and the fear and the terror gave way to harmony as the unknown masculine psychic element transformed into a courteous welcoming being. Thus she experienced herself as a beautiful woman, and became aware of her feminine sexuality and at the time a sensual approval of herself.

The dove which had sacrificed itself in her garden was the transforming symbol in her life. From the day of her return she ceased to try to please her mother. She sacrificed the lustful desire to put others before herself, and by so doing was able to realise that if one does not love oneself one finds that others do likewise.

THE FESTIVALS OF APHRODITE

Corinth was undoubtedly the most oriental of all Greek cities. In that city was the holy hill of Acro-Corinthos, devoted to the goddess.

The least un-Hellenic aspect of the Aphrodite cult was the practice of religious prostitution. The historian Pindar has described vividly the hospitality of young women in Corinth whom he portrays as the 'ministrators of Persuasion in rich Corinth'.[17] He described how their thoughts often flew towards Ourania Aphrodite.

Women who were bought slaves were consecrated to the service of the goddess. Corinth was the only city in Greece where these hetarae took part in the state ritual of the Aphrodisiae, the festivals dedicated to the goddess. Usually a whole day was reserved for them, and a separate day for the respectable women, virgins and married women. As the cult depicted, Aphrodite became the patroness of married life, but this aspect was not present in the eastern form of the cult – the Ourania.

Because of its situation and its energetic enterprise Corinth became a dangerous and notorious city in those days. Lascivity and licentiousness were rampant during these festivals. Plato made a distinction, now well known between Ourania Aphrodite who personifies the intellectual life of the soul, and Aphrodite Pandemos who personifies the sensual love of the body. It is precisely this title Ourania 'Heavenly' which is the clearest sign of her Eastern origin. However the Platonic distinction was not recognised in the State religion, and the moral and spiritual meaning of the title is of late growth. Again, the 'Pandemos' aspect was not an independent Hellenic development, but a survival and development of the oriental conception.

The great Aphrodisia at Paphos was the most celebrated of all these festivals, and had no parallel in Greece. Human victims were slain for purposes of divination on one altar, and a parallel altar was used for perfumed incense. Gardens were associated with Aphrodite, and bearing in mind her association with adonis it should be recollected that frankincense and myrrh together with thyme were used almost exclusively in the sacrifices, and in the pleasures of love. The plant Little-Myrtle an aromatic shrub found all over Attica was used to weave crowns worn by marrying couples. The name of this plant which is consecrated to Aphrodite is used also to refer to either the clitoris or the pudenda of the woman. This perfume Little-Myrtle signifies the ultimate expression of the seductive attraction emanating from a woman totally committed to Aphrodite.[18]

In the Aphrodisia a ritual dance and mimicry were part of the mysteries. The initiates usually received in exchange for money for the Temple's treasury an image of a phallus and also a lump of salt. The former depicted the pleasure and the fertility of the gifts of the goddess, whilst the salt added savour to life, and also symbolised its bitterness. There is always bitterness in the tears both shed and unshed in the lechery innate in homo and hetero-sexual love, at one time or another.

At Argos, the great festivals of the Hubristika were unique in that swine were sacrificed to Aphrodite. The reference here is to Adonis who was castrated and killed by a boar. Adonis is the Greek term for 'My lord' but in the Phoenician language the word for the same term is 'Adoni', and Adonis was the title for the god Tammuz, but in Hebrew it was the name of God. It signifies always the masculine partner of the goddess.

SPICES AND PERFUMES
ASSOCIATED WITH LUST

Trees and shrubs symbolise vegetal life. Aromatic shrubs give us spices used to enhance the flavours of our food today. Formerly they were used to disguise the stenches of life, and were usually burned to promote a scented smoke obliterating the smells and odours of decay and putrefaction. Perfumes obtained from flowers were used in conjunction with spices in religious rituals, embalming and anointing of bodies. Naturally these substances were regarded as being endowed with mysterious powers.

Flowers symbolise feelings. Jung once described them as 'God's thoughts.' Rare mountain or alpine flowers are symbols of rarified, delicate or fragile feelings, but au contraire, the red rose often symbolises the essence of sexuality – lustful desire. Perfume then is the spirit of the feeling itself.

Now let us for a while explore the meaning of the perfumes which are associated with lust.

When the gods attempted to rescue Hera from the invisible fetters of an enchanted throne, only Dionysos the god of women and wanton abandon succeeded by persuading Hephaistos the Smith to drink wine, and to rub his limbs with myrrh. By so doing the perfume of the myrrh cast a smell over him, and he was lured unresistingly to unfetter Hera on Olympus. Dissolute pleasures are inseparable from clouds of frankincense, and heady perfumes. It is said that Hēdoné, 'Sensual Pleasure' is the name under which Aphrodite smothered in perfumes appeared at the judgment of Paris.[19] She was described as 'all proud of the power of desire'. However the perfumed Aphrodite is not only the patroness of sensuality (makhlosuñe) but also of courtesans when 'with their hair and breasts covered with perfume they would arouse the desire even of an old man'.[20] She is seen as the protectress of marriage who stands with Hera and Demeter and who on a religious level represents sexual desire in the marriage, and the pleasures of love (aphrodisiae) without which man and woman's union in marriage could not be fulfilled.

Myrrh played an immense rôle in the marriage ceremony along with other perfumes. In the play the Lysistrata of Aristophanes there is an interesting episode in which all the women of Greece in an endeavour to bring the war to an end pledged themselves to refuse to make love with their husbands. They dressed in gauzes, diaphanous robes, applied paint and perfume to excite the lust of their husbands and then refused them. A girl called Myrrhina[21] which means 'Little Myrtle' permitted herself to be coaxed into an alcove by her husband. She pretended to yield then made a thousand excuses to delay him. She recalled that they had not anointed themselves with balm. They did so, and her husband was consumed with desire, at that moment Myrrhina slipped away. The name carries with it as we have seen, erotic overtones.

A similar idea is innate in the myth of the King of Assyria's daughter Smyrna, or Myrrha, who did not honour the goddess Aphrodite, and was punished by the goddess who in her great anger caused Myrrha to conceive a passion for her father. With the complicity of her nurse she shared her father's bed without his knowledge for twelve nights.

When the King realised that incest had occurred he drew his sword to kill her. She fled but was overtaken, in her fear she prayed to the gods to become invisible. In their compassion they turned her into a tree called Smyrna or Myrrha.

Ten months later the tree burst, and Adonis, as he was called was born. Because he was so beautiful Aphrodite hid him in a chest unknown to the gods. He was the fruit of the union which had occurred because of Aphrodite's curse.

She entrusted his care to the goddess of the underworld, but Persephone likewise became enchanted and refused to give him up. Adonis was thus a god of enchantment. The dilemma caused by the jealousy of the goddesses was solved only by Zeus. He decreed that Adonis should stay alone for a part of the year, with Persephone for another part, but the remainder was allocated to Aphrodite. Needless to say Adonis disobeyed, (who could resist Aphrodite's charms) and allocated his own portion, in addition to Aphrodite. His punishment was swift, he was killed, gored to death by a wild boar.

Adonis as the masculine component of sensual seduction is also connected with Hēdoné, 'sensual pleasure', 'perfume' and 'love'. He represents the perfume of the male lover. It is stated quite specifically that Aphrodite's passion for Myrrha's son was provoked by the sap of the Myrrh tree, a juice whose perfume makes the drinker burn with passion. Adonis who is both the son of Myrrha and the product of the Myrrh tree is literally and figuratively 'the lover and the perfume', at once.[22]

This myth is one of seduction and lust of the daughter for her own father, and late of her son and the two goddesses. Adonis is trapped by Aphrodite into disobeying the Father God Zeus. As soon as he exceeds his lustful appetite for her he dies. Indeed in excess, lust withers away since eventually it is sated. This myth is also one of spring-time and its inevitable death. The boar as the animal of Demeter mother of Persephone, must as Mater Magna punish all excess.

Sometimes when one observes the passivity of the faces of very old people, one may be permitted to wonder what hellish passions seized them in their youth, passions which have like the spring-time given way to the sterility of autumn, and eventual death.

THE FLOWER OF LUST

There is a wild flower in the Northern Hemisphere which is called Arum Macculata or 'Lords and Ladies' in the English language. It is undoubtedly the flower of sexual desire. Sometimes it is called Devil's Ladies and Gentlemen, or Devil's men and women, Jack in the pulpit, Cuckoo pint or pintle. This name is to do with the word penis. The association between cuckoo and the cuckoo pintle points to lust, or ardour and zeal in sexual seduction.

In the Middle Ages the flower was always connected with the act of making love which accounts for its multitude of unusual and rather strange names.

The flowers are contained in a broad sheathing hood called the spathe. Inside there is a club-like structure, the spadix. Interestingly enough the flower gives off a smell of decay which together with a slight heat (always present) attracts flies in order to pollinate itself. The berries in the late summer are brilliant red, and very poisonous, usually described as adderberries or serpents' food. Adder is derived from 'Attor' and simply means in the Anglo-Saxon tongue 'poison'.

So full circle has turned to the poison lust of Aphrodite. It may not be out of order to remind oneself of the vast and indeed monumental materialism behind the commercial sales of perfume in the cosmetic world today. It mirrors the ubiquitous nature of lust itself, and also the seductive power of seduction.

In some of the Aphrodisiae, Aphrodite was worshipped as a divinity of death. For example in the city of Aegina. It is opportune to remember that the Arum Macculata has also the odour of decay.

A still beautiful woman of sixty years or more came in distress because she had fallen in love with a man much younger than herself.

In the course of analysis she revealed that as a young woman she had been a great beauty and much sought after by all manner of men. this I could well believe. She told me she could attract and bewitch any man, but she could never keep him. For some reason the man always abandoned her in the end. Indeed in this manner she had lost both her husbands. Her problem was primarily a father complex, but I suspected a deeper underlying deeply unconscious problem.

As a young woman she had deceived her husband, and had committed acts of the utmost depravity with a number of unknown men.

She was stricken by a devastating illness and remained confined to her bed for almost a year. She recovered slowly but had lost a great part of her beauty as she had also undergone a certain bodily disfigurement.

The exquisitely lithe and radiantly beautiful girl had disappeared. It was as if she had died, and been replaced by a sensually attractive, but deformed woman, who found even walking difficult.

161

In those times of licentious lewdity she had lost her footing as a woman. The foot confirms our direct relationship with the reality of the earth. It is also phallic, and is regarded in some areas as a symbol of the soul. In Greek legends, lameness usually symbolises some defect of the spirit, some essential blemish. Because of the footprint, the foot (and also the shoe) often has the association of 'going away'. A woman dreamed that her lover sent her a shoe, one of his old shoes. A few days later, 'he went away' – he died.

To return to the lamed woman. She was possessed by her own beauty and powers of seduction. As an 'anima' type she was easily able to seduce and win over any man. She was 'gripped' as it were by the wanton goddess, and treated herself as a whore and found therefore that others treated and used her for their pleasure.

She was not a whore, but she was caught eternally in lust for men. In her innermost being she was simply the phallus of a father rendered impotent by a dominant wife. She was without any consciousness of her human feminine self. Her dreams and her illness brought her to the reality of her problem which was to understand the autonomous possession. She came to see that the male she sought was an inner masculine being, the animus in all his divine majesty, and whose dark side exists in the seamiest underworld.

Aphrodite has a dark side and is a jealous goddess.

In the fairy tale of Amor and Psyche, Aphrodite does not permit a mortal woman to be so beautiful or seductive as she. To parody her divine sensuality, as did my erstwhile beautiful but presently lamed patient, is to mock the goddess, and for that she was punished severely. But she did not lose her life. Aphrodite imparts her beauty to both the living and the dead. She protected Hector's body from the dogs after Achilles had disfigured it.

In the long illness in which the patient was isolated she had suffered deeply for her behaviour, and this consciousness of the deed probably saved her from total destruction.

Aphrodite is not the loving one, there is no love in lust or seduction. She is the one who enraptures, she is the irresistible attraction which draws into the ravishment of union. What is often mistaken for love is a willingness to surrender, a yearning which in itself is irresistible. This is 'charis' a word which denotes gratitude, but which in a woman means specifically granting that which a man desires. At Delphi, Harmony in myth was the goddess's daughter where she was called Harma, which points to loving union. Yet in the heart of harmony separation has already begun.

This chapter is about lust, it is not about love, but mention must be made of Eros the son and companion of the goddess of irresistible attraction.

Like Hermes, Eros was originally a Boëotian god and was worshipped in the same manner as a stone or wooden phallus. In fact the two gods in earliest times were almost identical. In antique art he is often represented as a winged being who sometimes shows his genitals and is frequently hermaphroditic. At times he appears as a winged youth smelling flowers with a zither in the right hand, or a winged phallus with a head on it, a small boy with a divine snake, or a grown-up winged youth with a bow and arrow.[23] He is sometimes portrayed as a protecting spirit of the dead, or holding a torch downwards, the symbol of death. He is also represented as a butterfly, and shown sadistically burning it with his torch which repeats the idea that Eros the god of love is a great torturer of the human soul, yet at the same time its purifier.[24] Eros forces one to become conscious.

'Love with its passion and pain becomes the urge towards individuation, which is why there is no real process of individuation without the experience of love, for love both tortures and purifies the soul.'[25] Eros as the child of Aphrodite is born or may be born, every birth is in fact a miracle of life, out of Harma, loving union. It is the inherent possibility never a probability.

Many years ago a mature woman told me of an event which occurred in her extreme youth. In those long ago days of the Victorian era when she was about seventeen years old she became engaged to be married. Sexual impropriety was not to be tolerated during the betrothal. The fiancée was older, a decent and honourable man, but he had a severe mother complex which seemingly rendered him inert when dealing with the opposite sex. Such was the awkwardness of the relationship that the girl felt she could not go through with the marriage.

During the period of betrothal she accepted an invitation to stay with friends abroad. One evening at a dinner party she encountered an interesting man, who appeared to be quite free from inhibitions. In the course of several days they basked in the bliss of Harmony. She returned home and married her fiancée who became, as she had already perceived unconsciously, an excellent husband and father for their children. She never revealed her secret, and told me of it when she was about a hundred years old. She explained that she could only settle down and marry her husband because she had lived through and experienced lust or as she described it 'sinful pleasure' with another.

In her marriage she came eventually to experience Eros with her husband – he who is the great binder and loosener, because she has already obeyed the god Eros with another.

Love which is vast, all encompassing and impossible to define has everything to do with kindness, if there is none there is no love. The central essence is an unwillingness to cause hurt or pain. In lust there is no kindness unless a psychic relationship intervenes.

Jung used to say that 'sexuality has two aspects, reproduction which is carnal sexuality, and the other aspect which could be used to worship the god Eros, that is relationship'. It was the latter aspect that the Christian church condemned as sinful.[26]

It was during Jung's visit to India that he beheld the mausoleum built in 1632 AD by the Emperor Shah Jahan for his wife Mumtaz. The sight of the

Taj Mahal which he believed to be the most perfect temple of love ever erected led him to the understanding that the religion of Islam was founded on the Eros principle, the feminine principle of relationship whereas Christianity, and all the other great religions are founded on the principle of Logos, that is the masculine principle of discrimination.

'Logos and Eros' wrote Jung[27] 'are intellectually formulated intuitive equivalents of the archetypal images Sol and Luna. In my view the two luminaries are so descriptive and so superlatively graphic in their implications that I would prefer them to the more pedestrian terms of Logos and Eros, although the latter do pin down certain psychological peculiarities more aptly than the rather indefinite 'Sol and Luna.' The use of these images requires at any rate an alert and lively fantasy, and this is not an attribute of those who are inclined by temperament to purely intellectual concepts. These offer us something finished and complete, whereas an archetypal image has nothing but its naked fullness, which seems inapprehensible by the intellect. Concepts are coined and negotiable values; images are life'.

Hannah[28] writes, Jung pointed out that if we had lived in the time of Sophocles we would have realised 'the great god Eros, god of relatedness', and 'Logos the god of Form.' Jung[29] was to explain 'that the principle of Logos does not produce logical or intellectual thinking for Logos is an experience, a revelation'.

Hannah[30] makes the point with regard to the question of lust, 'Today modern mankind indulges itself far too much in carnal sexuality. They barely know that real relationships between the sexes exists, or that it has anything to do with sexuality. There is no recognition anymore of the 'great god Eros', god of relatedness.'

THE PROBLEM OF LUST IN THE MODERN WORLD

Since real Eros has disappeared, not only has man lost contact with his fellow human beings but also with his earthly roots, he no longer understands the living being of the planet and that he is merely of one single species amongst many, albeit he perceives himself as superior.

The earth itself, the sea, plant, aerial, terrestrial and submarine life have all been bespoiled by man's unconsciousness brought about by his hubris and lack of relatedness to living things. Modern man sees only in his narrowness of vision his needs and lusts. This divorces him from Nature as Magna Mater, and his own nature that is his instinctual feeling life.

Without thought or sense of mortality he can pollute, destroy, maim and kill, because he is no longer in touch with his own inner living world, he has lost his soul, and does not believe in a god. Ego-consciousness believes itself to be the master of its own house.

If modern man cannot consciously limit his procreative reproductory habits mankind will be lost. Over-population is probably the greatest problem facing mankind today. Already there is dissolution of the family as a unit, an ever increasing rate of divorce, disappearance of the sacrament of marriage, abundance of single parent families which means quite simply failed relationships or no relationship at all. Often a child is born to a woman who primarily lusted to leave home, have an apartment or a house of her own with freedom from responsibility of family or even occupation. Such a child, with an absent indeed unknown father, is born into a world without Eros.

The children of all these failed unions have no guide for psychic relationship since one parent is absent from the home. From this morass of failure there is a vivid perception of the emergence of a cold and brutal society, without compassion, humility or humanity or that which we believe to be human.

In the homosexual world which has burgeoned of recent decades, one cannot escape the conclusion that it is part of Nature's wise plan of compensation to restrict the fearsome spectre of over population.

In the nineteen sixties, when the contraceptive pill was engineered for women, a ban was lifted against the prevailing customs which had hitherto existed. Women had for the first time an undreamed-of sexual freedom which brought lascivity and licentiousness of unparalleled proportions. Sexual gratification was easy, short lived affairs abounded, relationships fell apart, marriages broke up and Eros departed.

Since those years we have as a species, unlike any other on the planet, feasted in wantonness which brings its trail of darkness, sexual deviation, perversity, rape and murder. As a parallel current to the hedonistic loss of soul, and contact with the body, runs the danger of disease.

There has always been disease attached to lechery. Venereal disease is an ancient scourge. For centuries it was syphilis, originally a heterosexual disease. Since the late nineteen forties it has been curable because of the development of antibiotic therapy. Consequently it is generally forgotten that it was a disease of horrifying destructive potential to the physical and intellectual organism of the subject, the marital partner and the children. The social stigmatisation was so intense that cases had to be treated in secret. There was no real cure until penicillin, and later other antibiotics.

It seems therefore that the sixties with the sexual liberation and freedom from disease was apparently the stillness before the storm. In the seventies it became apparent that all kinds of new venereal infections were occurring often due to viruses, and hitherto unrecognised organisms from the Orient, the sub-continent and so on.

Sexual relationships had been too free and easy, a brake had to be applied, and of course it came as it always does from the Unconscious. The homosexual community because of the new openness, and the instigation and extension of the 'bath house' for purposes of pleasure was attacked by innumerable disease organisms, and it was by no means rare to find homosexual men who had suffered several recurrent attacks of syphilis, gonorrhoea, herpes or chlamydia and so on.

Meanwhile in Africa, where heterosexual license and prostitution had been a problem for some time, a new disease appeared in the late seventies. At first it was apparent only that men, women and children became emaciated, lost a great deal of weight, suffered diarrhoea constantly, and died – It was called 'Slim'.

In the early nineteen eighties, on the other side of the world at a Medical Congress, it was revealed for the first time to the Medical profession that a new disease, insidious, unusual and devastating had made an entrance into the homosexual community. The actual significance of its potential was not immediately grasped, nor has it been fully comprehended even today.

It is the same disease which has spread through Africa, America and Europe and is now in India and Asia. It is a pandemic, and at the present time there is no cure.

It is primarily a disease of prostitution, a disease of lust. No one at this time can foresee the outcome. If one looks at it from the point of view of the unconscious, it would seem that it is a compensation to balance the ubiquity of sexual licentiousness and profligacy.

Acquired Immunity Deficiency Syndrome (AIDS) Sida, or Slim, destroys the immune system of the subject. There is much controversy as to whether or not the HIV virus is causative. The facts appear to be that those who develop the disease have no immunity to the effects of the virus, and the virus does appear to be present in their bodies. Often in the case of the homosexual victims of the disorder, they have suffered a number of sexually transmitted diseases, prior to the onset of the infection. Undoubtedly they are subjected to a ferocious bombardment of all manner of infecting organisms during the specific sexual act, which weakens the individuals resistance, and thereby their immunity.

The end result of excessive lust, lechery and lewdity in former times usually led in the normal course of events to a dissolution of the personality and sometimes psychosis and destruction of the body through disease. Causes of such physical disintegration usually evolved from concomitant addictions to drugs or alcohol.

Behind the modern problem is a deep and collective unawareness of the pervasive insanity of unbridled lust released by the fervent interest engendered through the money-oriented, video and general media transmitted pornography, and its covert partner, ubiquitous pedophilia.

The actual nature of the epidemic of the destructive spherical sixty-four sided retro-virus reflects or mirrors a dark shadow of a self image which fragments the body cellular structure into dissolution. The disease itself reflects the insidious psychosis which has beset the collective consciousness of our day.

Man in general is out of balance, he has lost his instinct for self preservation because he has lost contact with his soul. He has erred far from his humanness and as primitive man well knew loss of soul brings mortal danger.

And there for the time being we leave the shadow world of sensuality, the incredible dark side of Aphrodisiac lust which has its roots in the deepest realm of Mater Magna, whose goal was always, and is always to promote life, one would be justified to describe a lust for life in human phraseology. She is concerned, not simply with human life but 'all life'. She as wild raw Nature can be unutterably savage in human terms when she deals, without mercy, with those phenomena which in her all-life processes are contra-life. She is the dynamic life-urge.

Man's lustful wanton destruction of our earth over the last decades of this century already begins to demand a high price. Land has become sterile, drought seizes continents, trees are diseased in epidemics and desiccated by water impoverishment resulting in their death on the one hand, whilst on the other man savagely destroys them with the satanic chain saw. Animals are subjected to mysterious viral infections or epidemics caused by polluted foods manufactured for material gain.

The oceans of the world have become cess pools for the excrement of man's chemical and nuclear industry. Thousands of species of sea life have disappeared yet this blight is perhaps only the precursor of a global nuclear blight yet to come.

Only Nature in her infinite, and ineffable majesty can save us as a species. No conscious human being can avoid the reality of the potential catastrophe which Nature may (in her mercy for all-life) propose for us, not you may note, to us. If we have the hubris to appropriate the divine Aphrodite's gift, which she received from the Mater Magna for ourselves as unconscious lust, we must by the natural law pay the price.

RESUMÉ

Now perhaps we may take a look at the Abbe de Rancé, with whom we began. Lust is in fact an existence without consciousness, 'a being in the dark'. As such one could well be described as being devoured by a monster or a demon. Likewise Eros is an unseen (invisible) fascination. There is a chilling aspect to lust, it is dangerous, and brings destruction not simply to the subject and the object, but to all others drawn into its orbit.

De Rancé was a profligate and a libertine. He was caught by the profligacy and the danger of, and the seductive sensuality of, the beauty of Madame de Montbazon. She represented his own invisible anima, the dark goddess of sensuality in her numinous and dangerous fascination.

When de Rancé beheld the horror of her diseased and decapitated head in that silent house of the dead there is no doubt he gazed at himself and saw the frightful head of the Gorgon – the Medusa. It is a wonder he survived. But, remember at 13 years he had written a treatise upon the dignity of the soul, somewhere he had contact with the inner spiritual world. The image of the severed head brought him as it were to his senses. He gave up the vanities of worldly desires at every level to become an inward spiritual being.

One could say that in that image of the head presented to him at the moment he expected the beauty of the beloved, he was shown his own future fate to be – the dissolution of his soul, in potentia.

Such a shock is often the means by which lust is overcome be it, alcoholism, smoking, drug addiction or whatever. But it does require the participation of the Self – divine help, which may come in an unusual manner, or from an unexpected quarter. Therefore au fond it is Deo Concedente.

REFERENCES

1 Rowsell, Mary, Ninon de l'Enclos, Pub. 1910.
2 Johnson, Samuel, A Dictionary of the English Language.
3 Ibid. (Exodus XV: 9.]
4 Ibid. (Bacon, Francis].
5 Ibid. (Old Testament, Psalms 63: 7].
6 Ibid. (Numbers XI: 4].
7 Jung, C. G., Collected Works, Vol. 5 para 188.
8 Ibid., n 31.
9 Davidson, William, L., Encyclopaedia of Religion & Ethic, Vol. I p. 643, Ed. J. Hastings, T & T Clarke, Edinburgh, 1926.
10 Spinoza, Ethics V Prop. 3.
11 Boëthius Consol, Phil. Lib. III Prosa 7.
12 Dante, A., The Divine Comedy, Part II Purgatoria, Canto XXV verses 121–122. Penguin Books.
13 New Testament, Gosp. St. Luke I: 34.
14 Du Bois Goiband (Janséniste) Note: Delong, Claude L'Amour au xvlle siecle p. 149, Librairie Hachette, 1969.
15 Bachofen, J. J. 57, 192, Myth, Religion and Mother Rite (Bollingen Series) Princeton University Press, 1967.
16 Ibid.
17 Pindar, prg. 87, Ed. Boeckh.
18 Detienne Marcel, The Gardens of Adonis ([Spices in Greek Mythology) p. 63 The Harvester Press, 1977.
16 Ibid.
17 Pindar, prg. 87, Ed. Boeckh.
18 Detienne Marcel, The Gardens of Adonis, (Spices in Greek Mythology) p. 63, The Harvester Press, 1967.
19 Ibid. p. 62 n 8.
20 Ibid. p. 62 n 10 Archilocus F. 38 ed. Lasserre and Bonnard.
21 Ibid.
22 Ibid.
23 Von Franz, M-L Apuleius' Golden Ass, Spring Publications, 1970, Chapter V.

24 Ibid.
25 Ibid.
26 Hannah, Barbara, A Biographical Memoir, Jung His Life and Work, p. 151, Putnam, 1976.
27 Jung, C. G., Collected Works, Vol. 14 para 226.
28 Hannah, Barbara, op. cit. p. 144 & Chapter 8 n 6.
29 Ibid.
30 Ibid.

6

THE DEADLY SIN OF AVARICE

Avarice means quite simply 'an inordinate desire for wealth'.

The word has been in use in the English language since the 13th century.[1] It is derived from the OF 'avarice', which in turn stems from the L. 'avaritia' and the subsequent French word evolved from the Latin 'avarus' which means greedy. 'Avarus' itself is related to 'avid', 'audacious' and 'ave'.

In the 14th century the word 'avaricious' became extant. This word is closely related to the OF, 'avaricieux' which in itself has been preceded in the 14th century by 'avarous'. OF, 'averos' means wealthy from the word 'aver' which means possession. The Latin 'habere' means 'to have or to hold'. Later, 'aver' from 'avere' which has the meaning of miserly or greedy. Avarice like gluttony and lust is a sin of the flesh. The synonyms for avarice are possessiveness, acquistiveness, cupidity, monopoly, rapacity and avidity or greed.

Allied to avarice is desire, venality and mercenariness. Associated conditions are parsimony, which means to scrimp, pinch, scrape, together with the nouns meanness, stinginess and miserliness. Certain phrases which appertain to the hand go with this condition. They are tight, close or hard-fisted, or close-handed. The meaning is that the hand closes on the gift or the money and refuses to release it.

This leads to the idea of retentiveness, uncharitable, ungenerous and churlishness. To be avaricious means to be grasping, greedy, selfish or extortionate. To be parsimonious means to retain, begrudge or withhold. Certain phrases worth while remembering are, to fleece, to haggle, to beg, to borrow or to hoard. 'Skin a flint' or 'live like a pauper' point to the same idea.

Avarice may be defined therefore as an absorbing passion for material possessions and things. Or a selfish gratification in their retention. Avarice includes both the search for and the acquisition, as well as the keeping of wealth. An avaricious person is unwilling to be brooked by anyone or anything in obtaining his personal desire, be it money, possessions or whatever. Once he has got that which he wants he is not concerned with putting it to any particular use. The chief thing is to have it, own it, or possess it. He may never look at it again, but he has it, that is the central point in the psychology of the avaricious person.

Avarice is largely restricted to the actual feature of possession whilst the passionate desire that betokens the person with an avaricious nature is usually described as covetousness. A distinction between parsimony where wealth is retained and stored, and rapacity, the seeking after wealth is helpful. Also rapacity signifies exorbitant greediness of extortionate practice. Envy or covetousness induces a state of discontent which aims to seize what others possess, but the miser, he who is caught in avarice, hoards greedily that which he already possesses.

When avarice seizes or takes possession of the mind or human being, it appears that the person in question becomes another. He is driven by a desire or a passion to seek or make money, or acquire possessions. It seems as if the money or the possessions constitute the goal. Yet this is not exactly so, there is a doubt as to whether the possessions or the money is the aim, or whether behind it is simply the means to gratify the love of pleasure in attainment or the love of power which that entails.

One of the age-old images planted upon the mind from the days of the first nursery books in that of the face of the miser, looking down upon, and illuminated by a conical pile of golden coins. It is not difficult to recall the intentness of expression, or the sharply focussed glittering eyes connected by an invisible thread from the directed mind to the pot or pile of gold. That is the face of the miser. Behind such an image one has to endeavour to perceive the reason for those psychic drives which in the simplest of terms denotes the possibility of acquiring ease or satisfying ambition. What then exists in his imagination as he gazes so raptly at his treasure?

Perhaps he dreams of security against poverty, insurance against his old age, to secure the presence of a warm house, and enough food to last his whole life. Or perhaps, and this is by no means uncommon, he visualises the amount of money he will leave to his heirs, or the size of the foundations which he bequeaths to posterity so that his name may linger on into the years to come. So behind the amassment of riches is an appeasement to the desires of pleasure or sensuality, and ambition. The love of pleasure, and the love of power, or the hybrid love of sensual power where power unites with sensuality is at the root of avarice. Avarice itself starts perhaps as a small seed, and like a tree it may in the end, dominate, overpower and totally engulf a life.

I always remember reading an anecdote when I was a young girl. I read about a multi-millionaire whose great ambition was to possess the most up-to-date racing yacht attainable which would carry off all the most prestigious prizes of the sailing world. In describing the origin of his great wealth, which had permitted him to indulge himself in the sensual pleasure and appease himself in this worldly ambition, he told the following story.

As a child of humble origin his parents made their living in a small shop. One day he noticed that when his father counted out the eggs his hands were big and the eggs seemed small, but when his mother held the eggs in her small hands they seemed to be bigger. As a boy he told his parents to let his mother sell the eggs, and since the eggs appeared thus to be larger the price could be increased. That is the seed which when planted was to produce for him the vast fortune.

When I read of his boyhood ruse I remember thinking, and I would be of the same age at that time as he was when he made the comment – how cunning and how deceitful! It was of course, but not to him, the morality was not to be considered. Even then in those early days of his life money was the thing, the future was all. Yet behind it was a love of immense power, and sensual indulgence. One often finds this in men who have acquired immense wealth in their lifetime. At base one sees quite simply – a miser! Of course one could argue, but some do put their money to good use and charitable purposes. But do they? Usually it is often for tax avoidance, to make more money, or philanthropy to promulgate further personal aggrandisement with bonds, lands or ancient and new titles. Or again perhaps to arrange suitable marriages associated with the above, for children and/or heirs.

Usually the central obsession the actual miserliness may become totally repellent, and the utter degradation of the soul is usually revealed in the life of the miser in the end. The worship of materialism signifies an absence of spirituality, and a loss of soul. The healthy instinct of the unconscious is always against such deviation from normality instigated by obsessions of this nature.

THE SIN OF AVARICE IN THE
DIVINE COMEDY

As we have observed in this poem Dante deals with the mortal sins, the sinners who commit them, and the way in which they expiated them. For a deeper understanding of the sins and of their meaning this poem is invaluable. It is as relevant today as it was 700 years ago.

In the early hours of the morning of the third day in Purgatory[2] Dante is confronted on the Fourth Cornice by a Siren. He then climbs to the 5th Cornice and meets the souls of the avaricious and the wasters. As he ascends he hears the souls recite examples of true liberality. It is here just at this point that Dante equates avarice with the ancient she-wolf of the dark forest. The wolf is often quoted as symbolising avarice and greed. One speaks of the greedy intake of food or gluttonous eating as 'wolfing it down'.

THE WOLF AS SYMBOL

Long before this poem was written, before the arrival of Christianity, the northern peoples of the circumpolar tribes believed that the end of the world would come in ice, and that there would be three frozen winters, then the lakes the rivers and the sea would freeze. As the sun would grow colder summers would cease and snow would fall endlessly. Then one long endless eternal winter would come, and finally – the wolf called Skoll would devour the sun and darkness would descend. This was the advent of the Fimbul winter. It signifies the opposite pole to a time of plenty, describing the cold darkness which faces a lost soul.

The wolf has a not dissimilar meaning in both European and Indian mythology. Essentially he is a robber, a thief or an outcast. He takes food, property, and as death dealer he takes one's life in one way or another. He is said everywhere to be avaricious and greedy, but one must recall that the wolf has to carry the onerous burden of man's projected non-human shadow.

On the positive side he is clever, cunning and sagacious. The wolf as a phenomenon represents something which takes away something which can only be regained with divine help from the sun, the moon and the stars.It is a factor in psyche which induces unconsciousness and reduces conscious awareness. An unconscious psychic content as is avarice would undoubtedly be responsible for such a state. The Lunar, solar or stellar light is equivalent to a high degree of illumination or increased consciousness necessary to become aware of the problem of the darkness obscuring one's perception of the situation.

It is because of the purported rapacity of the wolf that ravening hunger and insatiable greed are attributed to it. The prophets Jeremiah[3] and Zephariah[4] spoke of the 'wolves of evening' in reference to avarice and corruption. Nocturnal wolves were shadowy and could only be seen with some difficulty in the darkness of dusk when they appeared insatiably hungry. This points to ideas of cunning, deceit and danger.

Sometimes one observes a singular type of animus of a lupine nature in some women. The woman herself in her persona may appear to be generous and not at all rapacious in her womanly nature, but somewhere in spite of outward appearances one senses a deep greed.

A modern woman dreamed constantly of wolves. It was some considerable time before it became clear where the dream-wolf resided in her psyche. She had a pleasant agreeable personality and was not ungenerous. However she had a defective moral sense. It is always important to recognise one's own faults in preparation to discerning them in others.

Her rapacity lay in an unusual quarter. She was very proud of her intellect and if any of her colleagues informed her of new researches in the field of study which occupied their minds, she always replied 'I know that!' or 'I knew that!' She found that the others began to brand her as conceited and poked fun at her apparent academic superiority. This brought on a depression which concealed a furious rage against her peers.

The criticism levelled against her was justified only to a point. She was not conceited she had a greed to possess facts. She did not truly pursue knowledge for its own sake, nor did she value knowledge, she wanted only to possess it for purposes of self-aggrandisement. She had a rapacious lupine animus which sought to devour any morsel of information which was then assimilated as the wolf carries the dead in its entrails.

Her problem lay in the realms of the father complex. Her father an intellectual had constantly denigrated his daughter's ability to think. The compensation to bolster self-esteem against her inferiorities in this area was only possible because of the wolfish animus. This aspect of her psyche would have been difficult to unravel without the benefit of the 'dream wolf'.

Wolves have always been associated with death and incarnation since they were carrion eaters and scavengers. Formerly it was believed that they carried the dead in their own bodies to the pagan heaven or hell.

A very disagreeable woman, who hated everyone in her circle suffered a severe illness which progressed to the point where her life was endangered, and a successful outcome was virtually impossible. Virtually, but not absolutely. If she had been able to change her attitude to the world in general, and herself in particular, a resolution of the illness would perhaps have been possible.

Then she had the following dream in which she was in the actual hospital bed which she occupied. She leaned over to withdraw her looking glass and comb from the bedside locker table. As she gazed into the mirror, she realised that her face had changed into that of a dog with a muzzle, and as she peered more intently the realisation came to her that it was the muzzle of a wolf, and she was looking directly into its eyes. She woke up.

She told me the dream, and added at once that she was going home. That day she discharged herself from the hospital. As she left I knew it was a death dream, and I learned that she died a few days later.

When she took out the comb and mirror in the dream I was reminded of the wonderful image of Hermes in his rôle as god of death, in which he waits patiently and slyly at the inevitable psychopompos as he watches a woman prepare herself ostensibly for her lover, but in reality it is for her own death.

The wolf is sacred to the great goddess and is also one of the transformations of the goddess, and it is this aspect also which Dante[5] encounters in the second dream, and which is pertinent to this theme. It will be recalled that the ancient sorceress was the 'dolce sirena' the sweet siren in the dream. She is unmasked by Virgil as the image of corruption and putrefaction. The siren hag reveals herself to be the essence of lust, avarice and gluttony, the sins of the flesh. The three are symptoms of excessive perhaps even idolatrous love for the fleeting materiality of objects be they of whatever nature. Avarice represents material desire and in the poem it is stated 'Non-manti acquista l'or ma l'oro loro.' 'It is not we who possess the gold, the gold possesses us.' Dante describes this 'mad desire' be it carnal as in lust, or for goods as in avarice, as 'Folle volere' including those possessed to run after that which never can give satisfaction.

There is a translation of a poem[6] concerning avarice.

'The miser runs, but peace flees away faster.
Oh blind mind whose mad desire
cannot see that the number which it
seeks always to pass, stretches to
infinity. Now here is the one who
makes us all equal, tell me, what
you have done, blind undone miser?
Answer me, if you can, other than
'Nothing'. Cursed be your cradle
which flattered so many dreams
in vain, cursed be the bread lost
on you, which is not lost on a dog
For evening and morning you have
gathered and held with both hands,
that which so quickly distances itself again.'

A miser is the slave to a base desire, that is the fact which must not be forgotten. The miser is entrapped in the wolf, and exhibits wolfish greed or the voracious rapacity of the wolf.

A woman of sixty years told me of her daughter-in-law. After several years of marriage the daughter-in-law apparently revealed her true colours. It was Christmas time, a time when a great many of our complexes become intrusive. The analysand as was her wont, invited her son and his wife for the festive season. Again as was her wont the analysand furnished the family with various, generous and appropriate gifts. The daughter-in-law in her turn gave the analysand a tiny box which contained various coloured wood shavings, a tiny bottle of synthetic scent, and there was an ornament in the box of a half carved unpainted wooden apple. The cost of the gift was negligible. Its nature revealed a poverty of spirit.

That night the analysand had a dream, and in it she was standing at a bus stop waiting for the bus. It was raining hard, but she was wearing a mackintosh and underneath she had on her fur coat. Then she realised that she had been lost in thought, and suddenly she saw the red London bus she had been waiting for just drawing away from the bus stop. She realised she had missed it. Then she awakened and realised 'she had missed the bus', which means that she had missed an opportunity.

I asked her for associations, and she said that when she had been standing lost in thought in the dream, she realised that she had been absorbed in angry thoughts against her daughter-in-law's meanness. She related the dream at once to the fact that in earlier years the same thing had happened time and again. The previous year she had vowed that she would not buy a present for her son's wife the following year. She forgot, and fell into a collective 'Christian' pattern of giving, and once again gave a generous gift in spite of her own good intentions not to do so.

She admitted that it was her Christian 'turning of the other cheek'. Clearly the dream was against the proposed and eventual completed action on her part.

In turning to the personality of the daughter-in-law, the recipient of the generous gifts, it seemed from the giver's point of view that she was both a miser of material things but also of the spirit. She had not accepted her husband's family, and she always omitted to enquire after their welfare. She was also undoubtedly representing a mean-spirited aspect of the dreamer's shadow.

In the dream the dreamer was well protected against the rain, (mackintosh) and the cold (the fur coat underneath). The protection was at last the arrival in consciousness of her daughter-in-law's rapacity, and the dream was a warning for her not to repeat her folly.

The apple is the fruit of the tree of knowledge, of good and evil in the Christian myth. In the dream it was carved and made of colourless wood which has a feminine symbolic nature. A wooden half signifies only half of the potential knowledge which depicts unconsciousness of the dark side. Undoubtedly the daughter-in-law had a miserly shadow and her Eros was deficient, eaten up by the wolf. However the mother-in-law was not guilt-free, she had not heeded the signs and likewise was unaware of what she was doing, until the dream rescued her.

On the 5th Cornice the spirits of those who were envious or covetous are fettered face downwards. It is exactly at this point that the siren-hag appears in Dante's dream.[7]

> 'In dream a woman sought me
> halt of speech.
> Squint eyed on maimed feet
> lurching as she stept
> with crippled hands and skin of
> sallowy bleach
> I gazed and as to the cold limbs
> that have crept,
> Heavy with night, the sun gives

176

life anew.
Even so my look unloosed the string that kept
Her utterance captive, and right quickly drew
Upright her form that all misshapen hung
And stained he withered cheek to love's own hue.
Then she began to sing, when thus her tongue was freed,
and such a spell she held me by, as had been hard to break;
and so she sung
Lo the sweet siren – yea – tis I
Who lead the mariners in mid sea astray,
Such pleasures in my melting measures lie.
I turned Ulysses from his wandering way
with music; few, I trow to me who grow
know how to go, longing I so allay.'

Then Dante sees a lady and she asked Virgil who was the Siren. With that Virgil strides forward and exposes the Siren, and rending her disguise exposes her belly which released such a foul stench that Dante awoke in surprise. Virgil calls the Siren that 'Ancient Witch' because of whose beguilements the souls do penance in Upper Purgatory. Obviously she does not represent the materiality of lust, avarice and gluttony itself. She represents the desire for another, or money or food. At first she is ugly and maimed and not seductive at all. She therefore carries a psychic projection, she betokens something which is unconscious and unrecognised.

It is the same within a dream – maybe an image is presented to us in the night. Unattractive and perhaps wholly alien, someone we absolutely detest. Then we work on the dream and slowly we come to see that the rejected 'other' is in ourselves, a part of our psyche. At first we feel sad or dejected, or deeply ashamed that such a being resides in our own soul, as an aspect. Slowly we come to accept this neglected isolated part of ourself. We take it in and then we become seduced by this being, we think about it, feed it with intuitions and feelings. We are seduced and not a little in love with this hithertofore unknown aspect of our innermost self. Then one day the reality of the shadow personality truly becomes conscious. The projection falls away, and one feels that one has emerged from a dream, which in fact is very near to the truth for we have been possessed by 'another'.

This is the meaning of this strange dream for Dante. He sees the ancient living old hag who becomes a beautiful alluring Siren, who sings to us and calls us away from reality where we remain until the day comes, Deo Concedente, (and it may never come) when the illusion falls away and cold reality intervenes. One as it were emerges from the trance. The possession may be one of lust, for another, lust or desire for money, avarice, or an insatiable greediness for food. Lust, Avarice and Gluttony all belong to the ancient siren.

A modern woman one day saw a man, in reality she told me she thought he was a god, he was so beautiful, so handsome, so kind and so generous. She could neither eat, sleep or work until she got him by the most cunning and calculating means. She lay in wait, plotted, planned and outwitted him.

There is an old maxim of great truth. 'Beware of that which one wishes for passionately.' Such prayerful wishes may come true.

She got the man and what did she find? Why she found a rapacious, cunning conscience-less miser. A man of such physical and material greed that his soul had warped into a kind of madness. She found herself, at least she found an aspect of her unconscious mind which had been projected upon the man: when the projection was withdrawn she saw him as he was in reality, and at the same time, her own greed.

She had met the inner wolfish animus through the wiles of her unconscious negative feminine, the sweet siren-hag, who had seduced the man in this case 'for much worse, and not for better'!

In analysis and fearful suffering she managed to get out of this entanglement in the outer world, and the inner entanglement where the siren-hag and the wolfish animus had formed a partnership behind her back, and she had been powerless, a puppet in the game.

You see the danger of these sins! The subtlety of our unconscious desires, and the meaning inherent.

A possession of whatever, nature is a loss of soul, greatly feared by all native primitive peoples who at once sought and still do seek the services of a shaman or medicine man. Today we rarely realise when we have lost part of our souls, if not the whole, for man today does not know his soul or the fact that he is without a soul. One has only to gaze at the faces in the streets, restaurants and football (and other) crowds, at the blankness or deadening of the soulless gaze.

The miser seeks to commandeer as much in the way of worldly wealth as he can glean. He is not aware that he is caught by a power which has grasped him, and so he in turn becomes grasping. He is entrapped and seduced by the seductive cries and songs of the siren.

Let us look at some examples which have come to us down the ages as revealed in the poem.

As I have said the penance on the Fifth Cornice, for the avaricious was to be bound face downwards in fetters, so that the face lay in the dust. Dust is the powdered residue of the substance of the earth, the lowest form of materiality. The face was as it were rubbed into the dust, to show to the sinner the essential nature of the residuum of the bag, the pile or the mountain of gold, or riches he had acquired during his lifetime. The acquisition of which had dominated his life, which in the last analysis ended with his soul bound to the dust. Avaritia is a peculiarly earth-bound sin looking to nothing beyond the rewards of this life. It is expiated in the poem by the endurance of its effects, the souls are so bound that they can see nothing but the earth upon which they have set such great store all their days.

The prayer of the avaricious[8] states, 'adhaesit pavimento anima mea' = my soul cleaveth to the dust.

If a soul however, had in life already confessed guilt and stain for the sin purged on any particular cornice, (this was so with all the cornices) there was no continued detention, and the soul passed straight on to the next.

In general most of our sins such as jealousy, sloth, lying thieving are relatively superficial in the personal unconscious, and consciousness of them can be grasped with out too much difficulty. Some however, as we have seen, and shall see in this instance are more complex and difficult to grasp.

In analysis when an analysand becomes really aware of his shadow, and perhaps in a dream meets a jealous monster or a miser, he or she has then the opportunity to take it in and digest it. It is never easy to do this and a moral sense is necessary. Supposing one meets in a dream an acquaintance who is in reality constantly penny-pinching in small ways or short-changing his employees or whatever. One has then to face the fact that this shadow figure may be a mirror image of the stingy miser in one's own self. If however a moral sense is weak or non-existent, the reality of the meanness, pettiness or downright miserliness in not viewed as it is, and the analysand is then incapable of assessing the darkness in his nature.

Once a woman came to me because she had terrible dreams. She had dreamed more than once that a vile old man who had committed murder held her prisoner. Her reaction to the dreams were not quite right, she could not accept the reality of the dream image. I said to her, what would you do if you knew such a man, met such a man, or were captured by such a man? Those you see were the telling questions. The objective psyche which reveals itself to us in dreams is absolutely objectively real and totally unconscious, and I do mean unconscious.

Such a woman as I have described was in the grip of a murderous animus whose reality she could not accept, and therefore she was not able to purge herself. A patient came to me many years ago not for analysis, but with some minor illness. She was about 60 years old. I asked her if she was married. She said that she was a widow. Then she told me that she had had seven husbands who had either died or left her. I did not have any opportunity to hear her dreams, but I suspect that she had a murderous animus who disposed of the unfortunate spouses in exemplary fashion.

It would be quite in keeping to assume that her wolfish nature devoured her husbands. She was quite inhuman in her attitude to the deaths of these men as she talked of the tragedies. Not a nuance of feeling blemished her passive face.

In the eyes of the collective it would seem at first glance that this woman was deserving of pity. But if one turns one's attention to the fact that seven men chose escape or death, rather than stay with her, one is given pause for thought. This theme has been analysed with great care by Hannah[9] using the biblical Book of Tobit to describe the religious functions of the animus.

I have enlarged upon this theme because many people find it very difficult to recognise and accept as a moral obligation their own shadow. The reason is a lack of insight regarding the nature of the personal unconscious contents, which could just as easily be conscious.

Very often persons of a mean-spirited or greedy nature use it as an excuse against the opposing sin of the prodigality of a too generous nature, profusion, luxuria and waste. Penance for opposing sins was performed on the same terrace in Purgatory. The same holds true of the generous in whom there is often somewhere a deep and unrecognised miserliness.

THE FIFTH TERRACE

Of the seven figures who constitute the Bridle of the 5th Terrace, King Midas is the one who is the best known. The story of Midas by Ovid[10] is a superb portrayal of the sin of Avarice.

THE AVARICE OF KING MIDAS

Publius Ovidus Naso was born in 43 BC, at Sulmo in Central Italy. He went to school in Rome and became a leader of that witty literate and erudite society. He was expelled from Rome for some unknown offence by the Emperor Augustus. His writings include the remarkable Metamorphoses.

In the story one recalls that the Phrygian peasants had captured Silenus the satyr whilst unsteady with age and wine, and tutor of the god Bacchus. They had bound him with chains of flowers and taken him to their King Midas, who had himself once been instructed in the Bacchic mysteries by Orpheus of Thrace. When Midas recognised Silenus as the god's companion and partner in his mysteries, he celebrated the arrival of such a guest in festivities, and restored the tutor to the young god. The god then asked him what he would choose as a gift for himself. Midas said 'Grant that whatever my person touches be turned to yellow gold.'

Bacchus though sorry that Midas had not asked for something better granted his request, and presented him with this baneful gift. The Phrygian King went off delighted with his gift, unaware of the grave misfortune which had befallen him.

Whatever he touched turned to gold, the earth itself, the ears of corn, an apple from a tree, the pillars and doors and when he washed his hands the water ran away glittering and sparkling with gold particles. At first he exulted in his good fortune, and his tables were filled with the choicest of foods. But as he touched them, the meat, the bread, the fruits all turned to gold, and the wine was reduced to molten gold.

The wretched King dismayed by this strange disaster prayed for a way of escape, 'Forgive me father Bacchus I have sinned, pity me and save me.' He became contrite.

He became conscious the moment he realised that he would starve to death, and the shining glittering beautiful world of gold was bringing his life to an end, and no earthly power could save him. Fortunately he realised his plight and he was able to submit and confess his sin.

Bacchus cancelled the gift, and advised Midas to go to the river which ran through Sardis, and to make his way to its source. There in the foaming bubbling spring he was bidden to plunge his head and body and wash away the crime. The sin of greed had to be totally expiated. Even today it is said this river still runs with gold.

Now that is not the end of the story, for in fact he remained a foolish person, and later he was involved in a dispute between the god Apollo and Pan the nature god as to who was the better musician. The mountain (Timolus) was asked to judge and decided that Apollo was the victor, his music was sweeter that that of Pan. Midas disagreed and set himself against the mountain which is symbolic of the Self, and praised Pan, whereupon Apollo lengthened his ears and made motable at the point where they joined the King's head so that they would twitch. He then had ears of a lumbering ass. In order to conceal his deformity the King wore a purple turban, but his barber found out his secret, though bidden to keep it, could not keep quiet and went off, dug a hole, and whispered into the earth the secret of the King's long ears. But in the months to come a thick carpet of trembling reeds covered the hole. The reed as explained reveals the secrets of the marsh land. When the reeds were fully grown they told the barber's secret to the winds, and it was relayed to the heavens. Everybody then knew that King Midas had asses' ears.

Apollo punished Midas for his stupidity, he had a stupid nature. He had been introduced into the secret of the Bacchic mysteries, yet when Bacchus suggested a gift all he could desire was unlimited gold. He was so foolish he actually resisted the god Bacchus whose essence is enjoyment of life or 'une joie de vivre'. Again when the mountain Timolus, after great consideration of the world of men and animals chose by serious judgment that Apollo's music was the sweeter, Midas failed the god, this time Apollo, and for which he was punished for a fool. The fool was the cover for the stupidity of avaricious hubris.

Only an ass would prefer to honour gold above and beyond the desire to honour a god. On the level of the intellect when viewed objectively, such phobias, compulsions or possessions are futile and foolish because they squander and waste both psychic and physical energy, and ultimately a life.

The sin of greed is age-old, most people are conversant with the play L'Avare, the story of a miser by the French dramatist Molière. This play which concerns a miser was adapted in all probability from an exceedingly ancient play by the dramatist Plautus, called 'Aulularia' which means 'Pot of Gold'. It was written probably about 204 – 184 BC.

Very little is known of the playwright, one Titus Maccius Plautus, who was born about 255 BC, at Sarsina in Umbria. He went to Rome at an early age, and worked it is believed at a theatre. He then returned from Rome penniless and found employment at a mill.

During his leisure he began to write plays, he wrote three at first, and these were to be followed by twenty more. It seems however that Plautus adopted the theme of the miser from an even older work by the Greek dramatist Menander who lived and worked in Athens approximately 317 – 307 BC. His play concerning a miser refers to smoke escaping from his house, who falls into a rage at the loss. This theme was then taken up by Plautus and approximately 2000 years later by Molière. It is therefore pertinent and recognisably true that avarice has fired man's imagination from earliest days, and is part of the human condition.

THE STORY OF AULULARIA OR THE
POT OF GOLD

The miser is a mean old man called Euclio, a man who would hardly trust his very self, always suspicious and terrified that he would lose a pot of treasure which he had found buried within his house. After the find he buried it deeply in the ground, and became a prisoner in his own house because he was so frightened that someone would discover it and purloin it if he was absent from its walls. So he set himself the task to watch over it constantly.

An old man called Megadorus is persuaded by his sister to marry and he asks the miser for his daughter's hand. The daughter Phaedria however has been wronged by a young man Lyconides, who is the nephew of Megadorus. The miser agrees, but fearing for his pot of treasure hides it, and moves it from one place to another. The servant of Lyconides plots against the miser, and Lyconides himself entreats the uncle to give up the girl and let him marry her because he loves her, and is the father of the child to be born. The play ends when Euclio the miser who having been tricked out of the pot of gold, recovers it unexpectedly and joyfully bestows his daughter upon Lyconides.

The play rotates round the extreme stinginess inherent in the grasping nature of the miser. The story opens with a speech by the Lar Familiaris, the household god. In Roman times he guarded the house, and it was customary to say prayers, light votive candles and sometimes offer food and fruits from the table. The god if placated and honoured took care of the house and the family within. The household god tells us that he had preserved the house for the father and grandfather of Euclio, the miser. He goes on to inform that the grandfather entrusted to him in utter secrecy a hoard of gold which he buried in the centre of the hearth, entreating the god to guard it. The lars are usually hearth gods.

When he died, the grandfather was so avaricious that he could not bear to reveal its existence even to his own son and chose to leave him penniless rather than inform him of the whereabouts of the buried treasure. All he left was a little land which the son had to toil in order to make his livelihood.

The Lar Familiaris then continues to inform us of subsequent developments. The son as well as the grandson did not honour the god, and the neglect grew even greater, so by the time the son died, his son the grandson Euclio, the old miser of our story, paid no attention whatsoever to the god since he was a man of the same mould as his father and grandfather before him.

This play, at least 2,000 years old is in fact exceedingly pertinent to our discourse. Much of the trouble in modern families usually arises through problems related to land and possessions, but mostly money, allied to greed. Wills are made, fortunes bequeathed, land and titles distributed, but always somewhere there is envy for one thing or another. The fact which is usually forgotten is that the attainment of the preservation of, and the continued safe-keeping of riches belongs to the gods. Great wealth and riches almost always no matter how hard the recipient has worked, schemed, scrimped, saved, gambled, thieved, cheated, murdered, raped or pillaged for the treasure, it is a gift from the god or goddess of fortune, or as the gambler always adds from 'Lady Luck'. As such it should be treated as a gift for which one is responsible, one is indeed the custodian. It should not be squandered, equally it should not be hoarded. But each of us treats a windfall as some kind of cleverness on our part, or a reward of some kind, and it is usually claimed as one's own property from the moment it arrives in one's conscious awareness. Here is the greed of ego which one sees in the earliest days of a child when ego-consciousness begins to develop, when he says 'Thats mine,' or me! me! me! 'My Mummy,' 'My Daddy,' 'My teddy-bear,' 'My cup.' It starts there as a natural process. Education, training and life then begin to teach lessons, but innately the sense of possession remains even with old age when the aged sometimes cannot bring themselves to leave their riches to their heirs.

I watched my cat the other day. I usually feed the birds in winter-time in the garden. I had given her some fresh fish earlier, and she had turned up her nose and ate something else. She frequently does this. Then when I put the food outside for the birds, I added the fish for the magpies and the occasional tawny owl or hawk which swoops down. But no, my cat went straight out and began to eat the fish. You see it was by rights hers, and even though she had refused it and did not want it yet she would not permit a bird to approach it. Although the food had come from me in the first place it was truly hers because she knew that from the moment she smelled it, although she could choose exactly whether to eat it or leave it, it would be forever hers. That is the animal instinct of possession.

In the plains of Kenya one can see the male lion snarl ferociously or even kill his cubs who approach when he is eating, although usually the lioness has hunted and killed, and provided the meat. In all the animal world one sees instances of this. Squirrels in particular, dogs who bury their bones, such behaviour belongs to the instinct for self preservation, and food is equated with life. Although this behaviour is not immediately apparent as relating to the sin of avarice, it belongs nevertheless to the same instinctual pattern before the boundaries become confused, and the instinct becomes distorted as in the human disorder.

To return to the play. The household god informed that Euclio had a devout daughter, who prayed to him constantly and presented him with gifts of flowers, incense and wine daily. Because of her devotion in honouring him he had made it possible for Euclio to find the pot of gold in order to provide a dowry for this dutiful daughter. She had been ravished by a gentleman of high rank, and although he was aware of her identity she on the other hand did not know his. It was essential because of her condition that she found a husband to avoid dishonour.

As revealed in the play, the miser upon finding the treasure lived in abject fear of losing it. He permitted no one to enter the house, use his water, borrow from his fire or use his tools. He even told his servant that if Dame Fortune herself came she was not to be permitted to enter. Yet it was she who had bestowed the treasure upon him!

Gradually the suspicions overwhelmed him, and he regarded everyone as a potential thief. In order to lay a smoke trail and deceive everyone, he pleaded poverty. This is the 'cri-de-coeur' of the miser from the beginning of time. His paranoia was the result of projection of his own robbershadow.

It becomes clear why the Lar wanted to help Phaedria, because with such a father she had little chance of any kind of dowry, since he was the personification of meanness, he would never pay for food, wine and clothes for a wedding, let alone a dowry.

His servants said of him, at night he tied string round his jaws in order to close his mouth. He was afraid to lose his breath whilst sleeping. Nor it was said would he even, 'loan his hunger'. He took home his nail clippings from the barber, and when a hawk flew down and took a piece of his food he went to the magistrate to report the theft! The more pronounced the obsession the narrower becomes the field of awareness, and ego-consciousness is slowly absorbed into the unconscious. He gave nothing, it is of course an extreme case, but meanness and pettiness is the characteristic stamp of the avaricious.

However when the gold was stolen, and later to be replaced, the miser had a kind of spiritual conversion and whether it was a change of heart or whether it was the influence of the household god, he gave the gold to the young couple as a wedding present.

As a symbol the pot of gold represents the treasure, the gold is the supreme value, it had been kept in the family under the care of the god – a household lar, or hearth god. Because of the miserliness which denotes a worship of the material which includes a meanness of spirit, and a rejection of spiritual values, the house had fallen into decline. The daughter of the house who alone pays homage to the genius of the place, or as we would say the Self-figure, has been ravished and is with child. This had occurred at the festivities at the great festival to Ceres, the goddess of grain and fertility of animals. Her counterpart in Greece was Demeter, the great mother-goddess of the earth.

Something new had to enter into the life of the family which was stagnant like the Fimbul winter, cold and ice-bound, empty of humaness and relationship. This had come about because the family had for some time turned against the gods, ceased to honour them, and had placed the gold in the seat of honour.

The unfortunate fact of the daughter's pregnancy was a blessing in disguise. Psychologically the new attitude, (the baby represented the future attitude) could only enter the scene by the grace of the gods. The household Lar and Ceres conjoined to break down the grip of possession by the demonic negative instinct of greed, the wolf, or the old ancient witch as the old she-wolf herself.

The miracle occurs and Euclio undergoes a change of heart, which as in the cases of severe addictions or compulsive obsessional neuroses, help from the Self is required to bring about a resolution of the inner conflict.

THE POT OF GOLD

Since the central symbol of the play was a pot of gold it may be helpful to explore its symbolic meaning.

The pot as a vase or krater is a feminine symbol and is an agent of rebirth since it is shaped like the uterus. In former times it was believed that ancestral spirits occupied the great pots, or kraters, found in the ancient household kitchens. These were kanapoi the spirits of the pots. This idea probably arose from the fact that the ashes of cremated bodies were conserved in them and sometimes buried under the hearth. Usually the pots fell under the protection of the lars or household spirits.

Gold is bright golden and is the heaviest of metals. It signifies excellence, perfection, purity, incorruptibility and wisdom.

Jung wrote[11] 'There is an old mythological idea that the heart of the earth consists of gold. It is an alchemical idea that the core of the earth is gold, originated through the movement of the sun round the earth. Since the sun is identical with gold, its continual revolution round the earth has spun the gold in the centre, and has created its image in the heart of the earth.' He continues, 'This is a recognition that there is in the unconscious something of great value – a kernel of gold an equivalent of the celestial sun in pure gold.'

Jung again, 'The real gold is symbolic, that is why it is so highly praised. It has definite value but the chief value is that which man has given to it; the use to which it is put in the ordinary way would never explain the fascination gold has in itself for man.'[12]

Gold is always used to designate something that is valuable. It is after all the essence of all money. There is a saying, 'the love of money is the root of all evil'. It is frequently misquoted as 'money is the root of all evil' but that is incorrect. One could just as easily say 'the love of gold'. Today gold is not often associated with actual money which nowadays consists of paper notes and metal coins. The idea is the same, its essence is gold.

Now it was seen all too clearly how the miser in the play Aulularia prized his gold above all else, it came to dominate his life, he in the end could not bear for it to be parted from him. Of course one sees its value, but surely here the fascination is excessive. We have seen that the alchemical sun is the astrological equivalent of gold, we know that the sun can be a substitute for gold. The definition of God would be the Summun Bonum the greatest value of all is certainly God, and the greatest value to life is the sun because it warms the planet and is the source of energy. But to the miser who stays indoors, does not go out, does not see the sun, becomes isolated from his family and friends, ignores and rejects the gods, the greatest value is the gold, but is it? It certainly seems so.

Let us look again, his daughter has been ravished and is about to have a child, and he plans to marry her to an old man who does not insist on a dowry. He is quite suspicious, indeed paranoid about his servants. He grudges they say the smoke escaping from the fire, even his own breath released from his body. These examples are extreme, but in analysis one can certainly find, not infrequently, that some miserly men are impotent. They will not share their essential masculine-being with their wives. Of course frigidity in women is often associated likewise to a selfish withholding of the sexual self. These states betoken an inner greed and a deep reluctance to share. Impotence and frigidity are personality problems. For the miser, who typifies avarice in its most overt form, mistakes money or the gold as the supreme value in his life, he does not see the gold or the money as a symbol. His unconscious fascination and his passion for value blinds him to the fact that it is really a symbol. Behind his fascination with the outer gold is an inward fascination to the Self – the great gold sun – or the supreme value within – the god image. Such persons have no inner life they are truly soul-less.

Now we can begin to understand a money complex. A great many people are afflicted. Some are misers, and some let money flow like quicksilver through their fingers. If a person has some idea of psyche then they know that their fixation is with money, and that they have a complex. They frequently believe the cause is too little money, or they are not paid enough, or taxes are too great and bills are too high. All of these may be true. I know a man and when I meet him he tells me of his family's earning capacity, and yet although he will admit to a money complex he does not realise that it is not the actual money which grips him. In a way of course it does, but the real problem is his 'love of gold'. He is really a miser, I know this for he begrudges having to pay the cost of a dinner. But the 'love of gold' points to a deep religious problem which he has not realised, and perhaps never will. But that is the problem which besets him. His unconscious fascination like that of Euclio is with the god within.

The pot of gold or the purse full of money represents the same thing, the treasure. The coins of gold or other metal money are symbolic of the rolling corpuscles of the blood, and so money has come to represent in a way a kind of lifeblood. Money then is simply coined energy, it represents libido, so a pot of gold, a purse of money or a deposit account in the bank represents psychologically an accumulation or a condensation of psychological energy. In reality the pot of gold would bring wealth if sold, but the symbolism of so much psychic energy affixed to the object is of equal, if not more value, and represents the unconscious magnetism of the central symbol.

THE SYMBOL OF THE MOLE

An animal long associated with greed is the mole, in the Middle Ages it was said that the mole was the steed of avarice. It is symbolic of earthly energy because it is black, a prodigious excavator and spends its life in the earth. Its short squat immensely strong body is ideal for a worker in darkness. Because of its blindness it was used for divinatory purposes.

In the Rigveda he was Akhus the demon killed by Indra, but he was also the animal of Rudra the healer god, as indeed he was in the Greek Asklepian mysteries. In Alchemy, Olympiodorus[13] told us that in lead was a demon who drove the adept mad. This was the mole who had been a man who had divulged the mysteries of the sun. For this he was cursed by God, made blind and forced to dwell in the earth. An alchemist would know the secret of gold making – that would be the secret of the mole.

Psychologically the mole represents a vital physical function that moves below consciousness. In an individual who dreamed of a mole it would mean the vital inferior function, furthest away from the differentiated or superior function. The mole as an initiator into the mysteries of the earth, death, illness and its healing was therefore a master, who led the soul through the obscure labyrinthine unconscious seat of passions and difficulties. Avarice is an illness, a dark disorder of the soul which must be brought to light.

As the steed of avarice the mole has a blind urge to seek to be fascinated, to be gripped by the lure of, or the love of gold. Avarice signifies one caught in the grip of a demon or a possession, and who is blind to the actuality of the situation. Mistakenly he believes that the physical gold he seeks is the valued treasure when in fact it is in itself a symbol of the highest value.

In world economy, universal fascination with money undoubtedly exhibits certain features akin to a demonic possession so described.

THE CORRUPTION OF MONEY IN THE MODERN AGE (AN ENTITY IN ITSELF)

I must add here that there is a world-wide fascination with money which has forcibly beset mankind of recent decades, since the Second World War its grip is collective like a vast net, and willy nilly we are caught and drawn into it. The markets, the stock and commodities, the rapidity of computerisation, the gambling, the roll of the dice, the lure of the casino, banking, insurance, pensions are all to do with materialism. Money has now superseded the god-image in consciousness, the Bank or Stock Exchange has become the temple.

The computer age with the wizardry of technical expertise has placed the machine in the chair of the master. The ebb and flow of the money tides are observed on a lighted screen as they cover continents in a twinkling of an eye. Money in the money markets, the stock exchanges and the international futurist commodities cease to be in fact real, it becomes illusory, because the machine removes all physical contact and relatedness to the object disappears. There is no Eros in the world of finance. As in all forms of gambling which is what most of it is, from the roll of the dice to the establishment of the diurnal bank rate, it is so, either unconsciously or consciously. The presence of Dame Fortune is all important as the unconscious or 'out of sight' goodness. How many of the money merchants would admit to such a weakness! But true nevertheless.

In the same way the credit or plastic cards erase the idea of real currency, and with it the consciousness of a relationship to the actual object itself. Money or gold represents the treasure and psychologically is simply coined energy. It carries an incredible mana, that is the latent hidden mana of the gold, and this is why the collective is so caught in the fascination.

If one thinks of money, stock and currency markets, banks, plastic money-cards, bonds, stocks and shares as ethereal or ghost numbers and paper money, then one becomes aware of the immense fascination with 'spirit gold'. But as we have seen the fascination is for the value of the gold as a symbol, so it is the loss of consciousness of the highest value which is the seat of the problem, the loss of contact with the soul of modern man, and with the Self. So we are caught in the blind unconscious compulsion to seek with passion, money, that which holds the secret of the highest value – with entrée to the world of the unconscious – our own soul and its relation to the Self.

Seemingly, the unconsciousness of the meaning of our fascination is profound and ubiquitous. As individuals we can most certainly not have any effect upon the collective attitude. But we can each in our own specific way strive to become consciously aware of the ever present dangers of unconscious engulfment in the monomania of avaricious possession, and be on guard against what appears to be our own trivial weaknesses of stinginess, meanness or parsimony.

As has been witnessed, in recent decades the hubris of the markets has been subjected to devastating collapse, producing economic depression, giving a foretaste of the devouring wolf, or the desolation of the feared Nordic Fimbul winter. It behoves us to be aware of the dangers inherent in the sin of avarice.

REFERENCES

1 The Shorter Oxford Dictionary of English Etymology. Ed. by C. T. Onions, Oxford University Press, 1966.
2 Dante, A., Divine Comedia, Pt. II Purgatoria, Canto XLX v. 7.
3 Old Testament, Jeremiah V: 6.
4 Ibid., Zephaniah III: 3.
5 Dante, A., op. cit. Pt. II Canto XIX v. 19.
6 Dante, A., Dante's Lyric Poetry II p. 305, Foster & Body, Trans. Ed. Jacoff, R., The Cambridge Companion to Dante, p.30–31.
7 Dante, A., Divine Commedia (2) Canto XLX 7.
8 Psalm 25, v. 119 Vulg. CXVIII 2: 5.
9 Hannah, B., The Religions Functions of the Animus in the Book of Tobit, Guild of Pastoral Psychology, No. 114.
10 Ovid, Metamorphoses, Bk. XL.
11 Jung, C. G., Neitzsche's Zarathustra, Bk. II p. 1223, Routledge & Kegan Paul.
12 Ibid., p. 795.
13 Jung, C. G., Collected Works, Vol. 14 para 183 n 326.

7

THE DEADLY SIN OF GLUTTONY

In order to understand gluttony one has first to understand hunger or thirst.

With regard to the question of hunger, the word is used in the English language to describe an unease or painful sensation caused by want of food. It also means a craving or an appetite for food, or something else. It is used to describe the exhausted condition which comes about from lack of food or sustenance. Hunger can also refer to a death, a famine or a starvation on a collective level. The great potato famine in Ireland 150 years ago is often referred to as 'the Hunger'. A million people died of starvation because the potato crops failed since a blight attacked the tuber. Because the majority of Irish had only the potato as a staple food the consequence of this disaster were overwhelming.

The 'hunger' lasted for five years from 1845 and was responsible for the emigration of a further one and a half million people before 1849. It is difficult to realise today the horror of those years when men women and children in a Christian country starved to death. But again in Russia during the pogroms of the thirties there occurred the same type of, but infinitely greater devastation. Such starvation was also endured by countless Jews in the German camps during and towards the end of the Second World War.

It is inconceivable that a mere 150 years since the 'Great Hunger', 60 years since the Russian pogroms, and 50 years since the German camps that in Europe the glut of food is now so vast that there is stockpiling of food.

The word 'hunger' stems from the OE 'hungor' or 'hungur'. Both are derived from the O. Teutonic 'huygru'.

A distinction must be made between the hunger for food and for some other object. Where there is no question of starvation because the food supply is unlimited the libido may then seek other gratification, tobacco, alcohol, drugs and so on. Various proverbs and phrases explain its essence. 'Hunger is the best sauce,' 'Hunger is good kitchen meat' 'Iln'ya sauce que d'appétit.' 'L'appétit assaisonne tout.' It is also said that Hunger (O. Teutonic) 'is the dish out of which the goddess Hel was wont to feed'.

On the other hand, of those who are sated it is said (Proverbs XXVII v.7) 'The full soul loatheth a honey comb' and again 'He who is not hungry is a fastidious eater.' One speaks of a hungry person as being 'as hungry as a dog . . . a hack . . . a hunter . . . a kite . . . or a wolf'. But 'to the hungry soul every bitter thing is sweet'.[1]

It was clear in those great famines mentioned above that the land had failed, the crops did not grow and blight had settled on the land in the case of the Irish and Russian famines, the latter because the Communist ideology of collective farming could not provide in the simplest of terms, adequate food for the masses.

In those years of half a century ago people ate to survive, there was no place for fastidious eating or petulant refusal for food. Food was necessary to keep the body alive and support its metabolism. The problem was to get enough.

Perhaps the following report will portray the nature of hunger as it affected one young girl in Stalingrad in 1949.[2]

'Directly behind the hotel and in a place overlooked by our windows there was a little garbage pile where melon rinds, bones, potato peels and such things were thrown out. And a few yards farther on there was a little hummock like the entrance to a gopher hole. Early every morning out of this hole a young girl crawled. She had long legs and bare feet, her arms were thin and stringy, and her hair was matted and filthy. She was covered with years of dirt so that she looked very brown. And when she raised her face it was one of the most beautiful faces we have ever seen. Her eyes were crafty like the eyes of a fox but they were not human. The face was well developed and not moronic. Somewhere in the terror of the fighting in the city something had snapped, and she had retired to some comfort of forgetfulness. She squatted on her hams and ate water melon rinds, and sucked the bones of other people's soups. She usually stayed there for about two hours before she got her stomach full. Then she went out in the weeds and lay down and went to sleep in the sun. Her face was of a chiselled loveliness, and on her long legs she moved with the grace of a wild animal. The other people who lived in the cellars of the lot rarely spoke to her. But one morning I saw a woman come out of another hole and give her half a loaf of bread, the girl clutched at it almost snarlingly, and held it against her chest. She looked like a half-wild dog at the woman who had given her the bread, and watched her suspiciously until she had gone back to her own cellar, and then she turned and buried her face in the slab of black bread, like an animal she looked over the bread her eyes twitching back and forth. And as she gnawed at the bread one side of her ragged filthy shawl slipped away from her dirty young breast, and her hand automatically brought the shawl back and covered her breast and patted it in place with a heart-breaking feminine gesture . . . It was a face to dream about for a long time.'

This is a portrait of starvation, she ate till she had filled her stomach. As the report indicates, she was no longer quite human but had retained her feminine modesty, she was a feminine being the instinct of hunger and femininity were intact.

It is not difficult to understand how in times of great starvation cannibalism intervenes into a society. The craving for food in such times is paramount, and must be fulfilled for the physical body to survive.

CANNIBALISM

In North American mythology[3] the greatest ceremonial significance related to the membership of the secret societies of native Americans of the North West Pacific coast regions. The fraternities of this area had a development of their own. They originated with the Kwakiutl tribes, and membership in the secret society was dependent in a way upon heredity. This was because certain of the tutelary spirits of the societies were supposed to appear only to members of particular clans and families. In the season of ceremonials the names of the society members were changed from the clan names to the spirit names, which they received at initiation. The spirits were genii or guardians of the societies.

The totem of the tribe appeared to be the ancestor, and revealed his mystery which then became the tradition of the clan. The spirits of the societies likewise manifested themselves to, and indeed had to take possession of each initiate. In the ceremonial season these spirits lived in association with the neophytes.

The most famous and most dreaded of all the tutelary spirits was the Cannibal, whose initiates practiced anthropophagy, biting the arms of other clan members who were not initiated. In earlier days undoubtedly the non-initiates were killed and eaten. The Cannibal of the society was a particular personage who was supposed to dwell in the mountains with his servants who were the man-eating Grizzly Bear and the Raven, and who fed upon the eyes of persons whom his master had devoured. The Raven was a long beaked bird who crushed the skulls of men and ate the brains. There were other spirits, the Warrior of the North whose gifts brought prowess in war, resistance to diseases and wounds. There was the Bird Spirit which permitted the initiate to fly, and the Dog-Eating Spirit whose votaries killed and ate a dog as they danced.

The initiate had to become possessed of the Spirit who spoke and acted through him. He was to become as glass so that the Spirit could be seen to enter into the body.

The poetry of the North West tribes like their mythology seems to have been pervaded with a spirit of overt gluttony, which finds its most unveiled expressions in the cannibal songs.

> Now I am going to eat
> My face is ghastly pale
> I shall eat what is given to me
> by Baxbakualanuchsiwae.

Baxbakualanuchsiwae was the name for the Cannibal Spirit and the appellation meant 'the first to eat man at the mouth of the river', i.e. in the north. The ocean was conceived as a river running towards the Arctic regions.

In some of the songs it is clear that the cosmic significance of the spirit is set forth.

> 'You will be known all over the world; you
> will be known all over the world. You
> went to Baxbakualanuchsiwae and
> there you first ate dried human flesh'

It is thought that the secret societies originated as warrior fraternities among the Kwakiutl whose famed tutelaries were as mentioned the Cannibal and the Warrior of the North. It has been suggested that the ecstasy which followed the slaying of a foe; the killing of a slave by the resulting cannibal society members was a victory celebration since the slave was war booty.

It seems perhaps that only certain clan members, initiates of the secret societies, would actually participate in any flesh eating which stemmed from the entry of the cannibal spirit, the spirit of gluttony into the bodies of the initiates. In this way it was the alien spirit who was responsible for eating human flesh. Before the formation of the societies no doubt cannibalism per se, was accredited to the invasion of the dangerous spirits described, and the formation of the societies would evolve in order to bring a measure of control into these dark areas.

Only in times of great hunger does it appear that the taboo against the ingestion of human flesh was overcome. However with it came condemnation mixed with an innate horror of the act.

Psychologically the spirit as an eater of human flesh would signify a possession by a perversion of the powerful animal instinct of hunger, which must be assuaged by no matter what means. The recognition of this powerful demon, together with the associated shamanistic rites, denotes a step in the elevation of conscious awareness of its alien attributes in the fraternity of the society members of the clan.

THE SIN OF GLUTTONY

As one of the seven mortal sins gluttony is the vice of excessive eating.

The English word glutton[4] stems from the ME, word 'glutunie' or 'glo-tonie' which in turn is derived from the OF, 'glutunie', 'glutonie'. The word is related to the noun 'glutton', one who eats excessively. From 'glutton' comes gluttonise to feast gluttonishly, This is the reason the cannibal songs described above are inspired it seems by a spirit of gluttony, because they celebrate the gluttonish feasting of the initiates at the celebrations in the winter time.

Gluttonish, glutton-like, voracious or gluttonous all mean excess in eating or excessively fond of a specific object or pursuit. For example one may be a glutton for punishment or a glutton for work.

From the root of the word comes the word 'glut'. To glut is to gulp or swallow greedily usually liquids or soft foods. It can mean to swallow at one gulp. It also means glutting, the condition of being glutted with food, indulgence to satiety or disgust. This latter where one has had one's fill or a surfeit.

Since 1594 it has meant the supply of a commodity which greatly exceeds demand.

Today we speak of a glut of grain, corn, sugar, butter or wine. We have thus come to possess grain or butter mountains or wine lakes. These gluts only occur in a society given to gluttony in high degree, where there is also a great excess, a time of plenty. This is undoubtedly the state of things in the western world at the end of the twentieth century, a far cry from the earlier years of global war.

To summarise, to glut means to gorge oneself, or to feed oneself to reple-tion. It also means to be filled with a ferocious or fierce desire to take one's fill of food, or perhaps of thinking or looking. It also has the meaning of to gloat, where one is excessively pleased at another's downfall. It has the deeper meaning of 'to long for something' in a greedy fashion. Finally it means to sicken. This occurs in patients with bulimia who episodically gorge themselves uncontrollably with food. Then they sicken either physi-cally because the stomach is overloaded, or psychologically with feelings of guilt because of their failure to control the appetite.

THE QUESTION OF APPETITE

Appetite is a desire or a relish for food or other gratification of the senses.

Psychologically it may be defined as a recurring sense of awareness of some bodily need. The sensation incurred by this want is associated with a craving for the object of need or a desire that the craving be satisfied.

It is the craving for satisfaction which initiates the effort or an act leading to the assuagement of the physical need. This brings satisfaction and ease from the sensation of discomfort inherent in the need. The majority of the appetites, thirst, hunger, repose, rest or sleep are concerned with the conservation and welfare of the person concerned. The sensual and sexual appetites are not, the sexual has concern only with the propogation of the species and its continuation. Appetite is an instinct, and it issues from the instinctual realm.

The bodily want may be described quite simply as an uneasy feeling. Many patients have described appetite as a sensation of 'hunger' or an emptiness difficult to define, moreover many have explained that it is difficult to know whether they desire food, drink, or sexual gratification. This indicates an unclearness as to the nature of the need. In a person who is starving for food there is never a confusion, the appetite must be assuaged by food, the craving is for sustenance.

The effort or the action aimed to fulfil the desire for satisfaction is reflex and instinctive, not deliberate or purposive. As soon as the discomfort is annulled by food, drink or whatever, the sensation of pleasure of fulfilment is apparent.

However the original wish to eliminate the unease may come to assume 'the desire for pleasure'. So that it is not the satisfaction of the craving to ease the discomfort of the bodily need, but the desire for the pleasure inherent in the act. This is seen in the gourmand and the epicure where the pleasure is the thing. Instead of food or drink being taken to allay hunger or thirst, elaborate measures may be introduced into the arts of cookery or perhaps an intense study of wine or spirits, in order to aid and increase the desire for pleasure. The acres of shelf space in book-shops attest this aspect of appetite for food and drink, as do also the institution of sex and pornographic outlets in the titillation of sensuality to promote the desire for pleasure in sexuality. This innovation results from the fact that sexuality has almost become a commodity like food drugs or alcohol.

The insidious development of the enormous increase in expertise in all the areas associated with food could only develop in a society of plenty. Since the days of starvation during the war, gradually want has given way to plenty and there is a surfeit of food. Consequently a monumental industry has developed, and since the goal is economic the sensuality in the field of food and wine has become the target of the power driven impulse for financial gain.

No longer can the simple act of eating or drinking be made to appease the sensation of hunger or thirst. Instead the pursuit of pleasure has become paramount in these acts, not simply the reflex pleasure of fulfilment. The pleasure that accompanies eating and the conscious deliberate pursuit of the pleasure are by no means identical, one may interpose thirst or rest, (leisure) or sexuality instead of eating.

If desire of the pleasure becomes the predominant aim, the normal

195

healthy craving in appetite may be displaced by an abnormal craving. Such a craving is seen in gluttony. Or an artificial craving which is called an acquired appetite may be produced instead of the normal craving. This condition is found in addictions due to alcohol, tobacco or drugs. Sometimes in pregnant women an abnormal craving for an unusual food occurs during the months of pregnancy prior to parturition. Such cravings should always be examined from a psychological point of view as they indicate the presence of an unconscious psychic content associated with the pregnancy.

In cases of the abnormal craving found in gluttony, or the acquired appetite for certain commodities of whatever nature, there is an induced desire. This state is prompted by the anticipation of the pleasure which has been experienced before by the individual.

Often the first drink of wine or whiskey, the first cigarette or the first introduction to heavy drugs in not a pleasurable experience. Another factor is the presence of fashionable pursuits at certain stages in life. The participation mystique engendered in group activities often paves the way for the development of induced desires and acquired appetites.

Appetite in summary is simply an instinctive craving for a given object. Desire of pleasure is a conscious process dependent on the memory of an individual pleasurable experience in the past, and a craving for that pleasure. This is repetitive, reinforced with time, and augmented particularly in the case of acquired appetites. The pleasure that the satisfaction gives is in proportion to the craving.

In the glutton, the drunk and the drug addict the strength of the abnormal craving for the pleasure is far greater than the pleasure of the gratification. The craving has the mastery, and so the victim in no longer appeased and the craving for the pleasure becomes eternally insoluble.

Since gluttony is concerned with the question of an abnormal desire or craving for food, it is clear that although today it is medically regarded as a perversion of instinct, the church fathers regarded it as a mortal sin. Moreover, as was seen in the North American native mythology, cannibalism also an appetite perversion, indeed an 'acquired' appetite occasioned either by hunger, gluttony or ecstasy, was also regarded as being due to invasion by a powerful or evil demon. Measures for 'control' of this demon became the aim of the secret fraternities.

As was seen in the Middle Ages, Dante in his poem The Commedia, described the demon of avarice as a she wolf who travelled it seems with the hag, who was in fact a sweet siren, the siren dolce who seduced men into the pleasures of the flesh, which also included gluttony as well as lust, the gluttony indeed is a lust for food.

On the sixth terrace of The Purgatorio the gluttons are found. Here the Beatitude of Christ's Sermon on the Mount is chanted. 'Blessed are they which do hunger and thirst after righteousness.'[5] This Beatitude is also appropriate for the 5th terrace where as was seen an insatiable thirst for worldly wealth was pursued.

On the sixth terrace[6] starvation is the penance for gluttony, deprivation of food resulted in emaciation of the shades. The words accompanied by a sound of sobbing which Dante heard on this terrace were 'Labia mea Domine'[7] 'Open my lips O Lord,' with the inherent meaning that my mouth may proclaim Thy praise.

This verse is apt for the souls of the penitent gluttons on this cornice whose mouths had been opened to less spiritual nourishment during their lives. Dante describes the appearance of these souls as being 'silent, devout, pallid of face, hollow and dark-eyed, so wasted that the skin had all its contours moulded on the bone'.

This is an image of emaciation of the body starved of nourishment, seen in starvation due to debilitating illness, times of blight-induced famine, war-induced famine, and war-induced lack of food.

Prominent amongst the shades on this terrace he sees the emaciated form of Erysichthon. In former life he had been a glutton renowned for his prodigious appetite. Ovid wrote of the sacrilege, and as it is one of the best descriptions of the disorder from classical literature it is worth examining more closely.

THE STORY OF ERYSICHTHON, THE GLUTTON AND HIS DAUGHTER[8]

Proteus in Greek mythology was the son of Poseidon. He was often called the Old Man of the Sea, he was fickle and he yielded only a force. He possessed the gift of prophecy, and to escape from foretelling the future he assumed various terrifying forms, but if his questioner maintained his hold throughout the transformations Proteus at last told him what he knew. The secret was to hold fast, and not let Proteus escape. He was the personification of the shifting winds and moods of the sea. His name is related to Pallas in the sense of being monstrous, and is an earlier spelling of the Greek word for early man.

The word 'protean' in use today means someone who is changeable and variable.

As the god of the sea he encircled the earth. He was known to take the shape of a young man, or a lion, sometimes as a raging wild boar and often as a snake, and now and again as a bull. Frequently he was a tree, or quite inanimate and appeared as a stone, perhaps as running water, a river or the very opposite, fire. Thus he was a living spirit, a nature spirit, universal and ubiquitous, he was an archetypal image of the spirit of the unconscious.

The story by Ovid tells us that the wife of Autolycus the thief, the son of Hermes and the Prince of Thieves, had the same power as Proteus.

Her father was Erysichthon a man who scorned the gods, and never made any offering of incense on the altars. This was the complaint by the Lar familiaris in Plautus' play Aulularia concerning the godlessness of the household in the drama.

Erysichthon used an axe to chop down the trees in the grove sanctified to the goddess of plenty, Ceres (Demeter). By doing so he violated the ancient and sacred woodlands where the goddess was honoured. This is reminiscent of the way the rain forests are destroyed today with the demonic chain saw, just as great a sacrilege today as in the time when Ceres was dishonoured by Erysichthon.

Amongst the trees stood a huge oak, sturdy and strong, which in the course of years had become a forest in itself. It was hung with wreaths, garlands and votive tablets. These were all tributes for prayers which had been granted by the goddess.

But although it was a sacred tree dear to the goddess, Erysichthon ordered it to be cut down, and when his servants were afraid to do so he said 'Should this tree be itself a goddess, and not just a tree the goddess loves, still its leafy top will be brought down to earth.'

We have seen how in Plautus' Aulularia, Euclio flouted the goddess of good fortune. Also with King Midas, how he denigrated the great god Apollo the far shooter, and now again Erysichthon does the same. It shows hubris, arrogant pride in all three where they put themselves above the gods.

In psychological terms we would describe a monumental inflation which always betokens unconsciousness.

The oak tree groaned and grumbled, the leaves and acorns began to turn white, and the living branches lost their colour. Then when his impious hand had made a gash in its trunk, blood flowed out where the bark was split open, just as it might pour if a mighty bull is slain before the altars as an offering. Everyone was horrified, but one man dared to prevent the sacrilege and stop the cruel axe. Erysichthon turned and cut off the man's head. Then he turned to the great oak, and dealt it blow after blow. Meanwhile in the heart of the tree a voice was heard. It was that of the nymph who lived in the tree, and was loved by the goddess Ceres because she had given the tree its life. The nymph was the guardian of the tree. As its living spirit she warned Erysichthon 'I warn you with my dying breath that punishment for your wickedness is at hand, and that thought comforts me in death.'

The Japanese film producer Akira Kurasawa who brings a fine delicacy of touch sometimes to his films has produced a series of short films called 'Dreams'. In it is the same archetypal motif of the tree spirit, or tree fairy in one of the film sequences of a peach tree orchard. All the trees of the entire orchard had been axed, save one. In this tree resided the fairy of the peach tree, and her appearance gave a hopeful prospect that perhaps another peach tree orchard would arise again. It is the same archetypal idea which is eternal.

In the case of Erysichthon, eventually the tree was brought down and all the sister dryads in the grove dressed themselves in black garments and mournfully approached Ceres, begging that Erysichthon should be punished for his evil deed, for such it was. When a great tree dies the home of thousands of beings is lost, all the tiny insects who lived on, in and under the tree. When a forest is destroyed the loss of natural indigenous life is monumental and catastrophic.

After deep reflection, Ceres gave thought to their request and decided to torment Erysichthon with Hunger. Since destiny does not allow Ceres the goddess of plenty to meet the demon Hunger, for they are opposites, Ceres sent her oreads or mountain spirits to the house of ravening Hunger. The demon lived in the house of Chill, Pallor and Ague, the three characteristics of starvation. The order given by Ceres to her spirits to convey to Hunger was this:

'Bid Hunger bury herself in the wicked
stomach of this impious wretch, and tell
her to fight to overcome my powers of
nourishment and to let no amount of food
defeat her.'

The envoy found Hunger, and the description is superb. The creature's face was colourless, hollow eyed, her hair uncared for and her lips bleached and cracked. Scabrous sores encrusted her throat, her skin was hard and transparent revealing her inner organs. The brittle bones stuck out beneath her hollow loins, and instead of a stomach she had only a place for one. Her breast hanging loose looked as if it were only held in position by her spine. The envoy oread, or the dryad the mountain nymph, did not go near to deliver the goddess' orders but remained at a distance. Even so she began to feel the pangs of Hunger.

Although Hunger is always opposed to Ceres, she obeyed. She was carried by the wind to the house of Erysichthon, and finding him asleep insinuated herself into his body breathing into his lips, his throat, his heart and spread famishing hunger through his hollow veins. When she had carried out her orders she left, and returned to her poverty-stricken home.

At first Erysichthon slumbered on, but then he dreamed he was feasting and began to chew uselessly at nothing, grinding his teeth together and cheating himself by swallowing a mere pretence of food. Instead of a banquet he gulped down air. He awoke and was furiously hungry; his famished jaws and burning stomach were utterly at the mercy of his craving. Without delay he gave orders for all the foodstuffs that earth, air and sea could provide be brought to him. In the midst of it all he ordered feast upon feast, but he could not be satisfied.

As the seas receive all the rivers, and as the greedy flames of fire consumes countless faggots and requires more, so it was with Erysichthon. He required more and yet more. All the food he consumed only excited his desire for food, and by eating he continually produced an aching void, his stomach was a bottomless pit, and yet in spite of all this his burning appetite was unabated. At length, when he had eaten all his wealth he was left only with his daughter, so he sold her. But she rebelled against having a master and called upon Proteus the god of the sea to rescue her from slavery. He changed her at once into the shape of a man, and looking straight at her asked her where the young girl had gone who had been standing there, and whose footprints stopped suddenly at the edge of the sea.

At once the girl realised that Proetus had saved her. She explained to the master that she had been fishing and had never taken her eyes off the sea, and had seen no one. To remove any doubts she said, 'I swear so may the god of the sea assist me in my livelihood that no one but myself has been on this shore for a very long time, and no woman has set foot here.' The man believed her, and walked away cheated of his slave. Then the girl's shape was restored to her.

The father however, when he perceived his daughter could undergo such transformations often sold her again to different masters to pay for his gluttony, but she escaped in the form of a horse, a bird, or again as an ox or a stag thus obtaining provisions dishonestly for her gluttonous father.

She aided and abetted the inner demon in her parent, and thus violated her feminine self by leaving one master to become the servant of another.

In men the demonic anima may collude with the shadow to form an unbreakable alliance so that ego consciousness cannot win. Here with Erysichthon, a greedy shadow issuing from a possession by the vice of gluttony and a semi-compliant anima had united. He was no longer a conscious being. When the violence of his malady had consumed all that was offered and aggravated his grievous sickness the wretch began to bite and gnaw his own hands, and then he ate his body.

EXPLANATION

The story illustrates with clarity the demonic possession which will not be sated in cases of addiction, be it to food, nicotine or whatever.

Some years ago I looked after an obese woman who was of such a size she could no longer walk unaided.

She told me that she had a poor appetite and ate very little. Obesity is certainly a symptom of gluttony. If one overeats one gets fat. The starving inmates of the German camps, and the serving German armies on the Russian Front in the Second World War bear witness to the fact that where there is no food there is no fat. Today the question of obesity is now tied up to the sin of sloth or inertia. Medical opinion has begun to hold the view that lack of movement or exercise is one of the prime causes for the general rise in obesity in the western world. It is of course not quite so simple as many factors are involved.

To return to the obese patient. One day I inadvertently had the opportunity to observe her whilst she ate her luncheon in the hospital. I was surprised to observe the quantity ingested, and the manner in which she consumed it. She aggregated it to her, and then engulfed it, there was no other way to describe it. It seemed she was caught by a demon. She was quite unconscious of the food either of its nature or the amount. She ate like an automaton. Then I realised the nature of the addiction, it was automatism she had an autonomous animus which gripped her. She became a different person when she ate. The animus lead her in the pursuit of a desire or craving for food, but she did not appreciate any satisfaction. It was the pursuit of desire to eat which gripped her. When I talked to her later I became aware of this inner unconscious voracity which was not to be appeased simply with food.

She was also a lesbian, a brilliant woman but gravely damaged psychically. She had tried all kinds of diets but without success. Her dreams were strange but interesting and pointed to immense changes to come in her life. She was not willing to continue with he analysis as the dream interpretations disturbed her. Many years later she returned, she was slim and happy and she had found great joy in an unexpected marriage. The hunger which I had witnessed was not for food it was in her case for heterosexual love and fulfilment as a woman. The dreams had predicted this, but it was something in those far off days she found unacceptable.

In the case of the glutton Erysichthon he had denied and dishonoured the feminine goddess Ceres, she was the sister as Demeter of the might Zeus. She it was who blighted the earth at a stroke when her daughter Persephone was abducted by Hades, and she did not relent until her daughter was restored to her. As a great goddess she exemplifies the instinct of the feminine in its matriarchal aspect. She as the goddess of plenty is responsible for the fruitfulness of man, animals and vegetation. Anything against her responsibilities as a promoter of life is an abhorrence to her.

An elderly woman told me that in her old age she only lived for a daily bottle of wine, or perhaps two. She sought nothing else, she wanted for nothing apparently except the wine. That she had to have. I saw in that something deeper. She had lost all her family and was quite alone, and lived a solitary life, she had as far as I gathered no inner life and very little awareness of the Spirit. Her daily companion was the wine bottle, and in that was the spirit of Dionysos in which she found for a short time each day the pleasure of anticipation, she sought the desire of the pleasure but she was never fulfilled, and eventually the bottle became her master.

The addict it appears seeks unconsciously the spirit in the object of his addiction. The poppy is the flower of Demeter so in fact the heroin or morphine addict is seeking the spirit inherent to the poppy, the spirit of the goddess herself. Likewise in alcohol, the spirit of the corn, the barley or the potato all gifts from Demeter – Ceres. Wine as we have seen is the essence of the Dionysian spirit. Most addictions reveal deeply hidden spiritual problems. Indeed the world-wide collective addictions betoken the unconscious clamourous search for a spiritual existence, be they cloaked in food, wine, drugs, fitness or health compulsions. As we saw with the miser Euclio, a spiritual conversion is required for a cure. This however can only be accomplished if the god or goddess offers divine help. If the archetype of order and wholeness, the Self, achieves the balance.

Since the great oak tree was the central feature of the story it might be helpful to study the tree as a symbol.

SYMBOLISM OF THE TREE

The sin of Erysichthon, and indeed it was a sin, was to cut down the great sacred oak tree in the grove of Demeter.

A tree is a symbol of the divine assurance of renewal, as such it symbolises the Spirit. It grows upwards from a seed or a kernel in a spiral form which is the way of all vegetal life. An animal grows to maturity, levels at its peak and then begins its slow decline to death, the animal body – our body does the same. We do not notice how slowly and imperceptibly our strength fails as we age. The spirit is likened to a tree. Spiritual life is eternally renewable, the tree – buds, flowers and fruits right on until it drops, perhaps even at a great age. We describe the eternal renewal of the Spirit in this same manner as a tree lives.

This vast oak tree in our story is not just a tree, it is we are told a great forest in itself. A tree in fact houses millions of creatures. When a mighty tree dies or is felled a great death occurs, and since Demeter is the goddess of all nature, thus a part of the goddess dies. A great sacred healing tree of such stature would of course be regarded as divine. In it we are told lives a spirit of the tree, a dryad of Demeter, who was killed with the tree by Erysichthon, and she cried out to warn him. A bystander tried to stop him, but he killed the man by decapitating him. This was a voice of conscience which also warned him, but he would not listen. He scorned the gods, and dishonoured the goddess. Such a man who dishonoured the goddess would of course dishonour women, as he did his daughter. Men who do not honour women as human beings speak slightingly of perhaps their physical appearance, their mental acumen, and their status or whatever. Such a negative assessment indicates a dishonouring of women as women, and also of the anima, the soul of man, the inner goddess. Au fond Erysichthon dishonoured his own soul. Such an egocentric being, and there are many who do not bend a knee, or bow the head to another, be it a god, goddess or another human being. We speak of hubris, arrogant pride a condition which betokens grave unconsciousness, such as was observed in the chapter on Pride. Lucifer the most beautiful angel who was thrown out of

Heaven was a prime example of this terrifying and dangerous condition.

A sacred tree represents deity's will and word, it is also a place of divine judgment and represents a ladder between the earth and heaven. These sacred trees have always supported votive offerings and votives from supplicants and pilgrims seeking divine help.

The oak tree signifies one of the oldest modes of divination, for listening to the rustling of its leaves one can divine the future or the will of the god. The oak was sometimes referred to as the door to heaven. It was also called the Thunderer, perhaps because it was usually sacred to a sky god Thor, for the Nordic peoples, and Zeus for the Ancient Greeks. Allah and Jehovah were also worshipped by offering sacrifices and gifts to the oak.

If as has been observed the felling of the oak deprived so much life, of food and nourishment, then it was a just though savage punishment given to Erysichthon. The goddess Demeter as Nature is never sentimental. She acts always in the best interests for the propogation of life and its support, that is her business. If a bird falls from its nest when learning to fly, and the cat gets it or it breaks its leg – that is Nature – the bird must have the wit to survive. – otherwise!

But if life is destroyed wantonly by human hand for no good reason that is another matter, that is a sin against Nature herself. Argument may furnish ostensibly good reason for such projects which include culling of animal herds, destruction of rain forests, deprivation of habitat and subterranean nuclear explosions. There are rational and valid solutions, but they do not justify or fulfil a feeling valuation of the taking away of animal and vegetal life of such magnitude.

To destroy life in this wanton way is the fashion of our time. If a society commits genocide, which has happened many times in this century it no longer possesses a respect for life, that is the earth, or the goddess of the earth responsible for life. Such criminal destruction occurs when there is a glut. Behind the apparent reason is the cold logic of the rational mind without Eros, or the feminine principle of psychic relatedness to cut down, to fell, to cull, reduce or simply to kill. It is the human mind which has severed all contact with its own unconscious instinctual roots. This is the problem of today, it is why the earth and its creatures are subjected to abhorrent disrespect and cruelty. Surrounded by a glut of food in the western world a respect for the land and its products has disappeared. A cold impersonality has invaded farming and the great collective farms have ousted the farmers who had a personal relationship to the fields, the animals and the people under their jurisdiction. There is a preponderance of vast machines which reap, cut, bind harvest and stack the crops in similar manner to conveyor belts in factories.

Over population likewise is a great problem, there is a glut of people in the world and individuals are no longer considered, everything must be judged on the scale of the masses.

In certain regions of Mexico water is still scarce, and if one requires water to wash the hands a very small amount about the size of of a small egg-cupful is provided. As it is presented for the purpose, the word 'Aqua' is said with great reverence. It is so scarce it is never wasted, it is more precious than gold and it is treated with respect. Tlalloc the rain god is revered and prayed to constantly to reassure him of devotion and gratitude. That is an attitude of reverence to the higher powers, an attitude we in the western world appear to have lost.

To return to Erysichthon, he disobeyed the spirit of the tree and he scorned his good conscience, he sinned and the sin perpetuated other sins.

The punishment exacted by the goddess was perfectly just, he was made to feel the unease caused by hunger, not just for a moment but for ever, day and night. That is Hell! He could never be satisfied, he ate and ate but was never replete. The indwelling demon of Hunger had visited him, and in spite of his burning appetite his stomach became a bottomless pit – unfillable. The account shows clearly the evolution of the demonic possession.

This story of Erysichthon is interesting psychologically. It portrays a being who has lost contact with the instinctual world, and the values inherent in the inner world are no longer of any worth to him. He derides, even denigrates the great inner figures. He is arrogant and puts himself above the goddess, even takes upon himself the right of destroying not just the tree, but the goddess herself.

Archetypes themselves are unknown, but from the archetypal image something can be gleaned of its nature. They are it seems foci of psychic energic impulses, age-old since eternity. The image of the archetype of the feminine may present as the goddess Ceres, Isis or the Virgin. The changing image is always pertinent to the time, but the archetype itself is unchanging.

In his dealings with the mighty goddess, Erysichthon forgot that man, albeit a king or an emperor, (a newspaper tycoon, a captain of industry, a pop star – dictator, a gold billionaire) is human and does not usually have more than ninety years on earth if fortunate. Men pass away and their circumscribed greatness fades with them like the petals of a rose leaving only the memory. But the vibrant dynamic archetypes whose images to us present as gods and goddesses remain to appear and reappear in prominence, according to the dictates of both the cosmic and microcosmic worlds.

To live a healthy adapted life it is as well to pay heed to these great figures, either in the external formal religions or in the inner world, as they appear to us in outer life sometimes or in our dreams.

It is important to possess a degree of humility and to be able to bow one's head or genuflect. Erysichthon did not, and he was punished by the very opposite of that which he had scorned, he fell as it were into the opposite. He became a poor man who in the end ate his own flesh and became the pimp of his daughter because he had already rejected and abandoned his inner daughter, anima. His sin was a mortal one because he had destroyed his soul and as such it was unpardonable.

Psychologically the tree is symbolic of the individuation process, the means by which one becomes an individual. Individuation is the general term that Jung gave to the process of getting to know the totality of the psyche, and to yielding the central place to the 'Self' instead of usurping it with the ego, just as Erysichthon did. In this process one learns what one is not who one is. Erysichthon was the son of a king, that he did know. He did not know though that he was an hubristic impious glutton because he was possessed by a demonic hunger, a great starvation had seized him for food seemingly. His need or the induced desire became insatiable and could not be assuaged. The loss which he sought unconsciously and with a blind gluttonous urge was for the knowledge of the eternal world of the Self, which he had dishonoured in the personage of the goddess Ceres. She who provided the food of the earth could be found as the spirit of plenty in that food, and that was his punishment, she was to remain eternally unavailable, yet forever sought.

THE GLUTTONOUS WOMAN

An obese woman came for treatment. She had undergone numerous dietary regimes in an endeavour to lose weight. She was forty years old and had a beautiful face. This was the factor which in the end helped her to lose weight.

She denied over-eating, and believed her obesity was due to glandular troubles. She was examined and investigated extensively. It was found that her endocrine system was perfectly normal. She was a fat woman, and she did over-eat, although this was not apparent at meal times. She ate the food provided as arranged without complaint. In many respects she was a compliant patient. She did however eat incessantly, she ate all day, between meals, before and after, and during the night. This was observed when she was admitted to hospital for the investigations.

It was decided that since the obesity was a symptom of a neurosis that psychotherapy was to be the treatment of choice. She agreed and treatment began. From the start it was clear that this woman, shy and retiring, always sought to be it seemed about to fade into the background. But because of her huge size this was impossible. The first thing that was decided was that her major hidden wish was not to be overlooked, she had to be more than just present. By eating she became 'big' and occupied a greater space than the thin person would.

Her two problems were first her mother, and the second was God, in that order. She hated her mother, and did not believe in God. Although the second problem was the most pressing, the problem of her negative mother

205

was treated first. The mother had been a tyrant who dominated her daughter, and insisted on controlling every aspect of her life. The only thing the mother could not control was the secret and constant vice of over-eating. The mother incidentally had been quite slim. The obesity of the woman was the outer form of the inner rebellion against the mother.

Outside this mountainous flesh was the world of which she was mortally afraid. This was the world from which she tried to hide or flee, but because of her bulk she was forced always into the central position. In this position she was ashamed of herself, and felt guilty because she knew she over-ate and she also knew that she was responsible for the obesity.

She did not believe in God because she had followed her mother in this respect, the latter also being an atheist. The whole problem lay in the realm of the shadow where a frightened abandoned little girl cowered in terror. A child starved of love, affection, warmth from her mother and starved of a knowledge of God. The nurturing in this case began with the beautiful face. This single fact which in the end she was able to accept permitted the beginning of a transformation. Slowly the frightened child was permitted a hearing, and the brutal sadistic irreligious animus exposed. The hunger which beset the adult woman was the inner hunger of the deprived and starving child, and which slowly over many years of psychotherapy came to the surface of consciousness.

The reason that she was able eventually to enter into a psychological understanding of the totality of the Self was that she had enough courage to face the fact that she was able to hate her mother for her unjust treatment of the child within. This courage later proved invaluable in standing firm against the opinions of the animus.

The inner child in this case reminded me of the starveling girl observed by Steinbeck at Stalingrad in 1949. However it was many years later that I came across the reportage.

FOOD AS THE ESSENCE OF GLUTTONY

The apparent object of the glutton is food. When dreams of food occur one has to perceive what kind of food has the unconscious portrayed. Is it a simple repast, food in abundance, a great feast or a cooking jamboree? When food occurs frequently in dreams or fantasies the question must be posed. Where is the dreamer starving, in what area of his/her life? What nourishment does he/she require?

In order for food to nourish the physical body it must be eaten, that means it must enter via the is, and be digested by the gastric organ (or the stomach) and the intestines. Nutrients are then conveyed to the liver to be processed and carried via the blood to every living cell as it requires it. So the stage after eating is the stage of transformation to be followed by assimilation. The stomach as the place of transformation is like the kitchen, or an alchemical cauldron or retort. A child is taught to eat correctly as soon as the teeth develop so that the food may be torn, chewed and masticated for absorption. A child is taught therefore to chew and swallow, he must not spit the food out or conceal it in the cheeks for later ejection, and he must not devour his food whole. This is the process which has to be learned. Any deviation leads to certain trouble between the mother and the child, and resistance begins. One of the commonest problems is that the child refuses to swallow the food, or refuses to eat it at all. What is happening is that the child is rejecting the mother's largesse, therefore something has to be changed by the mother.

Nearly all atopic children who suffer from the specific form of eczema called atopic eczema usually have horrendous eating difficulties. The archetype of the mother in her negative form is always centre-stage in this illness, and the eating problems merely reflect the mother-child rejection and latent antagonism.

THE DEVOURING ASPECT OF THE FEMININE

When food is swallowed greedily, gulped down or taken in whole without being masticated, in the manner in which Jonah was swallowed by the whale, it is said to be devoured. It indicates a certain way that food is ingested into the body.

When a particularly dangerous aspect of the maternal archetype is constellated one usually speaks of it as devouring. It may be present in both sexes and its effect is to devour ego-consciousness. The consciousness of the subject is assimilated or ingested into the unconscious; it is a very dangerous situation.

The Terrible Mother in her devouring aspect is a component of many myths. It introduces the idea of strangling, constricting, embracing and entwining. The devouring may be partial or complete. A man with a severe mother complex dreamed that as he was crossing a peat bog one of his legs caught fast in the shifting ground. Only with great difficulty did he manage to free himself in the dream. This reflected entirely the situation in his life. Peat bog, marsh lands or quick sands symbolise the devouring aspect of the maternal archetype.

The motif of entwining is a mother symbol and closely connected with trees whose branches like arms can uplift, embrace or choke one whence it becomes a tree of death. Sometimes the mother in her terrible aspect is portrayed as a voracious being, a wolf, a bear or a fish which devours. The aspect most to be feared is her lamia aspect. The lamia is a typical nightmare whose feminine nature is well known in that it 'rides' its victim – 'the nightmare'.

The siren woman of Dante's poem belongs to the category of devourer, who as the she-wolf brings a nightmarish quality to the dream. It is as well to remember the etymology of this word. A nightmare – signifies a horse which rides at night, it brings with it fear of the unknown, and a deeper hidden fear of darkness and death. The word 'mare' signifies a female horse, Gr. Mähre, or Mar. Mare is akin to OHG meriha (fem: of marah = stallion), OE myre (mire is a bog) is the feminine of mearh a stallion. ON merr. The supposed source of nightmare is the OE, and ON, mara: which signifies an ogress, incubus or demon. The French word – cauchmare, (night-mare) comes from the Lat. calcare, to tread. We have the calcaneum bone in the heel of the foot.

A child had fearful nightmares and awoke up every morning with pains in the heels of the feet just at the site of the calcaneii. The outer problem was an ambitious mother who 'rode' the child to become an expert runner in sporting events. The mother's secret was that the child was the result of a union with a man before her present marriage and who refused to marry her and then had left her. So you see the child had to carry a very heavy burden comprising the mother's disturbed emotionality. The 'treading' aspect has a sexual association, and a synonym for the nightmare is the 'troll' or the 'treader'! – the one who treads. The Indo-European root 'mer' or 'mor' means, to die. From it also evolves the L. 'mors' which is fate and is possibly related to the G. 'moira' –the goddess of fate. The Celts conceived the fates as matres or matronae who were considered divine by the Teutons.

Finally, mention must be made of Isis the Egyptian goddess of whom it is said 'In the beginning there was Isis, the Oldest of the Old.' She was the goddess from whom all becoming arose.[9] 'As the Creatress she gave birth to the sun when he rose upon the earth for the first time.'[10] But Isis as Creatress was also the Devourer. She played an evil trick on the sun god using a poisonous snake, and in likewise manner upon her son Horus. She thus earned the synonyms Terrible Mother, the Maw, the Lamia, the encircler, the embracer, the crusher and the cruncher. These attributes signify her aspect as a terrible death goddess, as the dark side of the archetypal feminine. It was the task of the hero to defy the danger, conquer the monster, overcome her and descend if necessary into the belly of the monster, and risk death face to face. At times he may have been imprisoned. The fight with the nocturnal serpent always signifies the conquest of the dark forces of the great mother as the collective unconscious.

The devouring aspect is usually contained in the maternal archetype behind the mother, but the father through the anima may sometimes have a similar effect upon a son where he wants to keep him, and not allow him to leave home or develop a true manly independence. This is a very subtle thing. It is a dark pull to keep a young man tied to the feminine without liberation, to take responsibility for his own life.

A man was a serious alcoholic. He came to me some time after he had sought to be helped with Alcoholics Anonymous, and when I met him he did not drink any more.

He told me that previously he had been unable to give up drinking, and tended to have long bouts in which he began to suffer from delirium tremens. One morning he awoke to find that his eyes were staring at the filthy runnels of sewage as they made their way between the cobble stones of a city alleyway. He could not get up, and he realised that he was in the gutter, he had no idea how he had arrived there. He found himself prostrated face downwards in what seemed to be a veritable sewer. He described how a rat approached him and looked at his face. (I told him that the rat was more conscious than he was!) Eventually he got to his feet, and from that day started the long climb back to find his humanness. He had lost it through his drunkenness. He had been possessed by a demonic perversion of instinct. He sought to drink spirits to assuage a thirst, but for the evanescent anticipated pleasure; the gluttonous addiction caught him and destroyed him as a human being. His health suffered and he developed both physical and mental symptoms directly attributed to the alcoholic saturation of his body.

There was a problem with the feminine, he had to fight the inner monster and to emerge victorious in order to save his life. There was no alternative.

As I recall the drink was rum – made from molasses. To drink rum one must be aware of its intoxicating power as it has the ability to warm the body instantly and prevent severe chills engendered by the cold sea winds. For this reason it was given daily to sailors in the Royal Navy in Britain.

He never drank again after his encounter with the rat, but he knew that if he took one drink he would be in danger of recapitulating to the demon within. Over the years his deep spiritual problem became his chef d'oevre.

That terrible night in the gutter he almost died because he came face to face with the unconscious as the death dealing devourer. Somewhere he gathered real courage to rise from the gutter and face the future without another glass of alcohol. Had he weakened, in all probability he would have died. I have seen many men emerge from that state of devastation after a long bout of alcoholism, and what I have observed to be present every time is a visible even tangible abject fear.

I suspect that basically the fear of all gluttons or addictives is an unspeakable terror. Of course there are degrees but the greater the fear the more mute the subject.

In many persons so afflicted with a severe addiction one may perceive in dreams figures which are threatening, or of a repulsive aspect that leaves the dreamer upon awakening in a state of 'in-terrorum'. If the figure has murderous intentions, as occurs not infrequently in dreams of severe dependencies, it must always be taken very seriously if the dreams are conveyed to one.

One of the problems of modern life is the advent of world terrorism. The terrorists are committed to torture, or to kill their victims after maintaining a state of terror for longer or shorter periods prior to the final act or murder. These men are often addicted to murder killing time and again. I have often contemplated what must be the nature of the unconscious psychology of those mass terrorists who arrogantly tread the corridors of the world. What frightful phantoms must rise out of their dreams?

Only after the victim of the demonic perversion of instinct has faced the unconscious in the guise of terrible Devouring Mother and stood firm against all the wiles by which she tries to encircle him or her, will he come to realise that the death-bringing demon as siren, or the ravening wolf who seeks food, drink, (or gold) has at last been recognised, and the possibility of quenching the insatiable greed has been reached. But the difficulty is to get to this point. Usually the encircling demon does not permit even a glimmer of consciousness outside the narrow viewpoint of the addiction in order to perceive the perversion of instinct. It is always a miracle when it happens as it was for my patient with the spectacle of the rat.

When he has fulfilled his heroic destiny only then can the victim turn to his human side. The dream of greed in the medieval poem appearing as a witch or a ravening wolf is an uncontrolled force of nature and must be transformed into a power that is at the bidding of the subject. It must as it were be tamed. Then he must seek the final deliverance of ego-consciousness from the deadly threat of the unconscious in the form of negative parents.

With regard to the two tasks mentioned, a transformation of the uncontrolled force of nature and ego-consciousness must seek final deliverance from the deadly threat of the unconscious, in the form of negative parents. Jung[11] has this to say, 'The first task signifies the creation of will power, the second the free use of it.'

Because the alcoholic man had suffered from delirium tremens in the past the question as to whether he encountered a real rat in the alley must be raised. He believed he did, and because of the sequence of events I believed him. In reality the question is immaterial. Whether the rat was a vision or a reality makes no difference since the rat appeared at the most dramatic moment of his life, the moment when he was caught in a death trap by the Terrible Mother, or the moment when the turning point was reached. At that moment the Self, or the wholeness of his personality entered into his life and changed it.

THE SYMBOLISM OF THE RAT

In fact it is not so strange that a rat should appear in the hour of this man's greatest need. In Christianity it signifies pure evil. The rat well deservedly does not have a good reputation. It is highly prolific and the rat population is at least five times that of the human population of the world.

Undoubtedly it is a great survivor. It is nocturnal, lives underground and is described as chthonien, because of its close relationship to the earth.

Late at night many years ago, whilst waiting for the night train to Paris on the Hauptbahnhof in Zürich, I watched a female rat with her three children making their way up the track. She carefully sought out and assiduously fed her children with tiny morsels of food. On that basis I can say that I have observed a very good rat mother. Rats do have prodigious appetites and they can and do eat anything. Sometimes they electrocute themselves by gnawing their way through electric cables. They are recognised as being very destructive for stored crops and property. Thus they are accredited with gluttony.

There are sayings concerning the rat, one of which is in common usage – it is 'to smell a rat' when something is suspicious, suspected to be wrong, secretive or deceitful.

The rat played a very important rôle in the Mediterranean civilisation in pre-Hellenic times, and was often associated with the serpent and with the mole. In the Iliad Apollo is evoked under the name of Smintheus. This word is derived from Sminthros a pre-Hellenic word for mouse or rat. The ambivalence of this name 'Smintheus' attributed to Apollo would correspond to a double symbol: the rat propagating the plague would be the symbol of Apollo of the plague: Apollo otherwise protects against the rats in so far as he is the god of harvests. One sees in the symbolism the same rôle of destroyer possessed by the rats is able to justify two different applications: utilisation of this rôle for vengeance, and suppression of that rôle for charity, whence the double aspect of the god called Smintheus.

This primitive and agrarian tradition of Apollo as rat god, who sends illnesses for instance the plague and who cures them, establishes a parallel with the Indian tradition of a rat god who is the son of Rudra and who also has the double power to bring and cure illness. Apollo Smintheus and Ganesha, the son of Rudra incarnate the beneficial and healing powers of the soil.

Because its activities are nocturnal and clandestine the rat apart from being associated with gluttonous eating is associated with ideas of cupidity, unlawful desire. This because the rat invades subterranean places and takes food as does a thief in the night. From this evolves the ideas of riches, wealth and avarice, the gains are ill-gotten and fraudulent but gains all the same. Also the accent is placed on its fecund nature, in Japan it is the companion of Daikoku the god of wealth. This same interpretation is found in both China and Siberia. As Shu in China the rat is symbolic of industry, prosperity, timidity and meanness. Because the rat appears greedy and has a voracious appetite and lives in the vicinity of food it is a symbol of rapacity. In China there is an ancient superstition that rats can transform themselves into male demons.

A rat is a symbolic image of an animal instinct present in human beings, an instinct to survive. When a dreamer dreams of a rat, or encounters a rat as the man did above it would mean that a 'rat instinct' was present in the unconscious of the individual whose ego awareness was reduced and narrowed to the extent that this unconscious uncontrolled force of nature had usurped to a certain extent, his humanness. In other words, in the grip of an inhuman greed for money, or an induced desire for food or drink he behaved like a bestial monster. It is easy to understand why the church fathers came to regard these sins as mortal. They are such that wilfully violate the divine law, destroy the friendship of God and cause the death of the soul. Mortal sins cut off the perpetrator entirely from his true end.

Jung said that every neurosis carried its own cure. I always felt that my alcoholic-addicted patient was very fortunate when he saw both the neurosis and the cure staring at him face to face as he lay in the gutter in the alley. 'I think we are in rats' alley where the dead men lost their bones.'[12]

Today in the United Kingdom there is an alarming and dangerous increase in the rat population, particularly in the cities. It is an increase carrying the potential of a multitude of infectious diseases. One of the easily discernible causes of this condition is the innovation of fast and take-away foods which result in many people eating in the streets, and throwing away containers with unused food. This is another symptom of plenty. This latter is the real cause since food is easily obtainable and relatively cheap, we have become wasteful, and show little respect for the fruit of the earth, its soils and the seas. There is an ominous deepening of unconsciousness regarding the necessity of good hygiene in our homes and public places. This is partly the result of modern medical training and teaching. There is not the proper concern regarding the nature of the causative bacteriae of so many ills since antibiotics are given freely, often without the doctor's knowledge of the exact nature of the invading forces in many instances.

The populace is bombarded with information concerning food, advertising is geared to promote gluttony, and is very successful. In times of plenty, pleasure induced in the partaking of food moves centre stage, and a collective gluttony ensues. The rats consequently prosper, and since they are survivors they propogate. Animals in the wild, and rats are wild animals, do not over-eat so the greediness or gluttony perceived in rats is a projection of the unconscious nature of the human individual. There is no doubt a rat will never reject food.

It seems fitting that the rat, a symbol representing pure evil in the Christian faith, and therefore the Western world for the past two thousand years should also symbolise the mortal sins of the flesh – lust, avarice and gluttony.

Upon reflection, this discourse of the nature of evil by way of seven deadly sins draws to its close.

REFERENCES

1 Old Testament, Proverbs XXVII v. 7.
2 Steinbeck, John, Stalingrad 1949, The Faber Book of Reportage, Ed. John Carey, Faber & Faber, London 1987.
3 Mythology of All Races, Vol. X: IV North American Indian Mythology, p. 245 ff.
4 The Oxford Dictionary of English Etymology, Ed. C. T. Onions, Oxford University Press, 1966.
5 New Testament, Gospel of St. Matthew, V v. 6.
6 Dante, A., Divine Commedia Purgatorio, Canto XXIII.
7 Old Testament, Psalms 51: 15.
8 Ovid, Metamorphoses, Book VIII.
9 Stone, Merlin, When God Was A Woman, New York, Dial Press, 1976.
10 Budge, E. A. Wallis, Gods of the Egyptians, Vol. I, p. 259, New York, Dover Publications.
11 Jung, C. G., Collected Works, Vol. 5, para 548.
12 Eliot, T. S., The Waste Land and Other Poems, Pub. 1940, Rep. Faber, 1972.

EPILOGUE

The seven deadly sins are as old as mankind itself, and in their manifestations so omnipresent and so much part of every day life, that no one in all truth can state that he is free of them.

Today there is hardly any access to teaching about them in the sense in which they were understood by the theologians of the early Church. However when they are understood to be psychological truths as representations of the dark side of man's being, as C. G. Jung defined this – they show themselves to be very pressing in modern society. Understood in this manner this truth no longer refers to a general list of values which was in fact jettisoned from the Church at the time of the Reformation in Europe.

Instead it has become the tutor in our ability to recognise the nature of the darkness of the shadow personality in ourselves, such darkness which destroys our relationships with our own souls, our fellow human beings and with Nature herself, whereby life itself indeed may be lost.

The twentieth century brought great devastation to the world soul of mankind; by means of the vast and still ongoing increase in collectivisation with its rational concomitant massmindedness and all that entails, involving almost half the population of the world.

In this malign contagion the individual is in danger of negation.

Today tragically, and to a very great extent the feeling for what is evil in people has been lost.

In this study a re-examination of the nature of the deadly sins has been undertaken by means of psychologically explained examples indicating their presence, how they express themselves, and how they reveal the subsequent consequences of their hitherto covert presence in individual lives.

The ability to perceive often unconscious destructive tendencies is the pre-condition for being able to combat the dark side of being, the shadow. This permits change to become accessible.

Since the deadly sins give form to evil, awareness of their nature and presence provides recognition and the possibility to deal with it, or attempt to do so.

Clearly man's consciousness is the vital tool.

In his biography written during the later years of his life,[1] Jung writes of his travels in Kenya in the early years following the First World War.

He visited the Athi Plains great game reserve, and there over the broad Savanna he witnessed gigantic herds of animals, gazelle, antelope, gnu, zebra, wart hog and others grunting, grazing, heads nodding as the herds moved forward like slow meandering rivers.

It was there at that place that the cosmic meaning of consciousness became overwhelmingly clear to him. He became aware at that time that Man in an invisible act of creation put the stamp of perfection on the world by giving it objective existence, by seeing it, feeling it and becoming aware of it.

'This act',[2] Jung continues (in his Memoirs) 'we usually ascribe to the Creator alone without considering that in so doing we view life as a machine, calculated down to the last detail, which along with the human psyche runs ceaselessly obeying foreknown and pre-determined rules'.

It was then that Jung fully realised the myth of mankind[3] 'it was that man is indispensable for the completion of creation: that in fact he himself is the second creator of the world, who has always given to the world objective existence, without which unheard, unseen, silently eating, giving birth, dying, heads nodding through hundreds of millions of years, it would have gone on in the profoundest night of non-being down to its unknown end'. Jung concludes 'Human consciousness created objective existence and meaning, and man found his indispensable place in the great process of being.'

Consciousness is the prerequisite for the understanding of psyche and the human spirit. The task of man as an individual is to become aware again of the existence of his soul, and also his own in-dwelling darkness.

Such a step taken by the individual brings the realisation of his own potentiality for destructive acts of an evil nature. It might be suggested that such a step is of as great if not greater significance for Mankind than that first step on the surface of the moon.

REFERENCES

1 Jung, C. G. Memories, Dreams, Reflections, Routledge & Kegan Paul, London, 1963, p. 239 ff.
2 Ibid.
3 Ibid.
4 Psalms, 111:10 of Proverbs 1:7.

BIBLIOGRAPHY

The Apocryphal New Testament, Trans. by M. R. James, Oxford Clarendon Press.

Aristotle, Encyclopaedia of Religion & Ethics, T & T Clarke, Vol. X, p. 276, Edinburgh, 1918.

As I Crossed A Bridge of Dreams, The Diary of Lady Sarashina, London, Penguin, 1971.

Avicenna and the Visionary Recital, Trans. Corbin, Henri, Spring Publications, University of Dallas, Texas, 1980.

Bachofen, J. J., Myth, Religion & Mother Right, Princeton University Press, 1967, Bollingen Series.

Bacon, Francis, Essays No. IX, Essays & Counsels Civil & Moral, 1597.

Boëthius, Consols, Phil. Lib. III, Prosa 7, Encyclopaedia of Religion & Ethics, lx, p. 74, T & T Clarke, Edinburgh, 1918.

The Book of the Dead, Trans. Budge, E. A. Wallis, 2nd Ed. London, Routledge & Kegan Paul, 1960, The Papyrus of Ani.

Budge, E. A. Wallis, The Gods of the Egyptians, 2 Bde., New York, Dover, 1969.

Butcher, S. H., Some Aspects of the Greek Genius, London, 1904.

Carron, J. S., Prisoners of Hope, An Exposition of Dante's Purgatory, London, Hodder & Stoughton, 1978.

Chaucer, G., The Canterbury Tales, "The Parson's Tale", 1993.

Chevalier, J., and Gheerbrant, A., A Dictionary of Symbols: 4 Bde, Paris, Seghers & Jupiter, 1973.

Clarus, Celtic Myth, Olten u. Freiburg, I Br: Walter, 1991.

Dante, Alighieri, The Divine Comedy, Trans. Charles Sisson, Oxford University Press, 1980.

Detienne, M., The Gardens of Adonis, Spices in Greek Mythology, The Harvest Press, 1977.

Eliade, M., Shamanism, Archaic Techniques of Ecstasy, Trans. from French, Arkana, 1989.

Eliot, T. S., The Waste Land and Other Poems, Faber (Rep), 1940.

Encyclopaedia of Religion & Ethics, Edinburgh, T & T Clarke, 1918.

Epistle-Romanus Inchoata Expositio, St. Augustine, London, Montgomery, 1914.

Etymologique de la Langue Francaise, O. Block et W. Von Warburg, Presses Universitaires de France, Paris, 1975.

Franz, Von M-L., The Golden Ass of Apuleius, Spring Publications, 1970.

Hannah, B., C. G. Jung, His Life & Work, Putnam, 1976.

—The Religious Function of the Animus in the Book of Tobit, Guild of Pastoral Psychology, No. 114.

Hays, H. R., The Beginnings, New York, Putnam, 1963.

Jones, E., Jealousy, London and New York, Penguin, 1988.

Jung, C. G., Collected Works, First published Great Britain, Routledge & Kegan Paul, London, 1979.

—Letters, Vols I & II, Routledge & Kegan Paul, 1973.

—Memories Dreams & Reflections, Routledge & Kegan Paul, 1963.

—Man and his Symbols, Aldus Books, London, 1964.

—Alchemy, Vols I & II, Modern Psychology, Lectures given at the E. T. H. Zürich, 1960

—Nietzsche's Zarathustra, Two Parts, Routledge & Kegan Paul, 1989.

Kerényi, C., Zeus & Hera, Archetypal Image of Father, Husband and Wife, Routledge & Kegan Paul, 1975.

—Gods of the Greeks, Thames & Hudson, London, Trans. from German, 1951.

Lederer, Wolfgang, Fear of Women, New York, Harcourt Brace Jovanovitch, 1968.

Leiter, F. Von H. H., Thal, Das Kamasutram des Vatsyayana, Wien-Leipsig, Schneider, 1929.

Lévy-Bruhl, L., How Natives Think, Chas. Allen & Unwin, 1926.

Maguire, A., Skin Disease, A Message from the Soul, Free Association Books, 2004.

—Vom Sinn der Kranken Sinne, Solothurn u. Düsseldorf Walter, 1993.

Mills, J. S., Essay on Liberty, London, 1859.

Morris, I., The World of the Shining Prince, Oxford University Press, 1964.

The Mythology of All Races, Bd 5, New York, Cooper Square, 1964.

Neumann, E., The Great Mother, Solothurn u. Düsseldorf Walter, 1994.

Ochs, Carol, Behind the Sex of God, Boston, Beacon Press, 1977.

Onians, R. B., Origins of European Thought, Cambridge University Press, 1951.

Otto, W. F., The Homeric Gods, Verlag Frankfurt, G. Schulte, Pub. Great Britain, Pantheon, 1954, Thames and Hudson, 1955.

Ovidus, Naso, P., Metamorphosis, E. Rösch, München und Zürich, Artemis, 1983.

The Oxford Dictionary of English Etymology, Ed. Onions, C. T., Clarendon Press Oxford, 1966.

Partridge, E., Origins, Etymological Dictionary of Modern English, Routledge Kegan Paul, 1958.

Patai, R., Myths of Modern Man, Englewood Cliffs, Prentice Hall, 1972.

Peck, S. M., People of the Lie, New York, Simon and Schuster, 1985.

Proust, M., The Captives, London, Chatto, 1957.

Roux, G., Ancient Iraq, George Allen & Unwin, 1964.

Rowsell, M., Ninon de l'Enclos, 1910.

Schwab, G., Gods & Heroes, Myths & Ethics of Ancient Greece, New York, Pantheon Books. 1946.

Sokoloff, B., Jealousy, A Psychological Study, New York, Carroll & Nicholson, 1948.

Sommers, P., Jealousy, London & New York, Penguin, 1988.

Spinoza, Benedictus de, Ethics V Prop. 3, Schniften und Briefe, Stuttgart, Kröner, 1982.

Steinbeck, J., Stalingrad, 1949, The Faber Book of Reportage, ed. John Carey, Faber & Faber, 1987.

Stone, M., When God was a Woman, B2, New York, Dial Press, 1976.

Thomas Von Aquin, Summe der Theologie, Bd 2 "Die sittliche Weltordnung" Stuttgart, Kröner, 1985.

Tolstoy, L., The Kreutzer Sonata, Verlag, 1985.,

Watterson, B., The Gods of Ancient Egypt, London, Batsford, 1984.

Zimmer, H., The Indian World Mother, Die indische Weltmutter, Frankfurt am Main, Insel, 1979.